The Impact of Public Policy on Environmental Quality and Health

The Impact of Public Policy on Environmental Quality and Health

The Case of Land Use Management and Planning

Amer El-Ahraf, Mohammad Qayoumi, and Ron Dowd

QUORUM BOOKS
Westport, Connecticut • London

Library of Congress Cataloging-in-Publication Data

El-Ahraf, Amer.
    The impact of public policy on environmental quality and health :
the case of land use management and planning / Amer El-Ahraf,
Mohammad Qayoumi, Ron Dowd.
       p.   cm.
    Includes bibliographical references and index.
    ISBN 1–56720–065–6 (alk. paper)
    1. Land use—United States—Planning. 2. Land use—Environmental
aspects—United States. 3. Land use—Government policy—United
States. 4. Environmental protection—United States. I. Qayoumi,
Mohammad H. II. Dowd, Ron. III. Title.
HD205.E4   1999
333.73′13′0973—dc21   97–13409

British Library Cataloguing in Publication Data is available.

Library of Congress Catalog Card Number: 97–13409
ISBN: 1–56720–065–6

First published in 1999

Quorum Books, 88 Post Road West, Westport, CT 06881
An imprint of Greenwood Publishing Group, Inc.
www.quorumbooks.com

Printed in the United States of America

The paper used in this book complies with the
Permanent Paper Standard issued by the National
Information Standards Organization (Z39.48–1984).

10 9 8 7 6 5 4 3 2

To my wife Loraine (Amera)—my partner in life; and to my children Ranya and Hadeel—my hope in life

Amer El-Ahraf

To my wife Najia and in memory of my mother-in-law Aziza Karim

Mohammad Qayoumi

To my students

Ron Dowd

Contents

Acknowledgments

We wish to acknowledge the support of the California State University, Dominguez Hills, California State University, San Bernardino, the Chancellor's Office of the California State University System, and the University of Missouri at Rolla and Portland State University. Our thanks to the California State University, Dominguez Hills librarians, particularly Dean Betty Blackman, Mr. Jim Hunt and Ms. Gail Cook, for their assistance with the literature search. Ms. Mary Moya, Ms. Myrna Griggs, Ms. Karen Becker, Mrs. Lucilla Malig, Ms. Karen Christiansen, Mrs. Cynthia Williamson, and Ms. Kathleen Garcia deserve our gratitude for their preparation of the manuscript, careful review of the material and other forms of support. Our deep appreciation is extended to our families who inspired us and appreciated our lifetime commitment to protect human and environmental health. We are grateful for the guidance we received from the Greenwood Publishing Group during the course of this project, particularly that of Mr. Eric Valentine, Publisher/Editor, Ms. Lisa Reichbach, Supervisor, Ms. Bridget Austiguy-Preschel, Production Editor, and Ms. Deborah Whitford, Editor, Publishing Support Associates. To all of the aforementioned and other colleagues and organizations who have assisted us in the course of this work, we express our sincere gratitude and appreciation.

Introduction

In 1997, Californians were reminded of the environmental, health, economic and social costs of land use decisions made in 1913. On December 17, 1996, the *Los Angeles Times* published a front-page story about Central California's Owens Valley multimillion-dollar plan to force the City of Los Angeles to return 13 percent of its cheapest water supply to Owens Lake. The proposed plan is a mitigation measure against pollution resulting from decisions made long ago to drain the Owens River before it flows into the lake.

The environmental editor of the *Los Angeles Times*, Marla Cone, outlined the plan which aims to control the dust storms that result in health and aesthetics problems through partial restoration of 35 square miles of the 110-square-mile dry Owens Lake. It will also cost the City of Los Angeles $69.7 million in construction and an additional $25 million per year in maintenance. The water rates charged by the city's Department of Water and Power would go up by approximately 9 percent or $1.78 per month per household. Los Angeles would have to buy additional water from the Colorado River and from the San Francisco–San Joaquin River Delta; water shortages may occur. The city vows to fight the plan but Owens Valley officials and pollution control agencies insist that environmental health and legal consideration are on their side. In this area lying at the foothills of the eastern Sierra Nevada mountains, the wind can be so strong that, every year it blows approximately four million tons of salty particulates off the dry lake into the air that the Owens Valley residents breathe. The Great Basin air agency noted that the people in the small towns of the area are exposed to unhealthy air that exceeds federal health standards for periods ranging from ten to twenty-five days per year. One day in 1995, the particulate level reached a nationwide record high (i.e., twenty-three times greater than the federal health standard allows). On such days residents and health personnel in the area report higher levels of visits to clinics, including emergency rooms, by individuals suffering from respiratory problems.

Additionally, Owens Valley officials point out that the federal Clean Air Act requires states to develop plans to clean up particulates by 1997 and to implement those plans by the year 2001. Failure to comply can result in federal economic sanctions, among other actions. Furthermore, a separate state law mandates that the City of Los Angeles pay for "reasonable measures" selected by the Great Owens Valley pollution control agency to solve the problems created by the diversion of water to Los Angeles and the consequent creation of the dry Owens Lake. But the Los Angeles Department of Water and Power does not agree that a plan that is so costly is reasonable, and they do not see that the health and aesthetic problems created by the dry lake warrant the measures proposed by the plan. The situation remains unresolved.

This report illustrates one case of a problematic land use decision taken in the course of U.S. environmental history. The other is across the world affecting the former Soviet Union which is described in Chapter 1 of this book. The two cases affecting two major powers in today's world illustrate the complexity of issues pertaining to environmental health, economics, and legal and regulatory considerations that impact on principles of land use management and planning. These issues are discussed here in the hope that sound management and planning will result from awareness of these complex issues, and prevent reoccurrences of these and similar examples of misuse of land and its valuable natural resources. In *The Closing Circle: Nature, Man and Technology*, Barry Commoner noted the four laws of ecology: everything is connected to everything else; everything must go somewhere; nature knows best; and there is no such thing as a free lunch. When it comes to land use, the so called free lunch is actually very costly; indeed, we cannot afford it. In retrospect one has to raise the question Why was it necessary to transform the sparsely populated land of southern California into a major human settlement with an unending demand for imported water from northern and central California and beyond?

By its nature, land use decisions represent key public policy issues impacting environmental quality and health, which makes it necessary for public health and environmental considerations to be among the basic elements in shaping public policy toward land use and management. This reciprocal relation must be clearly outlined, and the scientific facts as well as political considerations must be clearly understood and acted upon in the best interest of all concerned. Therefore, the purpose of this book is to examine the anthropogenic impact of land use and to demonstrate how it can be utilized as a determinant for a population's health and the quality of life. There is a myriad of actions that are essential in this regard. The emphasis here is on presenting a rational decision making process, for policy makers and professionals such as urban planners, land developers, and health scientists, in striving for environmental balance and creating economic sustenance for healthy communities.

Chapter 1, "Background and Overview," reviews the environmental impacts that affect land use and underline its relationship to economic activities, energy consumption, and public health. Presented here are the consequences of pollution, in terms of environmental deterioration and health impairment. Examples are given to underline the severity of the anthropogenic impact and importance of this topic. These demonstrate the current state of environmental chaos and why we need to be sagacious in land use for our utilitarian ends.

Chapter 2, "Legal and Regulatory Aspects of Land Use," gives an overview of environmental laws in the United States, such as the Toxic Substance Control Act (TSCA), Resource Conservation and Reclamation Act (RCRA), the Clean Water Act (CWA), the 1970 Clean Air Act (CAA), and other significant land use legislation. The 1991 Clean Air Act Amendment (CAAA), the Montreal Protocol and its amendments, and the 1992 Energy Policy Act are discussed in more detail. These samples demonstrate the regulatory role and the importance of compliance.

Chapter 3, "Environmental Health Issues and Land Use Determinants," shows how land use has a direct impact on the public health status of a community. This will enable urban planners to provide an improved framework which promotes an enhanced quality of life. The five major pollution sources being addressed here are air, water, soil, noise, and visual pollution. The discussion begins with the main sources of pollution in modern society and proceeds to their environmental health impacts on human society. This chapter demonstrates how systemic rational models can be utilized to present optimal solutions.

Chapter 4, "Methods of Pollution Control and Zoning," explains various ways of controlling the pollution sources that were discussed in the previous chapter. The main theme here is that energy, environmental, and economic concerns are not mutually exclusive. Moreover, it discusses how a comprehensive plan for land use should systematically consider physical, social, economic, and ecological factors, in other words, how their integration can serve as the cornerstone of a healthy society. The discussion includes land characteristics—geological attributes, landforms and shapes, climatic and weather conditions—as well as soil and vegetative characteristics. In addition, land use classification for agriculture, pasture and range, urban, and multiple or combined land uses, and zoning are discussed.

Chapter 5, "Legal and Legislative Framework of Environmental Protection," discusses the broad and overall legal framework concerning environmental issues. It explains the structure of the legal system and how environmental concerns are initiated, developed, and signed into law. The balance of the chapter looks at the legal liability of environmental laws and discusses some further aspects of environmental legislation.

Chapter 6, "Role of Government in Environmental Protection and Land Use," addresses key public policy issues. Since land planning and control has traditionally been exercised within the realm of local government, Chapter 6 examines the role of state, county, and municipal governments concerning land use coordination and control. Particular emphasis is given to the specific coordinating role of the states and the delegation of authority to the local governments. Besides municipal planning, zoning, and regional land use, federal environmental and land use programs are discussed.

Chapter 7, "Impact of Land Use on Environmental Health," examines the environmental and public health impacts of various land uses such as agricultural, industrial, transportation, and public recreation. Moreover, physical, climatic, social, and economic influences impacting land use are discussed. Special emphasis is placed on the relationship between land use and energy requirements and other related challenges.

Chapter 8, "Process of Land Use Planning," discusses numerous aspects of the land use planning process, the socioeconomic and political influences, and the omnipresent nature of planning. Special emphasis is given to the National Environmental Policy Act (NEPA) with its environmental impact reporting provisions. Also, the administrative processes of environmental impact statements (EISs) are presented in this chapter. NEPA is particularly significant in that it amounts to declaration of environmental rights for the people of the United States.

Chapter 9, "Toward a Sustainable Land Use Model," emphasizes the limited aspect of natural resources and demonstrates how proper stewardship of natural resources is an essential ingredient of optimum environmental quality and health within reach. The chapter examines various pressures on further exploitation of natural resources because of demographics and the aspirations of all nations to improve their standards of living. It shows that the only plausible solution is exercising responsible stewardship by all humankind. The conclusion shows how such a paradigm shift is happening as we move toward the next millennium.

Appendix A provides an outline of technical information required in the assessment stage of environmental impact reporting.

Appendix B is an example of an environmental impact report (EIR) prepared by San Diego State University in the course of planning the San Marcos Campus of the California State University. In addition to its generic value, it provides a specific example of tools used to plan new educational institutions. This should be of particular interest to students and faculty as well as other readers.

Thus, this book provides the scientific basis and public policy means to achieve the desirable objectives of sustainable economic development and a comprehensive approach to health and environmental protection. It is intended for use as a textbook for land use courses in Departments of Health Science, Human Ecology, Environmental Studies, Geography, Urban Planning, Public Policy, Public Administration, and similar disciplines. In addition, this work is intended to bridge the gap between health planners and land use planners by familiarizing them with common issues necessary to protect public health and the environment through the planning process. These issues are either left out or not addresssed sufficiently in books separately prepared for either group of planners. Policy makers and their staffs will find the book a useful tool to provide background information for planned actions affecting the communities they serve. The understanding and support of communities form the essential basis for sustained efforts to encourage an interdisciplinary approach to land use planning and its implication on the environmetnal health status of the population. For professors intending to use this publication as a textbook, the senior author will provide a "Teacher's Guide" including a model curriculum to be used in the classroom in conjunction with the book.

As noted earlier, the book examines the scientific basis and public policy considerations impacting enviornmental quality and health through land use management and planning. Human wisdom is an integral part of this process.

1
Background and Overview

Land is where human beings exist. It is virtually the reservoir that meets all material needs of humans. This is where we are born, live, and eventually die. About ten thousand years ago when the nomadic man turned from hunting to farming, this relationship was recognized in a very organic way. The strong and inseparable ties that we have with the land is a common metaphor that has been expressed vividly in all cultures and religions. Throughout history, humans have not only recognized land as a tangible asset to be utilized for their material needs, but they have also looked at the land with great respect and reverence. The obvious proof of this tremendous respect can be found not only in ancient mythology but in all major religions today.

As humans recognized the benefits of an agrarian life as compared to hunting, they began to establish roots in particular areas. This was the beginning of population centers and the dawn of subsequent civilization. With farming, it became obvious that not everyone was needed for producing the food required for survival of a community. This led to the creation of different trades and occupations. In many ways, this was perhaps the first time that land use became an issue. However, the world population was still very sparse; it did not pass 500 million until 1500. In addition, the main energy source was renewable and so human activities had not had a significantly long-term impact on the land.

The emergence of the industrial age fundamentally began to change the natural balance. The extensive use of fossil fuel provided the means for sustaining a rapidly growing population and an improved standard of living. For instance, between 1650 and 1900 the world population tripled and within another 80 years it tripled again to 4.4 billion. Today the world consumes about 250 quads (quadrillion) British Thermal Units (BTUs) of energy annually. The increase in the burning of fossil fuel has raised the concentration of carbon monoxide in the atmosphere from 280 ppm (parts per million) to about 350 ppm. Studies have shown that if this concentration reaches 600 ppm, the mean global temperature will increase by 1.5 to 4.5 degrees Centigrade, which will have disastrous consequences for mankind. Therefore, the environmental impact of energy has created a significant paradigm shift in energy deployment and land use.

As a result of excessive fuel use, today, over one billion urban dwellers in the world breathe unhealthy levels of sulfur dioxide and dust. In the United States (U.S.), presently we are spending more than $75 billion per year on air pollution, an amount larger than that spent on freeways, streets, and roads. Despite the heavy expenditures and environmental laws at federal, state, and local levels, about 30 percent of U.S. citizens live in an area where at least one of the federal pollutant levels is exceeded. Medical researchers estimate that as many as 60,000 people in the United States may die each year as a result of breathing particulate air pollutants, and strong evidence suggests that pollution caused by the burning of fossil fuel leads to 30,000 to 35,000 premature deaths every year. Similarly, according to a study by the former U.S.S.R. (Union of Soviet Socialist Republics) Academy of Science Institute of Geography, published in October 1991, approximately 20 percent of the entire population of the former Soviet Union lives in polluted areas. The problem is more severe in the urban and industrialized areas than in the rural areas.

One of the other major sources of environmental concern today is the release of chlorofluorocarbons (CFCs) to the atmosphere. Although the release of CFCs to the atmosphere is very small compared to carbon dioxide emission, CFCs retain up to 10,000 times more heat, molecule for molecule, than carbon dioxide, which is why it is a major source of global warming. Another major problem with CFCs is their ozone depletion impact. Currently, a 1 percent reduction in the ozone layer will result in a 5 percent increase in skin cancer cases, an additional 10,000 to 20,000 cases for the United States alone.

So, the excessive burning of fossil fuel and the lack of attention to environmental effects and preventive health measures have had an impact on our public health care costs. For instance, in 1991, the Ford Motor Company spent $150 million more on health care than on steel for manufacturing automobiles. Similarly, for every Chrysler automobile, about $700 of the price is attributed to the company's health care costs. These two examples just barely touch on the societal impacts of environmental cataclysm and the result of land abuse that we are experiencing in this post-industrial era.

These are not only problems in the United States, they are global concerns. As a matter of fact, in many developing countries and in the centrally planned economies of the former Soviet Block nations, the situation is much worse. To illustrate this assertion, let us briefly examine the condition of the Central Asian countries of Tadzhikistan, Kyrgyzstan, Turkmenistan, and Uzbekistan.

The Russians wanted to increase domestic cotton production, especially when the American Civil War made imported cotton scarce. The czarist empire decided on cotton self- sufficiency at all costs. Between 1885 and 1915, they expanded the area sown for cotton from 14 to 44 percent of the land in the Ferghana Valley of Kyrgyzstan, at the expense of grains and other food supplies. This ill-conceived policy resulted in Central Asia's dependence on imported grain from other parts of the empire. The First World War and the subsequent disorder caused by the Russian Revolution resulted in the diversion of Ukrainian grain supplies to the western front rather than to this Central Asian region. The disruption of food supplies brought severe famine, mass starvation, and social chaos to the area.

From the beginning of the first Five Year Plan in 1928 and the collectivization period, the Soviet planners emphasized the policy of self-sufficiency with respect to cotton production. Owing to the Stalinist modus operandi of *argumentum ad baculum*, the destruction of the ecosystem which resulted marks the beginning of the current environmental cataclysm. In order to accomplish this, vast irrigation canals were constructed and water from the Syr Dar'ya (Jaxartes River) and Amu Dar'ya (Oxus River) were diverted in such magnitude that today hardly any fresh water reaches the Aral Sea. (The disastrous condition of the Aral Sea is discussed later in this chapter.) Every kilometer of the Kara-Kum Canal destroyed 50 hectares of land suitable for irrigation. Moreover, 40 to 70 percent of the total water volume in this canal was lost through filtration and evaporation.

In an effort to increase cotton production, authorities cut trees and converted orchards to cotton fields. The overuse of tractors not only compacted the land but killed most of the soil's microorganisms and increased fugitive dust in the area. In addition, alfalfa, traditionally the rotating crop for cotton, was eliminated from production. By 1934 the soil became depleted and cotton production dropped. This was bad news to Soviet authorities. To improve productivity they started applying more chemical fertilizers. For instance, in Uzbekistan the quantity of fertilizer used increased from 65,000 metric tons in 1932 to 569,000 tons in 1937. By the 1970s, 100,000 metric tons of pesticides, defoliants, and other hazardous chemicals were applied annually.

The heavy use of chemicals and lack of adequate drainage increased soil salinity. Slight conditions of salinity reduces cotton yield by 20 percent while severe conditions of salinity can drop yield by one-half. Therefore, the practice of increasing chemical fertilizers resulted in reduction of total yield. Today more than 90 percent of the irrigated land has been contaminated. The salinization level is commonly divided into three categories ranging from (1) less than 20 percent, slight, (2) 20 to 50 percent, moderate, and (3) above 50 percent, severe. Slightly above 60 percent of Kyrgyzstan and Tadzhikistan are classified as slightly salinized while close to 40 percent of Uzbekistan and 10 percent of Turkmenistan fall into this category. The percentage of land classified as moderately salinized roughly ranges from 20 percent for Kyrgyzstan, 30 percent for Tadzhikistan, and over 40 percent for Turkmenistan and Uzbekistan. The rest of the land is classified as severely salinized which ranges from a few percent for Tadzhikistan to close to 50 percent for Turkmenistan.

More than 95 percent of the cotton grown in the former Soviet Union is produced by Central Asia. Uzbekistan is producing 61 percent of the crop followed by Turkmenistan and Tadzhikistan at 18 and 10 percent respectively. Uzbekistan, once viewed as the Beacon of the East by Stalin, is today the major victim of the cotton monoculture. In addition to increasing the soil salinity, the diversion of the rivers resulted in the drying up of the Aral Sea. Now the occasional salt and dust storms that blow as much as 100-150 million tons of salt have damaged human health and agriculture. In some areas, dust and salt cover the streets and houses like frost.

Another major problem created in these countries has been the accumulation of large stockpiles of hazardous waste. For instance, in Kyrgyzstan, the livestock industry has been a major contributor of hazardous waste. Today, open bodies of water in Kyrgyzstan contain dangerous chemicals known for their negative impact on wildlife and human health such as dichlorodiphenyltrichloroethane (DDT), phosphorus organic substances (POS), and hexachlorocychexan (HCH). Even in the resort area of Lake Issyk-Kul, one can find such hazardous chemicals. As Uzbekistan has used almost 100,000 tons of pesticides, defoliants, and other poisonous chemicals, high concentrations of DDT and other dangerous substances are found in the soil and ground water. The problem of nuclear waste is no better. Between 1949 and 1989 the Soviets detonated about 470 nuclear devices in the Semipalatinsk testing site located in Kazakhstan. Moreover, the amount of nuclear waste stockpiled in Kazakhstan is 17 million tons.

Environmental degradation has been a major source of excessive morbidity in Central Asia. This is particularly connected to the shrinkage of the Aral Sea, the nuclear testing of Semipalatinsk, the lack of safe drinking water, and air pollution due to industrial activities. Most of the inhabitants of Central Asia receive their water from irrigation canals which are increasingly polluted with salts, fertilizers, biocides, agricultural runoff, and other toxins. Consequently, they have high morbidity rates from typhoid, hepatitis, and gastrointestinal illness along with a high morbidity rate attributed to water pollution. For instance, the infant mortality rate in Karakalpak increased by 20 percent from 1980 to 1989, and in Tushanz Oblast, it rose by 43 percent during the same time period. In the settlement of Takhta, the water's sulfate content is 50 times higher than normal, chloride is 40 times higher, calcium 17 times higher, and magnesium 10 times higher than the normal rate.

In the Aral region, the incidence of typhoid has increased almost 30 times in the past 15 years. There has been a considerable increase in kidney diseases, gallstones, and chronic gastritis. The infant mortality rate is 50 per 1,000 and many newborns are weak and ailing. In Karakalpak, the infant mortality rate is highest in the world and grew from 47.3 percent in 1978 to 59.8 percent in 1989. The maternal death rate has tripled between the years of 1985 to 1990. Four out of five women suffer from anemia and one out of every three women give birth prematurely. Also, traces of pesticides and heavy metals have been found in breast milk of women in some areas. The aerosolized salt storms have been a major contributor to respiratory problems in the region. In Nukus, 120 miles south of the Aral Sea, there were 74 cases of throat cancer in 1959. By 1989, the number had risen to 366, a fivefold increase. Uzbekistan has the highest infant mortality rate among the former Soviet Union Republics, a rate higher than either Uganda or Nigeria.

In Kyrgyzstan, nearly half of all infant mortality is attributed to acute respiratory infections. In rural areas the numbers are higher in the winter due to indoor burning of wood and biomass and lack of adequate ventilation. The infant mortality rate is about 40 per 1,000 live births which is high when compared to other countries of similar income per capita. In short, cities of Central Asia have higher infant mortality rates than cities located in the European republics of the former Soviet Union. For instance, the numbers for Ashkhabad, Dushanbe, and Tashkent are 53, 38, and 28 per 1,000 births.

The conditions in Central Asia resulting from severe mismanagement of land and other natural resources will require possibly more than a century of remediation before many of them can be reversed. The purpose of this example is to demonstrate the severity of conditions that result from lack of attention to proper land management and planning. Unfortunately, there are many other regions in the world where conditions are not much better, that is, the Brazilian rain forest, the German Black Forest, and Siberian Lake Baikal, just to name a few.

It is fair to ask what went wrong to bring about the current crises. The answer is not simple. In the modern societies, the dominant social paradigm since the Renaissance has been shaped by overriding desire for economic growth, and exploiting nature for utilitarian ends. In other words, humans see themselves as separate and above the rest of creation. Moreover, due to the resilient aspect of nature, humans cannot inflict any enduring harm in the exploitation of nature. Consequently, the society has treated the land's resources with little or no sensitivity to future needs. But given the current environmental disasters, it is clear that traditional wisdom cannot solve today's problems. Today, a prerequisite for sustainable land use requires the understanding of complex ecological issues and the development of long-range comprehensive plans. It is clear that issues associated with land use management and planning must be among the highest priorities of national and international environmental protection programs.

2
Legal and Regulatory Aspects of Land Use

The concern for environmental and public health has always been a source of contention and perplexity among lawmakers. Sometimes, different laws have worked at cross purposes, and there even have been apparent conflicts within the same statute. Yet environmental design and regulations are not entirely new. The ancient Egyptians were the first to provide the world with sophisticated city planning and well-engineered and environmentally sensitive irrigation systems. In medieval England restrictions were imposed on the burning of coal. In the United States, until the 1960s, there were only local ordinances concerning environmental issues. However, in the early 1960s, the concern for the environmental and public health consequences of human activities, especially in the industrialized world, gained a lot of momentum. By 1970, the U.S. Congress adopted the National Environmental Policy Act (NEPA). NEPA amounted to a declaration of the right to live in a healthful and aesthetically pleasing environment. The motivation behind the act was to eliminate damage to the environment and biosphere and promote the health and public welfare of humankind.

The act established a Council on Environmental Quality (CEQ). Owing to the five-year efforts of CEQ, Congress enacted the Toxic Substance Control Act (TSCA) in 1976. This gave NEPA a better system for identifying and evaluating the environmental and health effects of chemicals. Other legislation has impacted positively on the environment and public health.

THE CLEAN AIR ACT (CAA)

The original CAA was signed by President Lyndon B. Johnson in 1963. Prior to its enactment in 1967, the responsibility of abating the anthropogenic effects of environmental issues fell to individual state governments. The federal government's role was limited to situations dealing with interstate pollution. Even then, enforcement was limited to when the governor of one state was asking abatement action against polluters in a neighboring state.

The CAA of 1970 with its subsequent amendments of 1975 and 1977 has been the basis of federal air pollution programs for thirteen years. Now with after over a quarter of a century of paying attention to environmental issues in the United States, there exists an emergence and acceptance of environmental ethics to be applied both domestically and internationally. In these latest amendments two sets of standards were established, primary and secondary standards. The primary standards set limits to safeguard human health, while the secondary standards protect animals and plants. Emission standards for six pollutants, specifically carbon monoxide, nitrogen oxides, lead, sulfur dioxides, ozone, and particulate were set. The Environmental Protection Agency (EPA) is required to review these standards every five years. This placed limitations of new sources in nonattainment areas, and areas which meet the current ambient air quality guidelines now have to follow prevention of significant deterioration (PSD) standards. Eight substances were listed as hazardous air pollutants—asbestos, beryllium, mercury, vinyl chloride, benzene, inorganic arsenic, radionuclides, and coke oven emission—and standards were promulgated for seven of these pollutants.

In June of 1989, President Bush proposed sweeping changes to the CAA. The underlying motivation for these amendments was to design a plan to appease major national environmental concerns relating to acid rain, urban air pollution, and toxic air emissions. Moreover, the amendments addressed the phaseout of ozone-depleting substance in accordance with international negotiations. (The revised Montreal Protocol is discussed later in this chapter.) The bill, with its final amendments, was passed by both houses with a significant majority and signed by President Bush in early 1991. The Clean Air Act Amendments (CAAA) consist of significant titles which are briefly discussed.

Title I: Provisions for Attainment and Maintenance of National Ambient Air Quality Standard

This provision addresses the urban air pollution problems relating to ozone (smog), carbon monoxide (CO), and particulate matter (PM-10, referring to a diameter of ten micron). It clarifies how areas are designated in attainment as well as nonattainment areas. Depending upon the degree of severity, the nonattainment areas will be classified as moderate and serious. Based on these classifications, among other requirements, these areas will need to implement reasonably available control technology measures (RACTMs) or best available control measures (BACMs).

Title II: Provisions for Mobile Sources

Although automobiles today emit 60 percent to 80 percent less pollutants than three decades ago, they still account for half of the volatile organic compounds (VOCs) and nitrogen oxide (NOX), and up to 90 percent of CO emissions in urban areas. The tighter standards will reduce tailpipe emission for hydrocarbons, carbon monoxides, and nitrogen oxides for trucks and automobiles. It also established a clean-fuel car pilot program, which began in California in 1996. Moreover, twenty-six of the filthiest areas in the nation are expected to start an emissions-limiting program for centrally fueled fleets of more than ten vehicles. [The alternate fuel vehicle (AFV) program is addressed in more detail later in the chapter.]

Title III: Air Toxicities

According to a 1987 industry report, an estimated 2.7 billion pounds of toxic air pollutants are emitted annually in the United States. It is believed that the actual release is likely to be two to five times this figure, and includes substances such as mercury, asbestos, benzene, arsenic, radionuclides, trichloroethylene, perchloro-ethylene, toluene, ethylene, propylene, methyl isothiocyanate, dioxin, and so on. The act provides a comprehensive plan to reduce the emission of 189 toxic air pollutants which, together, cause approximately 1,500 to 3,000 cancer fatalities yearly. Currently, any source emitting more than ten tons per year of any one chemical, or twenty-five tons per year of any combination of these chemicals will be considered a major source. The EPA is expected to issue maximum available control technology (MACT) standards for each listed source category with a prescribed schedule. Also, the Chemical Safety Board is mandated to investigate accidental releases of extremely hazardous chemicals.

Title IV: Acid Deposition Control

In the United States, approximately twenty million tons of sulfur dioxides (SO_2) are emitted annually from the burning of fossil fuels. More than three-quarters of SO_2 emissions come from electric utility plants. Sulfur dioxide has been recognized as the major source of acid rain, which has damaged lakes, forests, and buildings as well as causing adverse health in humans. The act will result in a permanent ten-million tons annual reduction of SO_2 in two phases. The first phase went into effect in 1995, which required an emissions reduction of sources above a certain output to a maximum of 2.5 pounds of SO_2 per million BTUs, multiplied by an average of their 1985–1987 fuel use. In the second phase, which will start after January of 2000, the emission rate will be 1.2 pounds of SO_2 per million BTUs, multiplied by the above average fuel use. Also, a source can trade emission allowances by selling or buying them to offset their excess emission.

Title V: Permits

The permit program under the act is similar to the federal National Pollutant Discharge Elimination System (NPDES). This enables the EPA to enforce the act effectively. Each state was required to submit a State Implementation Plan (SIP) to the EPA within three years after enactment of the bill. The EPA was required to review and accept or reject the program in one year. A permit issued for a facility will be valid for a fixed term of up to five years. Should a state fail to submit a satisfactory plan to the EPA, the federal government can impose two sanctions, namely, (1) remove federal funds from highway projects, and (2) drastically increase the emission reduction requirement to offset new source emissions. If these sanctions fail to produce satisfactory results, the EPA can impose a Federal Implementation Plan (FIP) to rectify the situation.

Title VI: Stratospheric Ozone and Global Climate Protection

In congruence with implementing the Montreal Protocol, the act outlined a complete phaseout of class I ozone-depleting substances, namely CFCs, halons, carbon tetrachloride, and methyl chloroform. Also, it established stringent regulations for class 11 chemicals, hydrochlorofluorocarbons (HCFCs). The EPA is required to publish a list of safe and unsafe substitutes for these chemicals in addition to banning the unsafe ones, establishing rules concerning the release of ozone-depleting substances.

Title VII: Enforcement

The act has given the EPA a wide range of authority to make the law more enforceable. It now has the authority to issue field citations of up to $5,000 and administrative penalty orders of up to $200,000. Criminal penalties for known violations have been upgraded from misdemeanors to felonies. Also, new criminal charges can be imposed on negligent and endangerment charges. Moreover, the act allows citizens to seek penalties against violators. The penalties collected are used by the EPA for compliance and enforcement activities.

Title VIII: Miscellaneous Provisions

Other provisions relate to offshore oil and gas operations, processing of stripper well oil and gas, research on causes and effects of air pollution, and job training for displaced and laid off workers as a consequence of compliance. Finally, it has provisions to improve the appearance of national parks and other parts of the country.

CHLOROFLUOROCARBONS (CFCs)

CFCs are fully halogenated man-made chemical compounds that have been widely used as refrigerants, solvents, and stimulants, propellants for insulation, and fast-food cartons. CFCs are halo-carbons made of chlorine, fluorine and carbon, which are nontoxic, nonflammable, and noncorrosive with a combination of desirable properties that are not often found in chemistry. Invented in the early 1930s by Dupont, CFCs affect virtually every aspect of our daily lives. CFCs are used by about 5,000 businesses that produce goods and services worth more than $28 billion per year.

Today, nearly everyone uses CFCs directly or indirectly. For instance, three-quarters of the food consumed in the United States depends on CFC refrigerant at some point in the production and distribution chain. The air conditioning in our automobiles as well as most of our building air conditioning depends on CFCs. CFCs have been used as a cleaning agent in most of the electronic appliances that we use daily. As a blowing agent, CFCs are used in furniture cushions, wall insulation, carpet pads, coaxial cables, and so on. They are used in sterilizing surgical equipment, catheters, and for cooling x-ray equipment. Finally, as a fire extinguishing system, halon is widely used in computer rooms.

CFCs are primarily divided into two classes, namely chloromethanes and chlorethenes. The two most commonly used chloromethanes are CFC-11 (trichlorofluoromethane, CCl_3F, commonly known as R-11) and CFC-12 (dichloro-difluoromethane, CCl_2F_2, commonly known as R-12 or freon 12). CFC-11 is used as a blowing agent for room insulation and as a refrigerant for medium to large centrifugal chillers used in commercial and industrial applications. CFC-12 is primarily used as a coolant for refrigeration systems, for automobile and small package air conditioning units.

The major class of chlorethenes are CFC-113, CFC-114, and CFC-115, of which CFC-113 (trichlorotrifluoroethane, $C_2F_3Cl_3$) accounts for 90 percent of that used in industrial processes. CFC-113 is mainly used as a solvent in the electronic and defense industries. However, it is also occasionally used as a refrigerant in small to medium chillers. Halons are mainly used in fire protection systems as a part of the CFC family.

Environmental Concerns

The Earth's stratosphere plays two important roles, namely absorbing ultraviolet B (UV-B), and influencing the circulation patterns of temperatures throughout the world, causing climatic and regional variations. The average concentration of ozone in the stratosphere is one ppm. As an unstable compound, ozone breaks down and builds up in the order of 300 million tons daily in the stratosphere; the key for this dynamic process is chlorine represented by methyl chloride, which is a naturally occurring substance. Hence, the interplay of ozone and chlorine plays a very important role.

In 1973, Stolarski and Cicerance from the University of Michigan hypothesized that under normal circumstances, a single atom of chlorine can initiate a compli-cated chain reaction destroying thousands of ozone molecules. In 1974, Molina and Rowland at the University of California at Irvine determined that since CFCs are not rained out as acid rain or broken down in the biosphere and troposphere, they migrate to the stratosphere (seven to twenty-eight miles above ground). Due to the chemical salinity of CFCs, they remain in the stratosphere for decades.

Solar radiation produces a photochemical reaction breaking off the chlorine from CFC. The chlorine atom attacks an ozone molecule forming chloride and oxygen (C/O). The chloride then combines with other compounds and the second reaction is repeated. Before the chlorine atom is stabilized a great number of ozone molecules are destroyed. In 1984, the National Aeronautics and Space Administra-tion (NASA), United Nations Environmental Program (UNEP), and the World Health Organization (WHO) formed a task force to examine the validity of this theory. They found that the concentration of CFC-11 and CFC-12 had doubled from 1974 to 1975. Based on their estimate, if the emission rate continued at the 1980 emission rate, ozone-depletion would be about 9 percent by the second half of the next century. This would create drastic climatic change and have severe implications for human, animal, and plant life.

Although serious doubts remain concerning the scope and scale of the problem, in 1985 British scientists reported that ozone concentration over Antarctica had dropped by over 50 percent since the 1960s. The springtime solar reaction had ceased, leaving an ozone "hole" larger in size than the United States.

Health Implications

The most significant effect on human health and welfare from CFC ozone-depletion is the increased cases of skin cancer. Currently, skin cancer amounts to about 400,000 cases annually. The EPA estimates a 1 percent loss of stratospheric ozone will yield a 2 percent increase in UV-B and a 3 percent to 6 percent rise in skin cancer incidence in the United States. These could result in 200,000 additional deaths from skin cancer in the next half century.

Increased UV-B radiation has a tendency to suppress the immune function, diminishes yields in many plant species by affecting photosynthesis. Aquatic ecosystems could be adversely impacted by disruption in the aquatic food chain, particularly in the polar regions. Although the evidence on immunological changes in humans is inconclusive, there is strong concern about the potential of UV-B to decrease our food supply and damage our health.

In addition to ozone-depletion, CFCs act as greenhouse gases; CFCs retain up to 10,000 times more heat, molecule for molecule, than CO_2. This makes CFC one of the major sources of global warming, although the release of CFC compared to CO_2 is very small. Though the effects of global warming are disputed, the scientific community agrees that an increase in greenhouse gases will not be beneficial to human health and the environment.

Montreal Protocol

To avoid the depletion of the stratospheric ozone layer, the Montreal Protocol on Substances that Deplete the Ozone Layer was established in September 1987 by sixty countries. Coordinated by UNEP, these countries (accounting for 83 percent of global consumption) agreed to freezing CFC production at 1986 levels by mid 1989, a 20 percent reduction by 1993, and finally a 50 percent reduction by 1998. In June of 1990, the London Revision to the Montreal Protocol significantly quickened the pace of reduction (50 percent by 1995 and 80 percent by 1997) toward a total production phaseout by the year 2000. By December 1991, a total of 81 percent countries signed on to the protocol. In the United States, the CAAA accelerated the CFC reduction schedule, with the year 2000 as the final phaseout.

In early 1992, NASA satellite information on ozone-depletion reported a 4 to 5 percent increase in the ozone layer over the United States since 1978, nearly twice the rate that was previously estimated. In response to the NASA report, ninety-three nations attended the November 1992 Copenhagen meeting which accelerated the phaseout to January 1, 1996. Moreover, a more accelerated phaseout schedule for

HCFCs was adopted. Beginning in 1996, the manufacturing of HCFCs will be gradually reduced to zero by 2030.

CLEAN WATER ACT (CWA)

The original federal law authorizing the regulation of the prevention of water pollution started with the CWA of 1956. Since then, the act has been amended in 1961, 1965, 1970, 1972, 1977, and 1987. The act now applies both to waste water and storm water discharges to either sanitary or sewer systems, or direct discharges to the rivers, bays, lakes, and the oceans. The act is implemented through NPDES waste water permit program. By 1994, the EPA had delegated permit authority to all but eleven states. In these areas—Alaska, Arizona, Florida, Idaho, Louisiana, Maine, Massachusetts, New Hampshire, New Mexico, Oklahoma, Texas, and the District of Columbia, and Puerto Rico—the regional EPA offices handle the NPDES program.

The act gave the EPA regulatory jurisdiction on direct point-source waste water discharges to surface waters in addition to indirect discharges of all nondomestic sewage into publicly owned treatment plants. Certain categories of direct point discharges are subject to effluent limitations and for requirements for pretreatment technologies. These limitations are based in part on allowable chemical concentration. In addition, there is a requirement for whole effluent testing, using bioassays to determine whether the composite of effluent is toxic to aquatic life. This is to account for any possible synergistic effects of the effluent. The indirect discharges must meet the local ordinances as well as any pretreatment requirements.

The latest amendments have authorized local districts to charge a fee for discharges of pollutants that increase the operational cost of these plants. Therefore, in addition to the sewage effluent volume they can assess charges based on biochemical oxygen demand or chemical oxygen demand (BOD or COD), total suspended solids (TSS), and treatment cost per pound of BOD, COD, and TSS.

In a related development, the 1991 amendments made very stringent provisions for the control of VOC emissions. Future regulations will most likely establish severe limitations to the discharge of solvents to sewer systems.

In 1987 the NPDES established a phased program for permitting storm drain discharges of industrial activity as well as municipalities serving populations of more than 100,000. One of the requirements is developing a Storm Water Pollution Prevention Plan (SWPPP). The plan includes a storm drainage system map, an inventory of exposed materials, a list of significant spills and leaks for a three-year period, and the evaluation of nonstorm water discharges to the storm system. Moreover, the plan contains an evaluation of best management practices (BMP) and other controls that will be implemented at the facility.

RESOURCE CONSERVATION AND RECOVERY ACT (RCRA)

In the four decades after World War II, the amount of hazardous waste in the United States jumped from 500,000 metric tons to 275,000,000 metric tons. Until recently most hazardous waste has been disposed of in landfills with minimal standards. Over time the chemicals leached through and hit the water table, once this occurred large areas were contaminated. So in the 1970s, the EPA encouraged Congress to develop a comprehensive cradle-to-grave program for managing waste by enacting the RCRA in 1976. The perception of some people is that RCRA for solid substance is analogous to CAA and CWA for gases and liquids. However, the intent of RCRA is far more comprehensive than it appears. First, the EPA not only regulates the disposal of hazardous waste but also its generation and transportation. Secondly, the EPA can take legal action to force the cleanup of existing sights that are believed to present immanent danger to public health. In 1984, Congress enacted amendments to the RCRA, which are commonly referred to as Hazardous and Solid Waste Amendments (HSWA).

By the late 1970s, with the advent of horror stories like the contamination of homes in Love Canal, the EPA needed a mechanism to collect the post-cleanup cost of such major contaminations. To meet this problem, Congress enacted the Comprehensive Environmental Response, Compensation, and Liability Act (CERCLA). Unlike typical environmental statutes, CERCLA is a regulatory framework that forces the cleanup of inactive and/or abandoned sites. CERCLA is also commonly referred to as the superfund program. According to an EPA estimate in 1980, $12 billion of federal funds will be needed to clean up the 2,000 identified sites. However, the Office of Technology Assessment (OTA) estimates the cleanup cost for the next fifty years to approach $100 billion, a major financial drain of our national resources. The total societal costs is an indication of the lack of adequate environmental concerns in the past.

FEDERAL INSECTICIDE, FUNGICIDE, AND RODENTICIDE ACT (FIFRA)

The first pesticide control law was passed by the Department of Agriculture in 1947. In 1954 the Food and Drug Administration (FDA) was given the authority to establish residue tolerances of pesticides on food and animal feed. With the establishment of the EPA, the FDA was setting limits on processed foods, the Department of Agriculture was setting limits on edible portions of meat, and the EPA was setting limits for raw, unprocessed meat and agricultural products. The United States has been using one billion pounds of pesticides and herbicides comprised of forty thousand products with approximately six hundred ingredients. In order to establish a regulatory vehicle to control these chemicals, Congress passed FIFRA in 1972. Under this law, no manufacturer or importer can produce or market any pest control product unless it is registered with the EPA.

TOXIC SUBSTANCE CONTROL ACT (TSCA)

The TSCA of 1976 gave the EPA a better system for identifying and evaluating the environmental and health effects of chemicals. The motivation for TSCA centered around the fact that although conventional pollutants such as sulfur dioxides, nitrogen oxides, carbon monoxide, particulate, fecal coliform, and so on are regulated by clean air and water acts, smaller quantities of other highly toxic chemicals are introduced into the environment. These chemicals often linger in the environment long after they are used. That is why today, thousands of tons of toxic chemicals are still haunting landowners. Toxic chemicals differ from conventional pollutants in at least five aspects:

1. Very low doses can produce adverse effects in humans, animals, and plants as compared to pollutants. For instance, with dioxins such as tetrachlorodibenzo-dioxin (TCDD), an exposure in the parts per trillion concentration range causes a toxic reaction, while with the ambient air quality the exposure limits of pollutants are in the parts per million range.
2. The impacts of toxic substances might not be apparent for many years after the exposure. This causes major controversies on the provisions or impacts of regulation.
3. Some toxic substances bioaccumulate and biomagnify in plants or animals. For instance, the concentration of a chemical will be much higher in fish than in their prey and higher in the fishes' predators than in the fish.
4. Some of these chemicals are very stable substances. Consequently, they fail to break down chemically for long periods of time, which increases the probability of their ending up in the food humans eat.
5. Most of these substances have ubiquitous sources. For instance, toxic chemicals like polychlorinatedbiphenyls (PCBs) have thousands of sources.

The TSCA has taken several steps to ban or control the manufacturing, handling, and disposal of many substances. For instance, the production of most forms of PCB was banned in 1979 and a phaseout of PCB-containing equipment was adopted. This had a major impact on the power transformer industry. Also in 1978 and 1982 rules were issued concerning notification and inspection of crumbling asbestos, which primarily affected buildings and construction.

ENERGY POLICY ACT

The 1973 oil embargo sparked great interest in energy issues at all levels to make the United States less dependent on overseas oil and gas. President Carter enacted a National Energy Plan that emphasized conservation, substitution of natural gas and oil with local resources such as coal, when possible, as well as the development of renewable resources such as solar and wind energy. From 1981 through 1988, with the drop of energy prices, the Reagan administration placed little emphasis on energy issues. In fact, there were proposals to merge the Department of Energy (DOE) with the Department of Commerce. Also in this period, the DOE shifted about two-thirds of its allocation of resources from energy conservation to defense and nuclear weapons programs. By the time President Bush took office, the political climate had changed considerably. For instance, the dependence on oil imports had increased to almost 50 percent of national consumption which carried national security implications. The CAA was a major priority that gave particular attention to the interrelation of energy and environment. So the CAAA contained initiatives that promoted reducing fuel consumption.

The Energy Policy Act of 1992 was ratified at a time when there was a great level of awareness and concern about the global environment; in the same year the United Nations Earth Summit was conducted in Rio de Janeiro, Brazil. The Energy Policy Act mirrors the nation's new perspective toward energy policies in fully appreciating the interrelationships between energy and the environment. The Clean-Fuel Fleet program, as mentioned in the CAA, will start taking affect as of 1998 in twenty-one cities. The act emphasizes greater focus on energy conservation, renewable energy, fossil fuels, and nuclear energy as well as initiatives to increase the supply of conventional fuels. Also, new statutory standards for appliances and some equipment have been developed.

Another important element of the act was the reformation of the 1935 Public Utility Holding Company Act (PUHCA). Under the Energy Policy Act, the wholesale generators of electricity will be exempt from geographic restriction imposed under the PUHCA. A controversial element of the act was the incorporation of integrated resource planning (IRP) or least-cost energy planning, in which environmental costs, national security costs, health effects, land use impacts, and so on will be taken into consideration. Some of the other provisions centered around promoting research and development and demonstration programs, initiatives to assist manufacturers in dealing with international competition, and the federal government being a pacesetter for energy efficiency and alternative fuel use. Finally, the act requires the federal government to assist in developing a market for AFVs by purchasing a certain number of them beginning in 1993.

Alternative Fuel Vehicle (AFV)

Beginning in 1996, the federal government should buy 25 percent AFV cars and light duty trucks. This percentage will gradually increase to 33 percent in 1997, 50 percent in 1998, and 75 percent in 1999 and thereafter. Centrally fueled state government fleets situated in metropolitan areas with populations of more than 250,000 must start the phase-in by buying 10 percent of the new vehicles in 1996, with the percentage gradually increasing to 75 percent by the year 2000. Municipal and private fleets of more than fifty vehicles with more than twenty vehicles in one location in a metropolitan area with a population of more than 250,000 are required to phase-in 20 percent of their new vehicles as AFVs beginning in 1999.

Since 60 percent of the petroleum consumption in this country is attributed to the transportation sector, the introduction of AFVs in large numbers will positively impact the air quality in many major urban areas. Currently, more than 100 U. S. cities do not have federal standards for ground level ozone and smog, and more than 40 cities fail the carbon monoxide limits. The ozone is primarily formed by the reaction of VOCs with nitrogen oxides in the presence of sunlight. In 1990, approximately 20 to 35 percent of VOCs, 20 to 45 percent of NOX, and 50 to 65 percent of CO emissions were attributed to gasoline powered vehicles. California has taken an even stronger position on this by creating the California Air Resources Board (CARB)which established the zero emission vehicle (ZEV) program. According to this program, 2 percent of cars produced for sale in California, beginning in 1998, will be ZEVs. This percentage will gradually increase to 15 percent by the year 2003. In addition to California, other states such as Delaware, Maryland, New Hampshire, New Jersey, Pennsylvania, Rhode Island, Vermont, and the District of Columbia have been looking into establishing ZEV programs.

CONCLUSION

By now, it has become clear that the bulk of legislation impacting the environment has been passed in the last twenty years. It will take a long time to undo the mistakes of the past, but there is enough progress that one can be optimistic. The impact of these laws is very significant for land use. The potential implications are arguably many. The cradle-to-grave approach of the new environmental legislation coupled with the comprehensive approach of EPA will significantly reduce "land abuse" and impact future land policies in this country.

3
Environmental Health Issues and Land Use Determinants

Proper land use can protect the environment and public health. However, improper land use such as locating polluting industries upstream, building community hospitals without proper mechanisms for disposal of infectious waste, or depleting water resources can result in the spread of disease. Diseases are grouped into two categories, infectious and noninfectious. Infectious or communicable diseases are transmitted directly by airborne, vector borne, and vehicle borne microbes. Air, water, and land serve as vehicles for the transmission of communicable diseases. Some typical communicable diseases are typhoid, cholera, hepatitis, and gastroenteritis. Noninfectious diseases are associated commonly with toxic pollutants such as poisons, carcinogens, and heavy metals. The primary sources of such pollutants in the environment are industrial based.

The cumulative knowledge of this impact should enable planners to provide an improved environment which promotes sound health and generally enhances the quality of life. Pollution from a variety of sources may be caused or controlled by land use planning and decision making. There are five major types of pollution which must be addressed if solutions to health problems related to land use are to be found: air, water, soil, noise, and visual pollution.

AIR POLLUTION

Air is the most important component for sustaining human life on the planet. Although a person can live without water for several days and without food for several weeks, one can hardly survive if deprived of oxygen for more than several minutes. Moreover, while humans on the average require about 1.5 pounds of food and 3 pounds of water a day to survive, they need 30 pounds of air daily to survive. About 99 percent of the ambient air is composed roughly of one-quarter oxygen and three-quarters nitrogen. The remaining 1 percent consists of a number of gases such as helium, ozone, hydrogen, carbon dioxide, and methane. Because of low concentrations, these gases are normally measured in ppm.

Air pollution consists of gases, liquids, and solids present in air to the extent that they are detrimental to man, animals, property, or plants. Although temperature, wind, topography, and sunlight are major causative factors, the use of land in combination with these can impede or encourage the levels of pollution in the air. Air pollution can be man-made (i.e., industrial pollution, vehicle, etc.) or natural (i.e, pollens, lightening fires, etc.) Environmental pollutants may take the form of gases, aerosols, microorganisms, or particulate. Moreover, odors, radioactive particles, and pesticides are considered air pollutants. Industrialization, mechanization, and large population shifts to urbanized residential settlements are perhaps the largest causative factors of air pollution.

The major substances present in air pollution are carbon monoxide, carbon dioxide, hydrocarbons, lead, nitrogen oxides, ozone, particulate, and sulfur dioxide. Carbon dioxide is primarily generated from the burning of fossil fuels, energy, and from forest fires. If the combustion process of fossil fuels is not complete, carbon monoxide is generated. The United States annually emits over 100 million tons of carbon monoxide into the atmosphere. Approximately 85 percent of hydrocarbons found in the atmosphere are generated from natural sources, that is from the decomposition of vegetation and other organic matter. Nitrogen oxides are formed when the combustion temperature of fossil fuel is high. The United States annually emits roughly 20 million tons of nitrogen oxides into the atmosphere. The hydrocarbons and nitrogen oxides go through a chemical reaction in the presence of sunlight and ozone is formed, which is the major component of photochemical smog in large metropolitan areas in this country, due to the high density of automotive vehicles.

Particulate is produced primarily by the burning of solid fuels such as wood, coal, and trash. Suspended particulate can range in size from a fraction of a micrometer up to 100 micrometers. According to the EPA, the U. S. emits over 10 million tons of particulate into the atmosphere annually. Sulfur dioxides are formed by the burning of fuels that contain sulfur; the main source of sulfur dioxide in the atmosphere is coal burned by large industrial plants. In this country, the total amount emitted into the atmosphere is about 27 million tons annually. Sulfur dioxide is believed to be the major contributor of acid rain. Acid rain damages freshwater lakes, destroys forests, negatively impacts yields of agricultural crops, and reduces fish life in freshwater lakes. Acid rain has been a subject of major controversy in the past two decades. In reaction to the problem, a joint U.S. and Canadian initiative was launched in 1986 to fund a $5 billion clean coal technology program. Finally, the presence of lead in the air can lead to lead poisoning and can severely impact the nervous system of humans, especially infants and youngsters. The problem of lead has been sharply reduced since the banking of leaded gasoline and the prevalent use of unleaded gas.

In Europe the existence of air pollution was first acknowledged as early as the fourteenth century when King Edward I decreed that coal should not be used during sessions of the Parliament. The impact of air pollution on health was first recognized in a paper written in 1866. In 1875 an air pollution episode was linked to cattle death in London. At the turn of the century, the term "smokefog" was coined, which in time was shortened to smog the term used today. The Engineers' Joint Council defined air pollution as follows "Air pollution means the presence in the outdoor atmosphere of one or more contaminants, such as dust, fumes, gas, mist, odor, smoke, or vapor in quantities, of characteristics, and of duration such as to be injurious to human, plant or animal life or to property, or which unreasonably interferes with the comfortable enjoyment of life and property" (Ehlers and Steel 1965: 74). This is a comprehensive definition that emphasizes outdoor air pollution. However, both outdoor and indoor air pollution in the residential or work environments share several common features. For example, air pollution may consist of single contaminant gas or particulate or a combination of several. Basic determinants of impact of air pollution include time of exposure, concentration level of any particular pollutant and atmospheric conditions.

Types and Sources

Pollutants can be natural or artificial, gaseous or particulate, or they can be classified by number and spatial distribution (point, area, or line sources). Pollens from weeds and plants, because they are responsible for allergies and hay fever, are the most significant form of natural air pollution. Other sources include airborne soil and sand, salt spray, gases emitted from earth fissures, smoke from forest or brush fires, and fog.

Fossil fuel combustion, mostly from motor vehicles, constitutes the most significant form of man-made air pollution. Other sources include attrition (i.e., emission of minute particles into the atmosphere through the grinding action of friction) evaporation, and incineration. Air pollutant types include nitrogen oxides, sulfur oxides, carbon monoxide, carbon dioxide, photochemical oxidants, lead, asbestos, beryllium, mercury, fluorides, odors emitted from a variety of natural and artificial sources, commercial and agricultural poisons, and radioactivity.

Land Use Determinants

Man's use of land directly impacts the types and levels of pollutants in the air. Large metropolitan areas generate their own impact on the atmosphere. Cities store heat through absorption of the sun's rays during daylight hours. This stored heat is then released at night, rising and causing an inversion layer, and carries a variety of pollutants with it. The warm air expands, moves toward the periphery of the city, then cools off and sinks. The cooler air, with all of the pollutants, flows back into the center of the city to replace the rising warmer air, thus perpetuating the pollution cycle.

Industry generates air pollution specific to varied manufacturing processes, including the raw materials, fuels, and processing techniques used. Although all industries contribute to air pollution, major polluters are steel and iron mills, metal industries, power plants, petroleum refineries, paper mills, chemical manufacturers, food processors, agricultural industries, and transportation. Most industries are fixed in a specific geographical location and, therefore, are more amenable to land use planning. The siting and spacing of pollution-intensive industries, particularly in regard to wind direction and temperature variation, can assist greatly in the reduction of air pollution influence on life and property. Pollution emitted from automobiles, trucks, aircraft, and other vehicles is associated with large concentrations of population. The concept of grouping residential, commercial, and light industrial uses in dispersal patterns vis-à-vis concentrated urban sprawl patterns reduces the likelihood of air pollution from auto emissions. Regulating the flow of traffic and minimizing traffic gridlock through engineered design of transportation systems also helps minimize the effects of vehicle emissions.

Health Impacts

Air contaminants can have deleterious effects on the lungs, heart, and eyes of man and animals. Indirect health consequences may occur as a result of the effects of air pollution on vegetation, property, and visibility. Pollutants in the air also find their way into our water supply, thereby creating another indirect hazard to health. Gaseous irritants and certain kinds of particulate are known to cause respiratory problems. These irritants can thicken mucous, cause swelling of cells, and constrict air passages. Breathing becomes more difficult in areas of air pollution concentration. Approximately 80 percent of the U.S. population lives in urban areas, where air population tends to concentrate; one can envision the impact on the health of the population.

Chronic lung disease, edema, hemorrhage of the lungs and specific lung problems such as bronchitis, lung cancer, emphysema, and asthma have been linked to various types of air pollutants. The presence of gaseous and particulate pollutants in the atmosphere causes eye irritation and reduces visibility. The close linkage between the circulatory system and respiration strongly suggests that heart problems may result from continuous and intense exposure to air pollution. Likewise, animals breathe polluted air and ingest feed which may be contaminated by residues of pollutants. Various manufacturing and smelting processes emit contaminants which find their way to grazing areas. Arsenic, produced as a result of copper smelting, lead and zinc dust from foundries, and molybdenum, produced in steel-making, all have deleterious effects on animals grazing on forage polluted by these contaminants.

The damage caused by air pollution extends to plants and property. Severe air pollution or chronic exposure to pollutants will destroy or retard the growth of vegetation. Sulfur dioxide, hydrogen fluoride, ozone, and ethylene have various harmful effects on plants, crops, and shrubbery. Chemical and physical reactions occur to building materials, finishes, drapery, clothing, leather, and rubber. Temperature, air movement, sunlight, moisture, and the concentration of pollutants all work together to cause varying degrees of damage to property in any given location.

Economic loss is sustained by society as a result of air pollution. The effects upon man and animals result in illness, injury and accidents, loss of productivity, increased repair and maintenance, loss of livestock and crops, higher costs of living, and so on. National efforts to clean up the ambient air rest in the provisions of the CAA and its amendments (see Chapter 4).

WATER POLLUTION

Water has the ability to dissolve an array of foreign substances. That is one reason why pure water can only be made in the laboratory and is hardly ever found in nature. When foreign materials are present in water that make it unsuitable for beneficial use such as drinking or recreation, it is considered polluted. Water may be contaminated with disease organisms from infected persons, dissolved minerals, decaying organic matter, pesticides, and industrial waste. Some of the most common water pollutants are oil, sediments, toxic substances, organic chemicals, plant nutrients, and pathogenic organisms. The improper disposal of human, industrial, and agricultural waste is one of the most significant factors impacting the health and well-being of individuals. More often than not, these wastes are discharged into our water supplies. Obviously, control of sewage is of paramount importance in the prevention of disease and enhancement of health among our population. The increase in demand for water, particularly in large urban centers, requires planned water collection and distribution systems and sophisticated water treatment engineering.

Nature of Water Pollution

Water pollution may be defined and classified in a variety of ways. The concentration of pollutants, time of exposure, and specific impacts are essential ingredients of most definitions. Some pollutants serve to restrict the availability of water supply for human consumption; some are considered a nuisance because they are aesthetically displeasing, and some are pathogenic because they are considered harmful to health. Water which does not meet various standards of quality in terms of physical, chemical, and bacteriological criteria may be considered polluted to one extent or another. Physical characteristics of water that relate to pollution include, solids, oils, grease, odor, color, and temperature. Solids can be further classified as suspended or dissolved, volatile or fixed. Volatile solids are organic, and fixed solids are inorganic. Color may be apparent (i.e., filterable) or true (i.e., dissolved). Chemical characteristics of water which relate to pollution can be categorized by organic components—acidity, alkalinity, hardness, salinity, chloride, metals, nitrogen, phosphorous contents. The BOD test is useful for identifying the organic makeup of water. Bacteriological characteristics of water which relate to pollution include viruses and bacteria, coliform, and fecal coliform.

Type and Source

Water pollution may be natural or man-made, as well as point or nonpoint in source. Natural water pollution is caused by silt which flows along water beds as a result of precipitation such as rain or snow carrying dust, particles, and other material into the water. Artificial pollution is due to wastes from domestic, agricultural, industrial, and military activities. Point-source pollution originates from specific industrial processes, while nonpoint-source pollution originates from various domestic and agricultural activities.

Industry depends heavily on water for cooling and processing. The effluent from industrial plants contains toxic and organic wastes harmful to health and aquatic life. Effluent from municipal sewage plants likewise contains potentially harmful wastes, although generally toxic wastes are not as dominant as industrial effluent. Organic wastes have the effect of reducing the amount of oxygen in a water supply, thereby upsetting the ecological balance, lack of oxygen kills fish and destroys aquatic plant life. Toxic wastes have a lethal effect on a variety of biological forms necessary for water quality and survival of fish and plant life. Wastes from pulp mills, canning operations, meat packing, textile industries, and milk production are prime examples of oxygen dependent organic pollution sources. Wastes from mines, chemical manufacturing plants, crop pesticide treatment, and steel-making operations are prime examples of toxic pollution sources.

Radioactive waste products from nuclear reactor cooling water, uranium ore mining and refining, and atomic bomb testing may find their way into the water supply and cause harmful effects. Soap production, pickling, and other industries may produce corrosive wastes harmful to fish and plant life, not to mention the effects it may have on ship hulls, bridge piers, and piping systems. Pathogenic wastes are instrumental in the spread of disease among man and animals. Livestock, tanning processes, pharmaceutical manufacturing, leaching from disposal sites, and food processing plants are prime sources of pathogenic waste materials.

Land Use Determinants

Pollution abatement regulations, chemical treatment of supply and source of pollution, filtration and related methods in combination with planned regional distribution systems hold the key to solutions of water pollution problems. Man's use of land directly impacts both the creation of pollution in our water supplies and our ability to control that pollution. Planned development of industrial, agricultural, and residential land use on a regional basis, which anticipates water needs, supplies and uses, and incorporates design of distribution and pollution control systems into that planning, is by far the most cost-effective approach to solving water pollution problems.

The trend in large urbanized areas has been to import water from unpolluted areas, rather than treat local, more easily accessible sources. Much of this is due to aesthetic factors—color, taste, odor, and hardness. There is a significant economic impact associated with this trend toward importing water supplies. The cost of collection facilities, storage reservoirs, transportation systems, and pumping stations represents a drain on the limited resources available to any community. However, regionalization and consolidation of water supplies remains the trend in the United States.

Land use patterns influence the impact of human uses as they relate to domestic, industrial, agricultural, or mining activities and the discharge of waste that may affect water quality. The density and concentration of residential land uses will determine consumption levels required, as well as the amount of discharge into sewage systems. This, in turn, will establish the types of pollutants likely to be found in the water supply, thereby establishing the kinds of potential hazards to health, plant, and fish life. The rate of conversion of land uses and the types of replacement uses planned will also determine future types and levels of pollution. Here, more than anywhere else, holds promise for the eventual long-range control of many types of water pollutants. Finally, the development of open space buffers between major types of land use in concert with planned development of water supplies, which considers pollution sources and impacts, will have a positive influence on land use determinants of water pollution.

Health Impact

Chlorination of water supplies and the establishment of water monitoring and treatment operations has greatly reduced many of the biological causes of waterborne disease. However, new organisms and chemical agents have been appearing on the scene, and old ones reappear from time to time. Pathogenic bacteria and viruses are present in varying amounts in the water supply. *Salmonella, Shigella, Vibrio, Brucella*, cholera and other bacteria present in the water cause a variety of infectious diseases in humans. Viruses which cause infectious hepatitis, polio viruses, echo viruses, and others which result in upper respiratory problems or diarrhea are often present in water supplies.

The presence of these organisms is indicative of contamination from humans and other warmblooded animals. Cholera is perhaps the most severe enteric waterborne disease. Infected persons contaminate the drinking water supply directly through fecal material or vomit transmission or indirectly by ingesting contaminated shellfish. Shigellosis, although rarely fatal, is on the increase in the United States, and can have serious consequences for the very young, aged, and infirmed. Salmonellosis, paratyphoid fever and other diseases can be traced to water-transmitted organisms. Outbreaks of infectious hepatitis have been traced to drinking water from contaminated water supplies. Adeno viruses, which are associated with eye infections and upper respiratory distress, have been isolated from chlorinated swimming pools. Waterborne enteric diseases such as giardiasis have been associated with summer resorts, raising concern about some recreational facilities generally assumed as natural and safe.

Potentially dangerous chemicals are being introduced into waterways and water supplies. Although much research remains to be done, statistical and epidemiological associations have been found among various chemicals in drinking water and cardiovascular disease, cancer, and chronic toxicity. Synthetic pesticides were known to kill fish as early as 1950 in the Tennessee River area of Alabama. Pesticides may be introduced as a result of runoff from agricultural lands and forests, or they may be applied directly to water sources (i.e., mosquito abatement).

Pesticides such as DDT represent suspected or known carcinogens. Chronic toxicity and its effects on human and animal populations over extended periods of time is the major concern at the moment. Other examples of significant water pollutants include nitrates, fluorides, chlorides, and sulphates.

SOIL POLLUTION

Solid waste disposal contributes not only to pollution of the land, but has significant impact on air and water pollution as well. There have been changes in solid waste disposal methods in response to environmental law and regulations, and, through efforts to upgrade technological approaches, sanitary landfills were developed as alternatives to dump burning and smoking incinerators, which contributed to air pollution. Landfill dumps, however, present other pollution problems through leachate, which pollutes surface streams and ground water surrounding landfill areas. Putrid odor and gaseous emissions are also problems. Although incineration is still a viable solution to solid waste disposal problems, sanitary landfill is preferred in highly populated areas. Chemical and biological treatment of wastes helps to control the potential spread of disease, gaseous emissions, and odors associated with landfill waste disposal. Site selection is an important factor.

Incineration of solid and hazardous waste has been viewed by some scientists and authorities as a mechanism to reduce soil pollution and preserve the land for other uses. Others have considered that the high cost and possible health risk of air pollution resulting from incineration as unacceptable. The experience of the United States and the international community with incineration of waste is worth noting. In the United States, Rhode Island banned solid waste incineration in 1992. This action was followed by West Virginia in 1993. In 1995, the United States as a whole used this technique to dispose of approximately 16 percent of its municipal solid waste and about 7 percent of its officially regulated hazardous waste. In 1985, Sweden decided to ban the construction of new incinerators. The Japanese modified the incineration process by first removing unburnable waste and hazardous material resulting in net reduction of bulk and toxicity of the ash. Additionally, Japan has instituted a series of occupational and environmental health measures designed to protect workers and the soil. Ash is removed via conveyer belts, transported in sealed containers, often formed in concrete blocks, and buried in heavily regulated and well-designed landfills.

Nature of Soil Pollution

The indiscriminant dumping of hazardous chemicals and other byproducts of industry, agriculture, and urban living have become the number one environmental priority for the decade of the eighties. Controversial occurrences in Love Canal, Lake Michigan, Elizabeth, New Jersey, and the bayou country of Louisiana during the seventies coupled with the nuclear accidents of Three-Mile Island and Chernobyl have heightened the level of public awareness of the dangers of ground pollution. Soils in different parts of the world are contaminated because of a long history of careless storage and disposal of solid waste material. Inappropriate location or operation of landfill dumps and illegal, capricious dumping causes a great deal of soil pollution. Insensitivity to this kind of pollution, lack of laws and regulations, and ignorance have created situations where irreversible damage has occurred or costs are too high to clean contaminated land. Different levels of soil contamination can be found even in university settings where underground fuel tanks were the norm in a previous era.

The production of underground methane gas, seepage of waste residue into ground water supplies, and airborne distribution of toxic chemicals create immanent hazards to health and the well-being of humans, animals, and vegetation. The residue from solid waste incineration, if not quenched and disposed of properly, is highly corrosive and will eventually become an air pollutant with the consequences mentioned previously. Refuse contains chemical or biological properties which are potential contaminants. Chemicals found in refuse may get into the surrounding soil, and organic materials decompose to contaminate the soil and underlying water sources. Leachate is generally acidic and may contain iron, zinc, phosphate, chlorides, carbon monoxide, nitrogen, methane, sulfate, sodium, and other chemicals which might permeate landfills and find their way into water supplies. Byproducts of the decomposition of organic matter include hydrogen sulfide, methane, and ammonia which also may find their way into underground water sources.

Types and Sources

Essentially, soil pollution is the result of biological, toxic chemical, and radioactive waste coming in contact with soil and contaminating it. These three general types of soil contamination can be found in a multitude of sources scattered throughout the U.S. The wastes are generated from governmental activities, industrial processes, hospitals and other health facilities, laboratories, nuclear power generation, uranium and other mining activities, refineries, and activities of daily living. Poor management of these wastes has resulted in significant environmental and public health problems.

Practically all nonradioactive wastes produced are toxic; usually inorganic toxic metals or bases of one sort or another. Synthetic organic wastes are flammable and may also be explosive. Halogenated hydrocarbon pesticides, PCBs and phenols are included in this group. Highly flammable pesticides, organic sludge, oils, solvents, and other chemicals present highly significant disposal problems. Military operations and explosive manufacturing processes will produce nitric acid, sulfuric acid, ammonia, and other explosive organic chemicals.

Radioactive wastes are classified according to the level and concentration of radionuclides they contain. A lengthy half-life of radionuclides will indicate a long-term hazard because of their decay rates. Biological hazards result from penetrating and ionizing radiation. Heat produced during the radioactive decay process can easily affect the viability of concrete storage structures. Hospitals and other health facilities and military production of biological warfare agents are major sources of hazardous biological waste materials. This waste includes material such as human tissue which may be diseased, animal remains, used hypodermic needles, medical supplies, drugs, and microbiological material. Although military production of biological warfare agents has been concentrated, stockpiles still exist which may cause concern.

An extremely significant soil pollutant is pesticide. Pesticides are frequently used for agricultural and domestic purposes. A variety of types are commonly used, including chlordane, parathion, heptachlor, diazinon, and dieldrin. They are used in houses and gardens as well as for agribusiness. Pesticides are pervasive and their use is growing. To farmers and homeowners they are hazardous.

Currently about 35 percent of the sludge produced in the United States is burned, 15 percent is dumped into the sea by coastal cities, 25 percent is buried in landfills, and 25 percent is applied to land as a soil conditioner. Sludge, which consists of about 50 percent organic matter, also provides some beneficial nutrients for soil.

Land Use Determinants

Perhaps more than any other type of pollution, soil pollution is more amenable to land use planning. Isolation of dump sites is a most effective approach to the solution of the problem, and this approach is well within the scope of recognized land use planning and control mechanisms. It is economically and politically attractive to select sanitary landfills from among undesirable plots of land such as swamps, ravines, and furrow pits. Once having filled the undesirable plot to grade, it can be developed for either public or private use. These sites are usually considered for public uses, such as parks, golf courses, and the like. Methane formation and differential settling of soils argue against use of saturated landfill sites for building purposes. However, building can be constructed on those sites after a few years of observation indicate feasibility of development. There are psychological barriers to this, and treatment of leachate still remains as a problem.

As technology advances in the field of solid waste disposal and as planned alternative uses of saturated landfill sites increase in popularity, it will become possible to integrate regional planning of multiple land uses with planning for the collection and disposal of solid wastes.

Ocean dumping has been viewed with increased disfavor because of its possible impact on aquatic plant and animal life. Alternative techniques and advances in treatment and disposal of waste must continue in order to protect the ocean environment.

Open dumps create all sorts of problems, including rodent infestation, extensive odor problems, spontaneous combustion leading to fires, and a general unsightly appearance, not to mention the hazards to the health of persons operating and maintaining the dumps. Land use planning for solid waste disposal must consider existing and planned land uses, potential conversion of open dumps to landfills, and potential impact on water supplies.

Health Impacts

Health impacts of soil pollution can be caused by chemical, biological, physical, psychological, and mechanical agents in nature. Chemical hazards are found in the use of pesticides, industrial waste materials, and municipal refuse. Since many chemicals are toxic to humans, the health impacts are direct and extremely dangerous. Sharp-edged objects such as glass, metal fragments, and stone shavings present mechanical hazards to humans, especially those individuals earning their livelihood in solid waste disposal associated trades. A cluttered, unsightly, and filthy environment most certainly has psychological effects on persons exposed to those pollutants on a day-in and day-out basis.

Flammable and explosive materials present an obvious and direct physical danger to humans. Insects and rodents are prime vectors in the transmission of many diseases affecting humankind. Flies, for example, carry a variety of enteric organisms from fecal material to humans. Numerous viruses, bacteria, and protozoa are also transmitted by flies, which breed and reside in dump sites. Mosquitoes, which transmit diseases such as malaria, yellow fever, encephalitis and dengue fever, also breed in areas where improper solid waste disposal methods are prevalent. Manures typically contain pathogenic soil fungi which cause mycotic infections in human beings. Additionally, since soil pollution is easily transformed to air and water pollution, all of the health impacts related to those pollutants can be reiterated here.

NOISE POLLUTION

Noise is a form of unwanted energy that is a byproduct of mechanical vibration. One way to visualize sound is a periodic change of air pressure density. The intensity of sound is measured by its amplitude and the frequency is measured based on how many full waves exist in one second. The frequency is measured in number of cycles per seconds or in Hertz (Hz). The human ear can detect sound levels ranging from 20 Hz to 20,000 Hz. However, for most people the best hearing range is between 200 Hz and 10,000 Hz, normal human voice conversation is between 300 Hz and 4,000 Hz. Living in highly modern societies, humankind has been subjected to a variety of noise sources and their hearing capability is not as good as that of people living in primitive areas. Noise can interfere with human communication, cause discomfort and disease, and actually contribute to hearing loss, not to mention the psychological and emotional impact of excessive noise in the environment. High density urban living coupled with high technology, industry, and transportation contributes to high ambient noise levels in the environment. There seems to be a constant "hum" in many communities. Individuals adjust to urban noise levels and seem to suffer withdrawal symptoms when removed from the urban environment.

Obtaining Sound Level Data

Sound travels in waves, and can be measured in terms of pressure or intensity relative to the atmospheric pressure. The pressure unit used is called a bar which is equivalent to one atmospheric pressure namely 14.7 psi (pounds per square inch,). Since the bar is a very large unit, normally microbar— one millionth of a bar—is used in practice. The lowest air pressure that humankind can detect is 0.0002 microbars and the highest sound that can be listened to without causing any pain is 1,000 microbars. So, the human ear can detect pressure level range of five million. In fact humans can listen to sound up to 10,000 microbars without any immediate physiological damage.

In practice the microbar is not a very good measure because the range of numbers that one deals with are very small, which makes them inconvenient. Moreover, the response of the human ear is not on a linear scale. In other words, a sound level with twice the pressure value is not felt as twice the strength by the human ears. A better scale to use is the logarithmic scale, which matches the human ear response more closely. Sound is measured in decibels; a decibel (dB) is a means of normalizing the sound to human hearing capability and converting it to a logarithmic scale. To obtain the decibel value from the air pressure, first divide the air pressure by 0.0002—the minimum threshold level for human ears—then take the log of the ratio, and finally multiply it by 20. Therefore, a decibel is $dB = 20 \log (P/0.0002)$, where P is the actual air pressure in microbars. This implies that if the air pressure is equal to 0.0002 microbars, the dB is equal to zero, and if it is equal to 0.002 or 0.02 microbars, the dB level is equal to 20 and 40 respectively. This means when the air pressure changes by a factor of 10, the dB level changes by a factor of 2. In other words, for instance the air pressure levels between 50 dB and 60 dB is a factor of 10.

When more than one source of noise is present the cumulative effect of the sources must be determined. To do this, one cannot simply add the dB levels of different sources. This approach gives the wrong result. The proper method is to calculate the individual air pressures from the dB levels, add the air pressures, and then intake the dB level of the total. The cumulative effect of various noise sources will be much lower than the summation of the individual dB levels. For instance, if two sources of identical intensity are combined, the cumulative effect will be only 3 dB higher. Also, if there is a dominant source present with a number of smaller sources, then the cumulative effect will be only slightly bigger than the largest source. This is the masking effect, since the largest source is dominating the other noise sources. Therefore, it is possible to obtain data regarding sound levels, compare this to established criteria for potential annoyance, interference with communication, and hearing damage, and make a determination of sources and need for noise reduction. Reduction of noise may be addressed through the regulation of personnel (in the occupational setting) or in the systematic planning of land uses which incorporates concepts of noise control. The common methods of reducing noise impact are protection from exposure to noise and interception of noise by blocking, increasing the distance from the source, or reducing the intensity of the source.

Nature of Noise Pollution

There is a subjective element in this kind of pollution, more so than in other types of contamination. Noise has been defined as "unwanted sound or sound in the wrong place at the wrong time." (Ehlers and Steel 1965: 512) Undesirable noise can be the cause of speech or hearing interference, annoyance, and actual damage, depending on intensity. Essentially, noise is vibration conducted via a variety of media, including liquids, gases, and solids. Pressure variations are produced by vibrating objects operating in a medium which conduct sound. Sound varies according to frequency, duration, intensity, and pressure. The more intense and frequent a sound, the more likely hearing impairment may result. The frequency of sound is the timing (rate) of a cycle of low to high pressures, which are produced by its source, and is measured in cycles per second. The quantity of sound is referred to as amplitude and is measured in decibels. Loudness is human perception of sound's amplitude. Human perception of undesirable noise levels can be a significant determinant of health and well-being.

Type and Sources

Noise originates from numerous sources in modern day society. These may be point-sources (i.e., stationary) or line sources (i.e., moving or sequential points). Point-sources are residential, commercial, industrial, recreational, and agricultural. Line sources are streets and highways, railways, shipping lanes, and airways. Decibel levels of sound emission vary considerably by source, from a point-source of 20 dB in a quiet movie studio to a line source of 140 dB emanating from a jet plane as it takes off. In between one can find a point-source of 50 dB in a private residence up to a high point-source of 120 decibels emanating from a hard rock concert. The latter, while annoying to most neighbors, could be exactly the reason for concert goers to pay the high price of admission.

Noise levels also vary by land use patterns and time of day. Highly concentrated urban areas exhibit a much higher level of noise than suburban areas, and suburban areas have a higher level than rural areas. Noise levels reach their peak during daylight hours and are at their lowest during the night.

Equipment used for construction contributes greatly to excess noise. The type of noise pollution may be persistent and seemingly unending in rapidly expanding urban areas, especially in big cities undertaking urban renewal projects. Industrial machinery is well-known as a prime source of occupational injury to hearing, as well as other physical injury. Likewise, agricultural machinery is considered potentially hazardous.

Noise produced by cars, trucks, buses, utility and maintenance equipment, motorcycles, and recreational vehicles is a never ending source of annoyance in those areas where most people reside. Indeed, with an expanding, highly mobile population and a vast network of streets and highways, it almost seems impossible to escape vehicular noise. Commercial and private aircraft, especially jet powered craft, are universally recognized as a source of particularly bothersome noises. Railroads and rail transit systems (particularly street cars and elevated systems) create high decibel noise levels and can be especially annoying within the confines of the inner city. Plans to expand and develop new mass transit systems which link suburban areas to the core will, out of necessity, require consideration of noise pollution and its impact on humans.

Land Use Determinants

Certain land uses, by design or necessity, produce noise levels in excess of what might be considered desirable or comfortable. Industrial areas, junk yards, mass parking, train and aircraft terminal areas, and business and commercial centers are all examples of noise-producing land uses which are a significant aspect of human activity. Elimination of these land uses would solve the problem of noise pollution, but certainly would create other problems which society would not tolerate.

Architectural design and building construction that places some emphasis on the need to buffer noise can be very helpful in this regard. Landscaped areas or other buffers which separate residential areas from transportation arteries are also helpful. Engineered control of equipment and machines is a prime device for noise control. A survey of "noise flow" in the community can be invaluable in the planning of control mechanisms. Many communities have developed noise control ordinances to deal with this problem.

Consideration of noise-producing elements in the master planning of communities, combined with appropriate building and control regulations, would be the most cost-effective approach in the long-run. Different land uses require different levels of noise sensitivity. The noise sensitivity of land use is divided into four categories: (1) very sensitive for facilities such as theaters, hospitals, and churches; (2) sensitive for facilities such as family dwellings, resort hotels, and outpatient clinics; (3) moderately sensitive for facilities such as restaurants, professional offices, and general merchandising; and (4) insensitive for land uses such as agriculture, auto parking, and mining.

Exterior and interior noise levels are classified according to general use. One such classification scheme has five categories: (1) Category A (60 dB limit)—public areas such as amphitheaters, open spaces, and large parks or portions of parks where security is a key feature of the environment; (2) Category B (70 dB limit)—residences, schools, playgrounds, hotels, libraries, churches, public meeting areas, and recreation areas; (3) Category C (75 dB limit)—developed property which is not included in the above; (4) Category D (varying limit)—undeveloped land; and (5) Category E (55 dB limit)—interior of residences, schools, libraries, hospitals, auditoriums, churches, and public meeting rooms.

The aforementioned general guidelines are helpful in architectural and land use planning. However, federal, state, and local guidelines generally presented as noise control standards include an exterior noise level of 65 dBA and an interior noise level of 45 dBA. These are the levels which are most commonly mentioned for residences, schools, hospitals, and so forth. An example of a noise ordinance is an ordinance developed by Los Angeles County and is considered as a "first priority" within the noise element of the county General Plan. Section 403 of this ordinance states:

(a)   Unless otherwise herein provided, no person shall operate or cause to be operated, any source of sound at any location within the unincorporated county, or allow the creation of any noise on property owned, leased, occupied or otherwise controlled by such person which causes the noise level when measured on any property either incorporated or unincorporated, to exceed:

Standard No. 1:   The applicable exterior noise level from Section 403(b) for a cumulative period of more than thirty minutes in any hour
or
Standard No. 2:   The applicable exterior noise level from Section 403(b) plus 5 dB for a cumulative period of more than fifteen minutes in any hour
or
Standard No. 3:   The application of exterior noise level from Section 403(b) plus 10 dB for a cumulative period of more than five minutes in any hour
or
Standard No. 4:   The applicable exterior noise level from Section 403(b) plus 15 dB for a cumulative period of more than one minute in any hour
or
Standard No. 5:   The applicable exterior level from Section 403(b) plus 20 dB for any period of time.

(b)   The following noise levels (dBA), unless otherwise specifically indicated, shall apply to all receptor properties within a designated noise zone:

Noise Zone I: (Noise sensitive area)	Anytime, 45 dBA
Noise Zone II: (Single, double, or	10:00 p.m. -7:00 a.m., 45 dBA
multiple family- residential)	7:00 a.m. -10:00 p.m., 50 dBA
Noise Zone III: (Commercial)	10:00 p.m. - 7:00 a.m., 55 dBA
	7:00 a.m. - 10:00 p.m., 60 dBA
Noise Zone IV: (Industrial or manufacturing)	Anytime, 70 dBA

Also, Los Angeles County has adopted the following noise exposure limits for the industrial settings where the sound level (dBA) allowed is dependent on exposure time, as follows:

Duration per day: 8 hours	Sound Level: 90 dBA
Duration per day: 4 hours	Sound Level: 95 dBA
Duration per day: 2 hours	Sound Level: 100 dBA
Duration per day: 1 hour	Sound Level: 105 dBA
Duration per day: 1/4 or less hours	Sound Level: 115 dBA

Source: Environmental Protection Agency (1978). *Los Angeles County Noise Ordinance Protective Noise Levels*, Washington, D.C. (550/9-79-100).

Health Impacts

Humans react to excessive noise levels in either physiological or psychological terms. Annoyance and chronic irritability are psychological effects of noise pollution. Sometimes this leads to rather vigorous community action, as found in communities sited near major airports. Other effects include interference with speech communication and general uneasiness. Changes in a person's ability to hear and actual hearing loss may result from prolonged, consistent exposure to excessively high noise levels. For example, research has shown that hearing loss may result if an individual is consistently exposed to noise levels above 105 dB for several years in an occupational setting. Consistent exposure to moderate noise levels will not result in "conditioning" of the ear to adjust to intermittent higher noise level exposure. Excessive noise may also cause sleep disruptions, reduced work efficiency, and interference with normal personal relationships.

It should be noted that individuals differ in their sensitivity to noise effects. For example, actual hearing damage may occur at levels considerably lower than 105 dB. As hearing ability varies from person to person, the EPA's recommendations are made in terms of a critical percentage of the population ranked with superior hearing over the remainder. These recommendations are based on a 96 percentile, that is, based on providing protection for 96 percent of the people. It is assumed that people with poorer hearing than the 96th percentile are not affected by noise of typical levels, therefore, the recommendations protect virtually the entire population.

VISUAL POLLUTION

The least discussed form of pollution is visual, yet it can have a significant impact on one's sense of well-being. Visual blight consists of the incongruous, garish, monotonous, and inharmonious structures and objects that offend and alarm our visual senses. It can be further recognized that human's insensitive use of nature's contributions to this planet result in pollutants that the eye perceives. Only recently have humans acknowledged that their treatment and use of land have created visual blight. In the 1950s, city governments across the United States, especially in California, took steps to develop qualitative design standards in matters of land use that are directed at our visual perception and range from the minor detail to the very broad in scope. Many jurisdictions are adopting policies that require or encourage the use of only two or three earth tone colors in sign and building finish, rather than permitting the use of a wide number and variety of garish and/or inharmonious paint combinations and the application of contour earth grading, whereby the natural shape of a given hillside or slope is recognized when an area is graded for development rather than indiscriminate grading that scars the land for decades to come.

Types and Sources

Visual pollution is perceived in a variety of ways and is created when humans build something out of harmony with its environment.

Signs. Signs and billboards erected without regard to the sites or buildings can create incongruous visual relationships. Excessive verbiage to identifying a product or an occupant of a building can be unsightly as well as confusing. The use of multi toned paints on signs can likewise offend the visual senses. Widespread use of banners and pennants for advertising is often repetitive and distracting.

Subdivision tract homes. Row after row of tract homes built in many of our housing developments today contribute to a lost sense of place and to monotony in our lives. The sameness with which we build our residential habitat can create lasting visual pollution for years to come.

Grading. Indiscriminate bulldozing of our hills, valleys, ridge lines, and arroyos is seen as a true rape of the land. Ugly scars are left to be viewed by future generations in many hillside residential developments. These grading operations often leave cut banks or fill slopes that pollute the views for miles.

Land Use Determinants

An inability to understand and a disregard for the nature of relationships between how land is used and the state of the land often manifests itself in a visually blighted environment. Blight can be mitigated or eliminated through sensible land development techniques. Design standards, acceptable to most as a common denominator, can be developed. Reasonable minds can arrive at that which is considered good design as opposed to that which is offensive. Reduced verbiage on signs, reduced height and number of free-standing signs, undergrounding of utility lines, soft earth tones on our buildings, planting of trees, shrubs, and ground covers, and contour grading can contribute in a positive way to our environment.

It is doubtful that the effects of visual pollution can be quantified since visual perception is by nature subjective and qualitative. Nonetheless, our mental well-being and our resultant social behavior are, in many ways, influenced by what we see in our environment. The effects of visual pollution, as in noise pollution, can have cumulative effects on our health. While these effects may be subtle, they can strengthen over time. The result can be apathy toward the community.

4
Methods of Pollution Control and Zoning

Environmental and economic concerns are not mutually exclusive. Historically, people in the United States have given a high priority to convenience, production, and consumption of the goods and services which result from a mechanized and industrialized society. Relatively little attention was paid to the effects on air, water, soil, and general living conditions of the industrial society, which embraced the work ethic as a value model. Early public health movements initially focused on environmental sanitation and hygiene in our major cities. These efforts were linked to epidemics of virulent and dangerous diseases. At first, quarantine of the infected and persons suspected to be affected by causative agents became the major vehicles of control. Later, as research and epidemiological studies demonstrated the relationships among microorganisms, vectors, and man, other methods of control were developed.

Immunization, therapy, prophylaxis, and vector abatement became the paramount vehicles for control of the spread of disease. During the Great Depression, the war years, and even throughout most of the 1950s, Americans relaxed their concerns about environmental matters. Events in the 1960s and 1970s gave rise to a new concern for environmental quality and cleaner surroundings. Traditional methods of pollution control must be reinforced and strengthened, and new ones must be developed to meet future challenges. The public is demanding cleaner air and water, relief from congestion and excess noise, and a more pleasant environment. At the same time, the public still wants the economic and convenience benefits from industrialization. Greater efforts must be expended to accommodate these conflicting demands.

AIR POLLUTION CONTROL

The decade of the seventies was a significant one in the environmental movement in air pollution control in particular. Between 1970 and 1975, levels of sulfur dioxide declined by 30 percent in urban areas throughout the United States. A vast majority of industrial and municipal stationary sources of air pollution are in compliance with air pollution regulations promulgated under the CAA of 1970. This law establishes primary air quality standards relative to the different types and sources of air pollution. The purpose of these standards is to prevent significant deterioration of ambient air quality in areas where the air is cleaner than the requirements and its subsequent amendments. These standards are established for each of five major air pollutants (carbon monoxide, ozone, nitrogen oxides, sulfur oxides, and suspended particles). Since the late sixties, there has been a reduction of 85 percent in the level of hydrocarbon and carbon monoxide emissions from automobiles. Other problems still remain, however. Excessive carbon monoxide in New York and ozone in Los Angeles are problems which seem to defy resolution.

Primary air pollution control is designed to prevent the formation of pollutants at their source. This is achieved by changing fuels, raw materials, or production processes in pollution-generating industries, or introducing equipment which eliminates pollution. If technology does not offer a means of preventing the emission of pollutants, then secondary air pollution control devices can be used to dilute the level of pollution in the atmosphere.

Source control, such as the use of car exhaust filters or conversion to less noxious fuels, is thought to be the prime mechanism for a solution to air pollution problems. However, a combination of land use planning and zoning and source control provides the most effective solution. Planning solutions would include siting industrial plants downwind of residential, work, and recreation areas; separating industrial land uses from other land uses; providing open space buffers; traffic and transportation control; regulating plant effluent and manufacturing materials and processes; and requiring environmental impact studies and reports relative to building projects and proposed land uses.

Similarly, prevention and control of air pollution involves a combination of approaches and methods as follows: education of the public on source, impact, and control of air pollution; constant surveillance and monitoring of pollutants; development and enforcement of emission standards; registration and inspection of major sources; land use environmental reporting and zoning regulation; land use planning which considers air pollution effects of projects; imposition of legal and monetary sanctions against persistent offenders; and technical assistance and training on the need for and use of source control methods and techniques. The joint cooperative efforts of local, state, and federal government agencies, private industry, and the general public is essential to the proper management and planning of air resources.

WATER POLLUTION CONTROL

The typical approach to water pollution control consists of sewage systems and water treatment plants. Sewers are receptacles for domestic, commercial, and industrial waste water, and feed water into treatment plants for eventual discharge into oceans, rivers, or streams or in some cases, for recycling. The primary function of waste treatment is to accelerate the natural processes by which water purifies itself. Basically, this involves reliance on bacteria to digest organic matter in sewage.

Primary treatment is designed to remove solid waste material from water. Initially, sewage is screened to eliminate floating objects. Sewage then passes into a chamber where sand and grit settle. From this chamber, sewage moves to a sedimentation tank where suspended solids settle out and collect at the bottom of the tank as raw sludge. The remaining waste water is chlorinated to reduce smell and eliminate any disease-causing bacteria.

Secondary treatment eliminates additional organic wastes. This may involve either a trickling filter or an activated sludge process. A trickling filter is a bed of stones or synthetic material through which sewage passes following primary treatment. Bacteria on the stone removes organic material remaining in the sewage. The activated sludge process involves the use of bacteria-laden sludge mixed with air to produce the same results as filtration. It is estimated that up to 90 percent of biological waste can be removed by a combination of primary and secondary treatment methods. Toxic wastes from pesticide use, domestic chemical refuse, and other industrial processes are not amenable to the above biological based treatment approach. Chemical treatment methods include coagulation-sedimentation, carbon-adsorption, and electrodialysis. These methods are briefly defined below:

1. Coagulation-sedimentation or clarification involves chemicals called flucculants, which serve to bunch particles together into larger masses which are then relatively easy to remove. Over 90 percent of phosphates can be removed by this method.
2. Carbon-adsorption involves activated charcoal, which is capable of removing practically all of the organic matter that primary and secondary treatments miss.
3. Electrodialysis reduces dissolved salts by employment of an electrically charged pole.

Among other methods of treatment now under investigation, the land disposal or "soil system" shows promise as a land use related approach. This is essentially a biological method based on the waste disposal capability of the soil. As a first step, sewage is held in shallow lagoons where it is aerated to hasten bacteria action. Sludge then settles out, and is used as fertilizer on the land. The liquid waste is chlorinated and sprayed on the land. Purification is then achieved in natural filtration through the soil to underground water tables.

The Water Control Act and its subsequent amendments have established basic goals and national policy with respect to water quality. The main goals and policies established are:

- Discharge of toxic pollutants in amounts harmful to health should be prohibited.
- A high level of quality which provides for the protection and propagation of fish and wildlife which will provide recreation for humankind both in and out of water, should be attained.
- The discharge of pollutants into navigable waters should be eliminated.

In addition, effluent standards and water quality standards have been developed for various sources, and schedules have been developed for compliance. Although much progress has been made, particularly with publicly owned and operated treatment plants, new industrial source performance standards still remain to be developed.

CONTROL OF SOIL POLLUTION AND SOLID WASTE DISPOSAL

Solid waste material in the United States has increased annually and it is estimated to be in the billions of tons. Approximately 10 percent of solid waste results from residential, municipal, and industrial sources. One-half of these wastes come from agriculture, and the remainder are mineral wastes. Today, it costs over $1 billion to depose of this waste, and the cost increases every year. Common waste disposal methods include dumping, burying, incinerating, and ocean submersion. Each of these methods is potentially hazardous to the public's health. Open dumping is a nuisance which creates noxious odor and encourages breeding of flies and infestation by other insects and rodents. Burying waste, particularly in controlled and scientifically planned landfill sites is by far the best of commonly used methods. However, if this method is not well-planned and controlled, it will result in the production of undesirable gases which are to say the least obnoxious. Additionally, leachate caused by settling may pollute ground water supplies. Incineration, although a highly efficient approach, has the drawback of producing air pollution. Ocean dumping is considered extremely undesirable because of the negative effects on marine life and the food cycle, not to mention the ever present danger of flow back to shore.

A variety of alternative methods are being devised and tested throughout the nation. Through chemical, biological, physical, and thermal processes, it is possible to extract useful materials from certain waste streams. Cyanide and chromium can be treated with an oxidation-reduction process. Organic waste can be rendered harmless by predator microorganisms. Solid waste can be separated from liquid waste and waste brines can be evaporated. Toxic metals such as mercury, cadmium, and arsenic can be extracted by sulfur precipitation. It is even possible to separate, recycle, and recapture some metals. Pretreatment of chemical wastes from industry is exceedingly important. With proper treatment at the source, industrial waste material can be fed into municipal sewage systems. Linkages between industrial, commercial, and residential land use, with proper attention to the flow and treatment requirements of waste, need to be a formal component of community planning.

Resource recovery facilities based on the concept of salvage and reuse of valuable byproducts of waste disposal have been successful in many communities since the late seventies. Sludge from sewage is well-known as a fertilizer and soil conditioner. Sludge has been used to fertilize abandoned strip mining land, thus transforming desolation into fruitful agricultural ground. For nearly a century, vegetables have been grown on untreated sludge in Paris, France.

Control of the manufacturing, distribution, and use of toxic chemicals through government regulation is a major thrust at present. The TSCA of 1977 monitors and reviews the production of any new compounds which might be introduced. A chemical compound can be banned from the market if the EPA rules that it presents a clear danger to public health and safety. Thoughtful consideration of the need for solid waste treatment management, recreation, and open space should lead to creative land use planning and decision making, such as the planned conversion of closed landfill sites to a variety of scenic settings for public enjoyment.

NOISE POLLUTION CONTROL

Millions of Americans are exposed to noise levels which may cause permanent hearing damage. Surveys have indicated that over a quarter of the nation's production workers, principally in textile mills, lumber industries, and food production, are consistently exposed to noise levels in excess of 90 dB. Most recently, noise levels in communities near airports have resulted in aggressive, public action to bring about abatement of the problem. Excessive noise from construction activities, highway equipment, and household appliances and tools are amenable to source control. Consumer pressure can bring about necessary changes in most cases. Industry has been responsive to demands of the market and has taken steps to lessen noise levels of products and manufacturing processes. The Federal Noise Control Act of 1972 requires the EPA to assess environmental noise levels and promulgate standards to protect the health and well-being of the population.

State and local government officials are expected to assume leadership and responsibility for development of noise abatement programs and noise control. To assist in local efforts, the EPA has developed a program called ECHO, Each Community Helps Others, which includes the appointment of community noise advisors in various communities throughout the United States and uses this pool of expertise to assist other communities in the establishment of noise control programs. The Federal Aviation Administration (FAA) enforces standards governing aircraft noise with technical assistance from the EPA. Federal noise abatement programs have been highly effective in reducing truck and highway project noise. A particularly successful method is the construction of various types of barriers alongside highways and freeways to deflect noise away from residential areas.

In addition to community action, land use alterations, and technical assistance to the communities, noise control at the source can focus on reduction of vibration, enclosure of the source itself, or attention by absorption. Elevation, depression highways, dense landscaping, grade limits, and highway site planning with respect to other land uses are prime techniques for reduction of vehicular noise. Changes in aircraft design and operations, architectural design features such as insulating buildings near airports, and proper land use zoning in the vicinity of airports help to diminish the effects of airplane noise. Mufflers, structural buffers, and changes in machine design are major techniques of noise abatement in industrial settings.

VISUAL POLLUTION

In order to mitigate and eliminate visual pollution and promote quality development design processes and standards, community review boards were inaugurated during the 1960s and 1970s. Many jurisdictions now require that all multiple family, office, commercial, industrial, institutional, and some single-family residential developments be approved by a local design review board before building permits are issued. These boards must establish procedures, standards, and policies of review so as to avoid arbitrary and capricious decision making. Having done this, better development is occurring in our environment. Some of the standards that can be adopted for better control of qualitative development include the following: sites should be graded with due regard for the aesthetics of natural terrain and landscape; buildings and signs should be related to their sites; open spaces, parking, and pedestrian ways should be interrelated and harmonious; adjoining properties should be properly related to avoid excessive variety and monotonous repetition; and mechanical equipment, trash, and storage areas should be concealed from view.

Standards should include the fact that a community, through its development permit process, should endeavor to include a review of exterior design, materials, textures, colors, and minimum illumination. However, there should be no concern with these items when they are not visible from the boundaries of the site.

CATEGORIES OF LAND USE AND ZONING

A comprehensive plan for land use must systematically consider physical, social, economic, and ecological factors and should attempt to integrate these into a single whole that will enhance healthful and productive living. Individuals are insisting on clean air and water, pure food, freedom from distracting noise, decent housing, adequate recreation, and unpolluted land. At the same time, these individuals want the flexibility of using whatever mode of transportation is most convenient, low rents and housing prices, and freedom to pursue individual expression of the rights associated with property. A sound land use plan must consider these sometimes incompatible needs and achieve a balance which serves the overall public interest.

Prevailing past practices such as single-purpose planning for transportation arteries, housing, or commercial development must be broadened in scope to include environmental, socioeconomic, and cultural aspects. Planning must consider potential adverse effects of various land uses, and ensure, to the extent feasible, that plans are designed to enhance healthful living and community well-being. Examples of factors to be included in a well-balanced land use plan include provisions for rest areas, buffer zones, landscaping, effects of ingress and egress on adjoining communities, and communication needs in the planning of transportation systems; environmental influences during and after major construction projects, including erosion control, flooding, water, and air pollution, disposal of natural vegetation, and waste disposal; effects of recreational uses on water supplies, vegetation, air quality, and wildlife; impact of noise-originating land uses on the surrounding community; and influence of industrial and agricultural waste products on air, water, and soil quality. To address these issues, knowledge of the various major classification schemes for land uses, knowledge of zoning classification, and appreciation of the differences between land use and zoning categorization is required.

Land may be defined as any portion of the Earth's surface which is capable of ownership as property, including everything natural or human-made which is annexed to it. This definition relies heavily on the concept of ownership and property rights. Both land (*terra firma*) and water are embedded in this general definition. Land is immobile, finite, and essential to human existence. Land and land-based resources are limited in number, but the number of people and their needs for the land may be infinite. Therefore, the uses of land, property rights, and land use planning and control are sensitive and many times controversial issues. Land can be used for a variety of purposes, either singular areas or parcels of land is an old concept which is considered highly desirable. The multiple use of land may be employed temporarily, such as crop rotation over certain time periods, or simultaneously, such as combined residential, commercial, and recreational uses on a single parcel at the same time.

There are reversible and irreversible uses of land which must be considered in land use planning and decision making. Reversible uses are those which do not involve significant changes to the land's soil cover or landform. Irreversible uses are those which change the original nature or character of the land to the extent that reversal to its former use is nearly impossible for all practical purposes. Urban and industrial land uses are rarely capable of reversal. Agricultural and pasture uses are usually easily reversed.

LAND CHARACTERISTICS

Classification of land according to its basic characteristics does not consider human's use of the land, but rather views land in its natural state. Geological attributes, landforms and shapes, climate, soil characteristics, and vegetative features are considered natural aspects of the land. The classification schemes usually account for land characteristics in one of the ways illustrated below:

1. Geological attributes include bedrock and surface geology. Physical and chemical makeup of bedrock and the depth of subsurface rock formations are highly significant geological attributes in terms of potential land use. Bedrock formation is essential to the adaptability of the land for construction purposes. The fertility and permeability of soil depends to a certain extent on bedrock depth. This has significant ramifications when agricultural uses are contemplated. Surface geology is concerned with sedimentation from water movement, glacier rift, estuaries, deltas, and lake deposits which, along with organic matter, determine the nature and characteristics of soil. The structural features, depth, and makeup of surface soils have great influence over the types of land uses available. Some other areas of concern may relate to seismic problems and liquefaction.

2. Landforms and shapes include valleys, mountains, plains, plateaus, rivers and streams, coastal flat lands, and other topographical features of the land.

Geomorphology, the knowledge of topographical land features, is a field that involves geographical mapping, measurement, and land description. Land is measured horizontally and vertically, and described in terms of its natural features, dominant land use, and politico-cultural characteristics. Land surveys and landform maps are essential in real estate development and recording ownership. Horizontal maps depict only distance and location relative to the Earth's surface and are called planimetric maps. Maps which also contain elevation measurements and land contours are called topographic maps. These maps are key features in land use planning.

3.   Climate and weather include measurement of precipitation (rain and snow), wind (intensity and direction), humidity, cloudiness, temperature, and air pressure. Weather and climatic conditions are measured in terms of annual and seasonal averages and ranges of extremes. Prevailing climate mapped with land topography provides valuable information in land use planning. The knowledge of air movement is important in siting buildings, devising techniques for the control of grass and wood fires, controlling the flow and distribution of air pollution, and placement of windbreaks to protect cropland. Information regarding extremes (hurricanes, droughts, floods, tornados, etc.) is obviously important to land use decision making.

4.   Soil characteristics include organic content and disintegrating rock. Soil formation is a slow and tedious process, established by the effects of wind and water movement, and the works of myriad living organisms. However, soil erosion through human-caused or natural means can be quite rapid and devastating. A system for classification of soils has been developed by the United States Department of Agriculture (USDA), and is based on the origin of soils and soil properties. The classification scheme is the result of continuous soil surveys conducted by the USDA Soil Conservation Service. For approximately 7,000 areas dispersed throughout the United States, the service has grouped various soil types according to texture, fertility, surface depth, drainage features, slope of the land, and other characteristics. For each geographic area surveyed, soil is analyzed and categorized in terms of its origin, physical and chemical composition, color and tone, permeability, shape and texture, and other essential properties. This detailed information is graphically presented in map form and is highly useful in assessing capability of land for a variety of uses.

5.   Vegetative characteristics of land can tell us a great deal about combined influences of soil, climate, and topography on the land. Types of shrubs, weeds, plants, and trees provide a good indication of potential land uses. A general classification of land based on vegetation would include: grassland (i.e., meadows and plains); woodland (i.e., pine, juniper, and other species); forests (i.e., coniferous and deciduous trees); wetlands (i.e., tidelands, swamps, marshes, and so on); woody shrubs (i.e., chaparral and alpine); and tundra (i.e., vegetation found in extremely cold climates).

LAND USE CLASSIFICATION

Capability of various types of land for different uses by humans forms the basis of classification schemes, which have entirely separate meaning from those based on land characteristics. A generalized classification of major land uses in the United States, includes agricultural, pasture and range, forest, urban areas, special, and other uses.

Agricultural land includes the land used for crops or in rotation, farmsteads and farm roads. The USDA Soil Conservation Service has developed land classifications based on two broad categories, namely land suited for cultivation, classes I through IV, and lands not suited for cultivation, classes V through VIII.

- Class I includes land which has few restrictions on use. Land is nearly level, well drained, and has easily worked soil with low erosion hazard.
- Class II includes land having restrictions that limit choice of plants and/or requires special conservation practices.
- Class III includes severely restricted land which reduces choice of plants and/or requires special conservation practices.
- Class IV includes land having adverse limitations which restrict choice of plants, and/or requires very careful management.
- Class V includes land having low erosion hazard, but which has other limitations which reduce use to pasture, woodland, or wildlife food and cover.
- Class VI includes land having limitations which make the land generally unsuitable for cultivation.
- Class VII includes land having limitations which make the land unsuited to cultivation.
- Class VIII includes soils and landforms precluding use for commercial planting and restricts use to recreation, wildlife, or aesthetic purposes.

Pasture and range includes nonforest pastures in farms, grasslands, and nonforest grazing land other than what is considered farmland.

Forest land, both on and off farms, is generally classified according to natural tree species, referred to as forest type, and growth capacity measured in terms of the quality and volume of wood.

Urban areas include politically incorporated or unincorporated (noncities) geographically defined places having a population of 1,000 or more.

Special use includes airports, highways, flood control areas, railroads, military bases, and reserves, government institutions, industrial areas, and other related uses.

Other land uses are those of low agricultural use or other value, such as marshland, tundra, desert, swamps, and rocky places.

Multiple or Combined Land Uses

Since land is often subjected to combined uses, either over time or simultaneously, it follows that singular land use classification and land characteristics do not paint the entire picture. Mixture of variable land uses can both create and solve problems for humankind. In the planned multiple use of land it is critical that a proper balance be achieved which ensures compatibility of uses and does not lead to a devaluation of the total land area involved. Problems of balance, compatibility, and value are similar in kind with respect to both urban and nonurban land uses. The primary purpose in nonurban land use is to produce or provide, a crop, timber, wildlife habitat, open space, recreation, and so on. Urban land, on the other hand, is used primarily as a physical base to support a variety of structures. Since humankind has adapted land to meet their structural needs, it follows that urban land use is highly flexible. However, urban planning is charged with intense feelings and emotions, and great complexity because of the number of people involved and the diverse interests to be accommodated.

Sound land use classification based on multiple or combined uses should not only distinguish between urban and nonurban areas, but should also consider the dominant use according to the best combination of compatible uses. Since compatible uses vary according to location and other distinguishing characteristics of the land area, the best combination and dominant use will change over time and from site to site. With these thoughts in mind, a useful classification scheme might include elements related to urban or nonurban land use. Urban use can include residential, commercial, industrial, recreational, open space, agricultural, mining/ refining, public services, and transportation elements. Nonurban land use may include agricultural, pasture and grazing, wildlife preserves, forests, national parks, recreation, public services, mining/refining, and industrial elements.

It is possible to classify dominant land uses in accordance with the aforementioned elements; relating them to geopolitical units and ownership parcels. For any relatively large (i.e., 10 acres or more) area, mixture of land uses could be identified and geographically displayed as a map or series of maps, for instance, an unincorporated area which contains 5,000 acres, a residential population of 200 persons in a rural setting which contains a government-owned wildlife preserve, an active sawmill and lumber cutting operation, and a county operated park.

ZONING

Zoning is the practice of allocating different areas of a city for particular use and imposing limitations for some other uses. Certain aspects of zoning regulation have been in existence in the United States since its very early days. In 1639, the town of Cambridge, Massachusetts, had passed an ordinance requiring consent from the town mayor before a building could be erected. Moreover, no building was allowed in the outlying areas until all vacant spaces within the town had been filled. The heights of all buildings in the town had to be the same. Needless to say, such ordinances will be challenged in the courts today as unreasonable and excessive. By 1692 all Boston buildings were required to be constructed from brick or stone with slate or tiled roofs. Early building and land use ordinances grew out of town fires and other disasters. For example, gunpowder manufacturing plants were located in highly congested residential areas and accidents caused major fatalities among the residential population. In the 1900s many cities established minimum construction standards to reduce the risk of fires and other disasters, and sanitary codes were developed to address health hazards.

Zoning rules in their current forms began in the late nineteenth century in Germany and California. The motivation in Germany was to keep abattoirs (slaughterhouses) out of residential areas. In California, zoning laws started for the discriminatory purpose of restricting the locations of Chinese laundries.

By the early 1910s zoning ordinances started to distinguish between residential and industrial uses. The widespread adoption of zoning laws began after New York City passed ordinances to control the development and spread of skyscrapers throughout the city. The city established commercial, retail, and residential areas. This was accomplished by dividing the city into various specific districts where only particular types of buildings with related height limitations could be built. The new zoning laws assisted New York City to transform itself from a fungus-like web into an orderly, efficient, and organized city. In addition, the other motivation behind the zoning laws were creating a coherent system of land use.

The constitutionality of the new height limitations in New York City was challenged in the courts. However, in 1919 the Supreme Court upheld the city's power to set height limitation and eliminate nuisances near particular zones. Until the 1920s the courts were overturning zoning laws that where prohibiting nonnuisance land uses. This led to the practice of invoking eminent domain in many jurisdictions, that is, the right of development was taken away from the owners by compensating them based on benefits assessed. Remnants of eminent domain exist today in some parts of Kansas City, Minneapolis, and St. Paul. The zoning laws were fundamentally challenged by the landmark case of the *Village of Euclid* versus *Amber Realty Company,* where the U.S. District Court of Ohio ruled that the Euclid ordinances were illegal and unsupportable. However, in 1926 the Supreme Court overturned the decision by ruling that the ordinance was reasonable and constitutional. The breakthrough led to the promulgation of Euclidean zoning laws all across the country.

Euclidian zoning divided a city into geometric patterns of use districts. There were a minimum of three use designations—industrial, commercial, and residential. Residential was considered the highest zone followed by commercial and industrial. Zoning was organized in a hierarchial cumulative fashion where the residential district was exclusive, residential use was allowed in commercial and industrial districts, commercial use was allowed in the commercial and industrial districts, but not in residential districts. Finally, the industrial use was limited to the industrial districts. Special facilities such as funeral parlors, churches, schools, and so on were decided as special exceptions which necessitated ad hoc determination. Administrative variances were utilized in cases where zoning laws were creating an undo and severe hardship.

Government regulation of specific land uses to prevent incompatible uses and arbitrate competing demands among interested parties is referred to as zoning. In practice, land use classifications are developed in comprehensive land use plans and established by local ordinances. For each zone, regulations which stipulate the type of land use permitted are adopted by the local governing authority. This might be the city council, board of supervisors, or a unit of special purpose regional government. Legal action is necessary to establish, amend, or waive zoning requirements and is based on the general police powers of the state, which is normally delegated to local units of government. Although zoning is applicable to nonurban areas, its use is more prevalent in the urban setting where land use issues are more complex and intense. Zoning may dictate housing density, parcel size, height and use of buildings, aesthetic requirements, open spaces, and types of industry and commerce.

Performance standards included in most modern zoning ordinances are only one of the other provisions to achieve environmental quality; health, safety, and environmental ordinances are other examples. Variances from established zoning requirements and standards may be granted when special or unusual circumstances prevail on a given parcel of land or are associated with a certain development proposal. A variance application can be submitted to the local legislative body or its assignee when a modification of requirements or standards is sought. Variance approval should only be granted when specified findings of fact are made in association with the land parcel or its development. These findings usually involve unusual circumstances or hardship inherent in the land or the project that prevents or thwarts the implementation of the project. A finding should also be made that approval of the variance will not be detrimental to others and would be consistent with the jurisdiction's adopted policy plans. Unfortunately, many jurisdictions allow the variance approach to be used to grant special privilege to the applicant rather than to allow equity of development. Some jurisdictions grant use variances which permit an applicant to develop a use not permitted within the zone classification. Variances should be granted only to permit variations or modification in development standards, for example, reduced building setback, not commercial uses in residential zones.

Likewise, the special use sections above could read as follows: certain uses are better approved on a discretionary basis within a given zone classification rather than permitted as a matter of right. Many uses do belong in a given zone classification, for example, churches and schools should be developed in a residential zone because these uses serve the population of residential areas. But the nature and scope of these uses tend to suggest that they should not be permitted just anywhere in a residential area. There are many such special uses that a jurisdiction may wish to approve based on the traffic generated and other environmental characteristics associated with the scope and size of the project. These approvals are discretionary and follow a public hearing process.

Another zoning technique that is used to regulate development is transferrable development rights or transfer of development rights (TDRs). This zoning approach is used when a jurisdiction wishes to establish open space, agricultural, or historical preserves. To compensate the owner of the property whose land is designated for low intensity use or essentially no use other than preservation, a jurisdiction may separate development rights from the land so that development rights can be bought and sold on the open market.

The jurisdiction first must prepare a land use plan identifying those properties proposed for development and those designated for low intensity use. Next the jurisdiction spreads or assigns the number of development rights per acre equally among all properties effected by the program. While development rights are spread equally among all properties within the program area, their application is uneven based on the intensity of development for each property as prescribed by the plan. For example, higher density areas will require more development rights per acre when the property is proposed for development. Presumably an owner seeking to develop their property for the designated higher use will purchase additional rights from the property owner whose land is designated for little or no use. Under this program the nonuser or nondeveloper is compensated for not building on land designated for open space or agriculture. It is obvious that a market must be created in order that the sale and purchase of development rights occur.

The heightened concern for energy conservation, the increase in better mass transportation systems, and sound use planning are calling for programs of mixed use development. Mixed use is nothing new. During the late nineteenth and early twentieth centuries, many cities witnessed tremendous growth, much of which involved the mix of residential, commercial, and industrial uses in close proximity. Mixed use is being applied again and in many instances under one roof. This phenomenon reduces sprawl and eases transportation haul. Overall energy consumption can drop because of better utilization of utility infrastructure. The new mix is decidedly different than the old, however. Contemporary and proposed performance standards allow for the compatible mix. Better sound insulation, innovative architecture, and good use of landscaping encourages the melding of uses.

When a municipality passes a zoning ordinance but does not develop a map showing the precise zoning areas, this is called a floating zone. Amendments to the zoning ordinance in the form of a detailed map, where specific use is defined, provides structure to the ordinance and fulfills regulatory requirements. Contract zoning follows a similar approach but differs in that covenants and conditions (contractual requirements) are added to the ordinance at the time of actual use. These devices provide a great deal of flexibility in the implementation of zoning ordinances. Subdivision maps are also useful in achieving appropriate land use, since they provide important regulation pertaining to environmental health.

Another important factor that helped the promulgation of zoning laws was the Standard State Zoning Enabling Act (SZEA) which was published by the U.S. Department of Commerce in the mid 1920s. This document has been adopted in almost all states. Today even a small town or municipality typically has more than twenty different zones. Cumulative zoning practices have been abandoned, industrial districts and agricultural areas are exclusive zones now. There are a multitude of different zoning types such as floating zones, incentive zones, X zones, Q zones, and so on. The SZEA and the Standard City Planning Enabling Act (SPEA) provide power for planning, controlling subdivisions, regional planning, and maintaining official area maps.

Zoning Authority

The authority to exercise zoning ordinances resides with the states. Although some statewide agencies have the task of controlling certain aspects of land use, almost all states have delegated the authority to cities, towns, municipalities, and counties. However, for special land use zoning such as airports, flood plains, and so on the states have retained the authority to deal with such matters by special state legislation. Airport construction in many cases can be subsidized up to 50 percent by the federal government, if the zoning provisions around the airport preclude any interference, such as height restrictions along the flight path for the operations of the airports. Flood plain zoning is heavily influenced by the Federal Flood Insurance Act of 1956, which created exclusions and limitations for buildings on flood plains. Unlike airports, there is no financial incentive program offered by the federal government to stimulate such zoning laws. Most of them have been put in place as a result of damages inflicted by flood disasters.

Unlike other states, zoning functions in Hawaii are reserved at the state level and not delegated to the local governments. The Hawaii State Land Use Commission classifies land use as urban, rural, agricultural, and conservation districts. Other states have retained certain aspects of zoning. For instance, in Louisiana, the state has retained the power to zone in order to protect housing and redevelopment projects. Similarly, all large commercial, industrial, and mining operations require approval from the State Environmental Improvement Commission, and in Wisconsin the flood plains come under the jurisdiction of the State Department of Resources Development.

Although zoning laws address general purpose and land use issues, they will be deemed invalid by the courts if they are enacted for purposes which are beyond the scope of police powers. In theory, zoning ordinances are supposed to conserve the value of buildings and properties by introducing some level of stability and predictability: when a zoning law lowers the value of a property it will still be valid in most other cases. The only exception will be in very rare situations where the zoning law will drastically reduce the value of a property. Zoning also promotes traffic safety and enhances the flow of traffic, that is the location and width of streets, although not controlled by zoning laws, are heavily influenced by them. For instance, running major arteries through residential areas are avoided because they endanger children who might be playing nearby and crossing the streets. Zoning helps promote health and general welfare by providing adequate air and light, avoiding congestion. However, there are cases where zoning laws have been used in certain localities to exclude people from socioeconomic conditions.

Agricultural Zones

In the past, zoning was primarily concerned with urban areas. Therefore, only incorporated towns, cities and municipalities were effected. As cities grew larger and larger and continued to encroach on agricultural lands, the need for establishing land use for agricultural purposes became evident, in other words, people came to the realization that agricultural land is not an inexhaustible source. Agricultural zoning limits land use for intensive stock feeding, canneries, and residential single-family home use. Agricultural zoning is the least intensive and most exclusive zone where, with the exception of single-family residence, all industrial and commercial as well as intensive residential land use is prohibited.

Zoning for Public Use

Local zoning laws do not have any enforcement jurisdiction on federally owned properties. However, the Federal Land Use Act of 1968 encouraged federal entities to cooperate with local planning and zoning authorities. The underlying idea behind this action was to open up lines of communication between the federal entities and the local governments, and, to the extent possible, comply with the zoning ordinances. If the federal government is the lessee of a property, local zoning laws do not apply. On the other hand, any lessee of federally owned property is governed by the local zoning regulations.

The state-owned properties are not governed by the local zoning authorities also unless the state delegates that authority. So state properties are also immune from local zoning provisions. The local government sometimes deals with the issue of zoning for its own properties expressly. The idea is to examine whether the local authorities believe they are subject to some of the laws which they hold for the general population. There are many instances where local governments endorse certain types of land use for themselves, while they will not tolerate similar use for the general public. In addition to the above, other types of needs that should be addressed comprise land for schools, houses of worship, utilities, hospitals, funeral homes, and so on.

Schools. Schools generate a lot of noise, confusion, and traffic for adjacent properties. Although people want to be close to schools, being very close to any public enterprise can compromise the marketability of a residential property. So people want to be close to schools for convenience, but at the same time not be adjacent to them. Despite the negative impacts, most ordinances allow schools even in restrictive zoning districts. In communities where influential members apply political pressure, the exception may be schools that serve the mentally retarded or disabled.

Houses of worship. From a zoning point of view, the problem for houses of worship is similar to schools. They are a source of traffic congestion, noise, and confusion, which negatively impacts the value of residential properties. Although the constitution guarantees the freedom of religion, it is erroneous to presume that zoning laws do not affect such land uses. Zoning ordinances treat such facilities as commercial use which is allowed in residential areas by special permit.

Public utilities. There is no difference between privately owned or publicly owned utilities from a zoning provision. Sometimes utilities are protected from local zoning rules because of provisions in the state constitution. The majority of control varies between utilities and local authorities and stems from aesthetic considerations. For instance, many electrical utilities, especially for older developments, maintain overhead power distribution because of lower cost and ease of maintenance, even though municipalities prefer underground distribution systems and the elimination of aerial blight. However, major public utility facilities such as high voltage switching substations for transmission lines or main water pumping stations are restricted to commercial and industrial areas and are not allowed in residential districts.

Medical facilities. Medical facilities such as hospitals provide a critical public service for the general public. Despite the noise, traffic, and congestion that such operations generate, they are generally permitted in some residential zones. Hospitals may be excluded from single-family districts, however, they cannot be totally restricted from or near an entire community. One of the objections that many people have against hospitals in their neighborhood is that facilities are a constant reminder of disease and death. So, although medical facilities provide an indispensable service, few neighborhoods are hospitable to them.

Cemeteries and funeral parlors. Cemeteries are regulated by state laws and as such are not affected by local ordinances. There was an old Supreme Court decision that precluded cemeteries in a city. Funeral parlors are not normally allowed in residential areas but are usually located in commercial areas. Despite the important service funeral parlors provide to the community, many commercial zones try to block them because of unwanted traffic congestion and the depressing reminder of death.

Zoning Limitations

Zoning is a powerful tool that can affect land use. Other factors such as public investment in utility infrastructure (i.e., water and sewer distribution systems, roads, and so on) have a stronger influence on land use. Zoning can reinforce a pattern of land use and community development. For instance, communities that did not impose zone restrictions for residential areas have smaller shopping centers scattered throughout the neighborhoods while those who had very strict zoning laws ended up with many residential neighborhoods void of many basic services. It should also be remembered that if an area is zoned for a particular purpose, there is no guarantee that it might be fully utilized for that purpose. For example, many cities in the United States designate large areas for the needed infrastructure that can attract a reasonable number of users. To the disappointment of such cities many such areas remain vacant.

This means that zoning needs to look at the general framework of land use deemed beneficial for public interest. The ordinances need to have enough control to restrain land users from doing what they desire. Also, zoning laws should not prohibit all possible beneficial uses of land. Finally, zoning can only be successful if it is conducted within the context of the social, economic and environmental parameters of a community.

5
Legal and Legislative Framework of Environmental Protection

In Chapter 2 a number of relevant environmental laws concerning land use were introduced. This chapter takes that discussion further by looking at the overall legal framework. Understanding the structure of the legal system helps one realize that the environmental laws in the United States are more than a collection of unrelated pieces of legislation. They need to be seen in the context of an evolutionary process that has gone through complex changes over the past several decades. This chapter examines these laws within the context of our legal structure. In other words the laws should be compiled from practically all legal sources namely the U.S. Constitution, federal and state laws, local ordinances, regulations promulgated by many federal agencies, prior court decisions, new interpretations by the courts, and any relevant treaties.

Federal laws are initiated in Congress by the introduction of a bill either in the House of Representatives or the Senate. The bill is then referred to the appropriate committee for examination, debate, and recommendation. When the committee chair feels they have reached a consensus, the bill is put in the docket to be considered on the floor of the House or Senate. If the House and Senate pass different versions of the bill, then a joint conference committee deliberates the topic further until the difference is resolved. Afterwards, when both the House and Senate pass the bill, it goes to the president to be signed into law. If the president does not agree with the bill, he vetoes it. A presidential veto can be overturned if a two-thirds majority in Congress supports the bill.

Laws passed by Congress and signed by the president are sometimes challenged in courts. Challenges usually deal with the constitutionality of new laws. The underlying basis of the legal system in the country is British Common Law. Common law addresses civil action as well as criminal action to redress the breach of any individual or the general public. Most land use related to environmental issues deals with tort laws as both civil and criminal liability.

TORT

A tort is a civil wrong which is committed by one party against another. It is commonly raised when one party has a duty to avoid causing harm to others because of an omission. So when a failure of action by a party results in inflicting harm through carelessness, it constitutes a tort action. The plaintiff can file action against the defendant and seek remedy for restitution. Many environmental wrongdoings are litigated as tort cases. It is important to note that the defendant action or lack thereof was not willful and with malice. The presence of will and malice may lay the grounds for criminal proceedings in addition to civil tort action. There are generally three categories of torts, namely, intentional, negligence, and strict liability. This chapter limits the discussion to torts related to land use.

Therefore, the intentional tort relating to our discussion primarily relates to trespassing. There are two types of trespass, namely, trespass to land and trespass to chattels. The first one addresses entering someone else's property without permission or a legal right to do so. For instance, a coal fired plant dumps dust and coal particles onto a neighboring property, or flying over someone's property at low altitude causing undue noise and interference are examples of trespass to land. Trespass to chattels refers to injury or interference with someone's ownership of a property and involves the destruction of property using force either by taking possession or refusing to surrender possession.

Negligence is defined by *Black's Law Dictionary* as "the omission to do something which a reasonable man, guided by those ordinary considerations which ordinarily regulate human affairs, would do, or the doing of something which a reasonable and prudent man would not do." The term "negligence" refers to a careless act on the part of a defendant that imposed unreasonable risk or harm upon another party. One of the main differences between negligence and intentional tort is with an intentional tort, the possibility of inflicting harm is almost certain; with negligent tort the defendant does not really desire to harm the victim. There are four elements in a negligence tort. First, the defendant must have a duty that would require a certain level of care to avoid undue risk. Second, the defendant fails to take the reasonable care. Third, the defendant's carelessness can be linked as the proximate cause of the harm suffered by the victim. Fourth, the victim actually suffered some damage. A typical negligence example related to land use may be polluting a neighboring property by not following expected environmental safety rules.

Strict liability relates to a special kind of negligence which states that, due to the dangerous nature of an activity, a landowner has a responsibility to exercise utmost care. For example, if a landowner keeps a wild animal and this animal attacks people or livestock, the owner of the wild animal is liable under strict liability. Similar actions have been filed against companies who deal with very dangerous substances such as lethal chemicals or radioactive materials and, through accidents, have damaged neighboring properties. There are many examples in the court dockets of federal, state, and local courts dealing with land use tort cases. A sizable number of these involve environmental laws.

ENVIRONMENTAL LIABILITIES

Environmental laws were established to safeguard against undue harm to humans and nature. Failure to comply with these laws results in civil or criminal liabilities. The primary reason for imposing liability is to create behavior patterns that encourage compliance to the law. It also serves as a deterrent for those who might be tempted to violate the law. Moreover, it serves to identify the guilty party and hold them financially responsible for damages. Finally, the law creates an avenue where responsible parties are required to compensate for damages inflicted on any single or group of individuals who sustained injuries. In addition to the compensatory damages, depending on the nature of the violation, there could be punitive damages assessed on a violator. This is determined based on the gravity of offense, the culpability of the violator, and the extent of the damages or injuries inflicted. Liability may be assessed against an individual, a corporation and/or the officers of a corporation. When officers of a company are in a position to prevent an accident, they can be held criminally liable even if they did not have any direct knowledge or role in the act. In the past decade the number of prosecutions of company executives have increased significantly. To put this in the proper context, let us look at the historical aspect of land management as it relates to environmental laws.

Successful land management and environmental protection require the judicious use of authority and governmental control. This means that both private and public rights must be duly recognized and that authority must be exercised in proper respect to balancing the needs of individuals and land resources. Supremacy of humans over the land is founded upon a long-standing Judeo-Christian-Islamic tradition. Yet this concept cannot justify improper conquest of the land or harmful exploitation of natural resources.

The same tradition that forms the basis of our notion of dominion over the land also requires that we exercise stewardship over the land. Stewardship, in the Judeo-Christian-Islamic sense, means assumption of responsibility to hold the land in trust on behalf of the Creator. Land is not owned, in the absolute sense of the word, but held in trust. The trustee is entitled to certain rights of use of the land, including access by tenure to the exclusion of the others. This concept of "ownership" has carried over to modern times. Present day landowners in the United States hold many rights to use of their land, but a superior power (government) holds certain rights in reserve. Government retains the right to tax property, to condemn property if it is in the public's interest (eminent domain), and to restrict freedom of landowners to use their land as they desire, if necessary, to abate a nuisance or ameliorate safety and sanitary hazards. These reserved rights are highly significant governmental controls and restrictions on private land use. Also, land which is not privately owned automatically belongs in the public domain. The government grands land title; land reverts to government if taxes are not paid, land is abandoned, or there is no heir.

Both federal and state governments have constitutional restrictions on their power over private property. The right to fair and just compensation under eminent domain, due process of law, equal protection under the law, and the right of unrestricted travel of citizens have an impact on land use laws and regulations. Eminent domain requires a finding that the taking of property (either in whole or in part) is required for public use. Exercise of general police power is contingent on the notion that the public interest will be served, that is, such action is needed to promote public health, welfare, and safety. Government may enact laws and regulations which restrict or limit an individual's use of private property, if such an action is found to promote or otherwise enhance public health and welfare. During the seventies, the federal government was quite active in establishing legislation affecting land use and environmental protection. As with most domestic legislation, federal initiatives provide guidance and financial incentives to enable and encourage the enactment of comparable state and local efforts.

NATIONAL ENVIRONMENTAL POLICY ACT (NEPA)

Perhaps the most significant legislation passed in our lifetime, which impacts on the health aspects of land use is NEPA in 1970. The purpose of NEPA was to develop a national policy that encourages productive and enjoyable harmony between man and his environment. NEPA called for the creation of a CEQ, charged with responsibility to analyze the environment, develop environmental policies and programs, coordinate federal efforts in the environmental area, assess environmentally related problems, and determine ways and means of solving them. A prime vehicle to ensure environmental consideration in government policy and action is the requirement that each federal agency must prepare a statement of environmental impact in advance of each major action, recommendation, or report on legislation that might have a significant effect on the environment. A wide variety of actions, programs, and projects are subject to this requirement, including but not limited to the following:

- Highway construction projects
- Nuclear power plant construction
- Jet aircraft runway construction
- Pesticide spraying over large areas
- River channeling and bridge construction
- Oil and gas pipeline development
- Disposal of munitions and other dangerous substances

Environmental Impact Statement (EIS)

An EIS must assess in detail the potential environmental impact of an activity and alert the public, the Congress, and the president of the potential environmental consequences of that proposed action. Federal agencies must prepare these impact statements on major and environmentally significant actions, such as proposals for legislation, analysis and reports on legislation, continuing activities and projects undertaken or supported by a federal agency, and policy decisions, regulations, and procedures.

Every EIS includes the following:

- Description of the proposed action, which includes specific data to allow an assessment of potential impact on the environment
- Evaluation of the possible influence on ecological systems which may result from the action
- Specification of unavoidable adverse environmental effects
- Discussion of alternative courses of action which could minimize adverse impact
- Assessment of the cumulative, long-range impacts in comparison to the short-term impacts in relation to productivity
- Description of any irreversible commitment of resources, which may result from a proposed action or program
- Discussion of problems or objections raised by the public or greater governmental agencies and private organizations which arise during the review process

Environmental Factors

The EIS process provides opportunity for the public and interested parties to participate in the decision making process. Many areas are considered important in the analysis of environmental impact. A comprehensive sampling of significant factors would include the following:

- Preservation of scenic coastal areas, rivers, lakes, streams, and refuges for waterfowls
- Use of herbicides, pesticides, and other potentially toxic substances
- Weather modification
- Air and water pollution
- Influence of electric, gas, and nuclear power generation and transmission
- Environmentally sound development of transportation arteries
- Reclamation of mineral lands
- Consideration of historic locations
- Development of fossil fuel and natural gas energy sources and distribution systems
- Handling and disposition of hazardous materials
- Solid waste disposal and sewerage
- Soil and plant life, erosion and sedimentation
- Noise abatement and control measures
- Contamination of food by additives and other chemical contamination
- Housing and other community development and planning
- Rodent and vector control
- Radiation effects on health
- Protection of wildlife

Highway construction, flood control, and energy-related projects have constituted the largest number of EISs to date. There has been minimal influence on land use planning in general, particularly in urban areas. Economic factors still prevail in planning and decision making in the development of urban and suburban communities.

NATIONAL CLEAN AIR ACT (CAA) OF 1970

The National CAA of 1970 calls for the development of air quality throughout the nation under the leadership of the EPA. The standards specify the maximum allowable concentration of major pollutants according to two designated criteria: (1) to protect the health of human beings and (2) to safeguard the public's welfare, protect plant and animal life, enhance visibility, and prevent damage to property. Pollutants singled out for control efforts include carbon monoxide, particulates, hydrocarbon, sulfur oxides, nitrogen dioxide, and photochemical oxidants. Under the CAA, each state is required to develop and implement plans for the purpose of meeting and sustaining the EPA standards.

Each state is geographically divided into air quality control regions, and each region is classified according to the level of air pollution found. State plans for regional air pollution control must include consideration of land use and transportation factors where these are related to ambient air quality standards. These factors come into play during review of construction proposals involving new stationary and indirect sources of pollution, development of air quality maintenance components of plans, and through programs for the prevention of air quality deterioration. Every state plan assesses the location of every new or significantly modified existing stationary pollution source. Stationary sources include steel mills, smelters, and fossil fueled power plants, which emit pollutants through a stack. Use of regulatory authority under the provision of the CAA can indirectly affect land use via a planning and review process which can influence the location of industrial plants.

Preconstruction review of indirect pollution sources relates to highways, airports, and other activities that attract mobile sources of air pollution. The planning and review process is much the same as that used in the preconstruction review of direct source. The EPA or a state-designated agency approved by the EPA is required to assess plans for proposed airports, highways, shopping centers, and parking facilities. Obviously, this authority allows tremendous potential for impacting land use plans and decisions.

The CAA not only requires that ambient air quality standards be attained, but that the standards be maintained and not be allowed to digress. Since population growth and urban development most certainly add pollution sources, state plans to implement provisions of the act must contain air quality maintenance components. The maintenance components should be developed in such a manner as to ensure that projected regional growth and development will be compatible with maintenance of national ambient air quality standards. For those regions where analysis indicates potential violation of standards, the state submits a ten-year plan of maintenance for the prevention of those violations.

Programs for the prevention of the deterioration of air quality must be developed by states and the EPA. Degradation of ambient air quality should be prevented through control of stationary pollution sources. Air quality regions are assigned priority ranking according to permissible levels of pollution by type of pollutant, and plans (including provision for monitoring) must be established to ensure that the levels are not exceeded.

Another element relating to the CAA is the development of the National Emission Standard for Hazardous Air Pollutants (NESHAP) program by the EPA. This program regulates the emission of asbestos in the ambient air by manufacturing, building, demolition, and renovation activities. Asbestos is a known carcinogen when the fibers become airborne and are inhaled by humans. Asbestos is found in nature. Because of the very desirable fire resistant characteristics of asbestos, the use of asbestos proliferated in a large number of construction materials. Today, there are more than 100,000 different types of construction materials that have been used in the industry for the past half century. This is one of the main reasons why the cost of many demolition or renovation projects in construction have been skyrocketing.

WATER POLLUTION CONTROL ACT

Historically, the first federal law dealing with the discharges of pollutants to surface water was enacted in 1899. These early legislations dealt with safeguarding navigation in waterways. Water quality standards were addressed for the first time in the 1965 Water Quality Act, which directed the states to develop allowable concentration levels for different contaminants. Later amendments to the Water Pollution Control Act in 1972 were designed to "restore and maintain the chemical, physical and biological integrity of the nation's waters" (Knopman and Smith 1993: 18). The act calls for a set of six national policies which, taken together, provide for accomplishment of the goal established under the act.

1.   Elimination of pollution discharged into all navigable waters by 1985.
2.   Achieve water quality which provides for the protection and propagation of fish, shellfish, wildlife, and for recreation in and on the water by 1983.
3.   Prohibit the discharge of toxic pollutants.
4.   Provide federal financial assistance to construct public waste treatment works.
5.   Establish areawide waste treatment management planning processes to control pollution sources.
6.   Provide for research and demonstration efforts to develop antipollution technology.

Responsibility for implementation of these policies is a federal-state partnership under the leadership of the EPA. The program designed to meet requirements of the act is divided into two parts: (1) point-source control, which focuses on sources such as sewage treatment plants and industrial sites where the source is confined and (2) nonpoint-source control, which focuses on sources which are dispersed in nature, such as runoff from mining operations and agricultural sites. The Water Pollution Control Act provides for a continuous state and areawide planning process and a program to fund planning and construction of municipal sewage treatment plants.

Point-source control implementation calls for the establishment of effluent standards for various types of polluters, the employment of control technology to limit pollution according to these standards, and the establishment of a permit program for enforcement and monitoring effluent restrictions. Nonpoint-source control implementation calls for the development of comprehensive areawide plans which provide for the control of nonpoint-source pollutants, protection which may cause pollution.

SIGNIFICANT LAND USE LEGISLATION

Land speculation and dishonesty in real estate development and sales relating to interstate transactions have moved the federal government to pass legislation for the protection of real estate purchasers and, indirectly, to protect haphazard land use. The Interstate Land Sales Full Disclosure Act (1969) was passed by Congress to regulate interstate commerce (especially mail advertisement and orders) involving the sale or leasing of subdivision lots. The law requires that any promoter, developer, or agent engaging in interstate land deals register with the U.S. Department of Housing and Urban Development (HUD) and file a report disclosing information about the subdivision in sufficient detail to give buyers full knowledge of the property, including any negative factors which may influence title or use of the land. This information and report becomes part of the official public record, and is available for review by any interested party. Although there are many exceptions to and exemptions from requirements of the act, and the law is limited to situations involving interstate commerce, it does present opportunity to review certain proposed land uses and allow some assessment of potential adverse impacts on health and the environment.

The Securities and Exchange Commission, acting under authority of the Securities Act of 1933, requires registration and a public report on any proposed condominium offering that presents an investment opportunity through use of rental pool arrangements. Under the law, this type of transaction is considered to be a security, and thereby subject to regulation by the Securities and Exchange Commission. Since condominium project development is becoming increasingly popular in the United States, and projects are found not only in urban and resort areas but in suburban and rural areas as well, the reporting requirements present yet another opportunity for public review and assessment of land use.

Coastal Zone Management

The Coastal Zone Management Act of 1972 was designed to protect and preserve resources along the coastlines of the United States. Essentially, this legislation provides funding to states for the establishment and maintenance of land and water use controls and comprehensive land use management plans for coastal areas. These plans, developed by affected states and submitted to the EPA for approval, must contain the following provisions:

- Identification of affected coastal zone boundaries
- Definition of permissible land and water uses within the zone which have influence on coast water
- Identification and description of land and water use control methods to be employed

- Priority guidelines on land and use relationships among local, regional, state, and federal agencies

National Flood Insurance Program

The National Flood Insurance Program, established in 1968, was designed to encourage flood protection via provision of flood insurance subsidized by the federal government. In addition, local community participation in the development of land use plans and controls within flood prone areas is encouraged through the provision of federal data and guidance. The lack of planning by localities in flood plains led Congress to strengthen the planning aspect of the program by adopting the Flood Disaster Protection Act of 1973. This act provided for sanctions to encourage land use planning. Under its provisions, federal financial aid will be denied for acquisition of, or construction on, property which is located in areas designated as having flood hazards, unless the local community participates in the National Flood Insurance Program, and complies with its land use planning and regulation provisions. A further sanction prohibits lending institutions from making loans on property unless the community participates in the National Flood Insurance Program.

Multiple Use and Sustained Yield Act

The first comprehensive public land use management legislation was the Multiple Use and Sustained Yield Act of 1960. Under this law, the secretary of agriculture is directed to operate and develop renewable surface resources of national forests for multiple uses and sustained yield of products and services derived from them. In the exercise of multiple use, the relative value of the various resources will be considered. In addition, interested state and local government agencies may work cooperatively with the federal government in the development and management of national forests. The concept of multiple use has become popular as an approach to bringing about harmony between human needs and resource use.

Underground Storage Tank (UST) Rule

The RCRA of 1976 called upon the EPA to develop rules to regulate USTs. By late 1988, the final rules relating to UST went into effect. At that time, according to an EPA survey, there were more than two million USTs nationwide. The motivation for the new law was to control and regulate leaks in underground tanks and, over time, phase out existing single wall tanks by the late 1990s. The reason why a separate law was passed concerning USTs is first, because of the large number of tanks, and second, when a tank leaks it not only pollutes neighboring soil, but the chemicals might migrate and pollute aquifers. Therefore, the negative environmental impact of leaky USTs can be quite severe. Two categories of tanks were exempted from the UST regulations—heating fuel storage tanks on a premise where the fuel is used for heating purposes and fuel oil tanks on farms that are 1,100 gallons in capacity or smaller.

The UST rule also empowered the EPA to impose civil penalties and assess fines of up to $10,000 per day per tank for any violation. Basically the UST rule required every owner and operator of USTs to report the presence of the tanks in an effort to develop a database for the location of all tanks. In almost all cases, the information is reported to the state, county, or other local government. In addition, the above entities are required to report any suspected releases, spills, confirmed releases, and any corrective action taken. For any damages to a third party resulting from an accidental or intentional release of chemicals, the owners and operators of the tanks are financially liable.

There are a number of other requirements that tank owners and operators must comply with. Records of fuel additions and dispensing must be kept and the tank level periodically measured to determine any possible leaks. To safeguard against any small long-range releases of fuel, the installation of detectors in the soil connected to a monitoring system is necessary. The law also requires periodic testing, calibration, and maintenance of the detection system. All single wall USTs must be removed by 1998. Finally, it should be mentioned that the UST rules also apply to all pipes and valves as well.

Oil Pollution Act (OPA)

The Federal Water Pollution Control Act of 1972 was one of the first major laws that addressed oil spills from tanker vessels. Later in the same decade, the Trans-Alaska Pipeline Authorization Act, the Deep Water Port Act, Port and Tanker Safety Act, and the Outer Continental Shelf Land Act Amendments addressed the strict liability and other compensation issues relating to major oil spills. Despite all of these laws, the debate continued for the next twenty years. In the meantime, California, Maine, and Pennsylvania enacted oil pollution laws at the state level. Moreover, the other twenty-four coastal states passed specific oil spill laws. In March of 1989, the Exxon *Valdez* accident in Alaska heightened public concern over the environmental impacts of accidents involving oil-carrying vessels, and, in response to these concerns and the outcry of environmental groups, Congress enacted the OPA in 1990.

The OPA consists of nine titles that deal in more specific terms with oil pollution liability. This is far more comprehensive than any other domestic or international law in existence concerning this topic. Title I specifically deals with strict liability relating to oil spills; it includes a comprehensive list of damages relating to spills. Title IV empowers the federal government to manage the cleanup process. The other seven titles deal with implementation and other general issues relating to oil spills, including appropriate international conventions. The civil penalty of the OPA includes compensatory damages relating to impacts upon natural resources, property and real estate, earning capacity, and other related matters. On the criminal side, the new law increased the prior fine of $10,000 and one-year imprisonment to a fine of $250,000 and five-years imprisonment for individuals and a $500,000 fine for institutions. Executives of corporations who are in a capacity to impose preventive measures can be held civilly and criminally liable for failure to exercise their fiduciary responsibility.

Safe Drinking Water Act (SDWA)

In 1974, Congress enacted the SDWA in an effort to ensure the quality of drinking water for all citizens and to protect underground aquifers from contamination. This law is different in a very important way from other environmental laws, that is to say, other environmental laws hold the polluters accountable for contaminating sources, here the suppliers of drinking water are liable and must ensure a prescribed level of quality. This law has a very direct impact on public health. Empowering the EPA to regulate aquifers is equally critical, as more than 50 percent of drinking water for the general public and 95 percent of drinking water for rural populations comes from these sources. In this regard the EPA was able to designate particular aquifers as sole source aquifers (SSAs) thus prohibiting projects that would contaminate these valuable drinking water sources. So in this regard, this law supplemented the RCRA and CERCLA in the protection of ground water from contamination.

This law empowered the EPA to develop two drinking water standards for the country. These were the National Primary Drinking Water Regulations (NPDWR) and the National Secondary Drinking Water Regulations (NSDWR). The first regulation dealt with health and safety aspects while the second addressed issues such as odor, appearance, and other aesthetic qualities. The act directed the EPA to develop guidelines and regulate eighty-three contaminants that could be found in drinking water by 1989. In 1988 Congress directed the EPA to identify twenty-five other contaminants that might be found in contaminating drinking water and negatively impact human health.

The EPA defines contaminants as carcinogenic or noncarcinogenic. Maximum contaminant level goal (MCLG) threshold for substances which have no known carcinogenic effect was set at levels where there is no known adverse health impact. For known carcinogens, the MCLG is set at zero. One of the contaminants that has received a lot of coverage in the media in the past few years is lead. The source of lead in drinking water comes from leaching out and the washing of lead in solder joints; Congress phased out the use of lead as an additive in solder and flux.

As mentioned earlier another role of the EPA is to regulate the underground water aquifers. It is important to recognize that the SDWA approaches the issue very differently than the CWA. The CWA controls contamination by holding the polluters liable resulting in controlling such problems at the source. The SDWA controls the integrity of water well structures as a means of safeguarding the aquifers through the Underground Injection Control (UIC) program. The EPA has divided the water wells into five classes based on the severity of the potential problems and the level of regulation. Moreover, with the SSA authorization, the EPA can bar federal financial assistance to any development project that threatens to damage the SSA.

Comprehensive Environmental Response, Compensation, and Liability Act (CERCLA)

The passage of the RCRA addressed the disposal of hazardous substances in the environment. After passage of the RCRA, the country still had hundreds of sites with very serious environmental liabilities totaling billions of dollars. In response to this concern, in 1980 Congress passed CERCLA, commonly known as superfund legislation. The motivation behind CERCLA was to tie hazardous sites to entities that owned hazardous materials, thus holding them liable for cleanup and remediation. To define CERCLA further, in 1986, Congress passed the Superfund Amendments and Reauthorization Act (SARA), which addressed the issue of response and remedial problems and the division of financial liability among individual polluters of a single site. Moreover, another provision of SARA was the Emergency Planning and Community Right-to-Know Act (EPCRA), which required the states to develop plans for possible accidents relating to large releases of chemicals and distribute the information relating to hazardous chemical facilities to the community. The highlights of CERCLA include remedial, liability, and settlement issues as well as reporting requirements.

An important element of CERCLA is the provision to exclude the cleanup of hazardous petroleum waste sites. This implies that any pollution resulting from abandoned service stations or underground fuel tanks are not covered by CERCLA. Based on this rule the EPA was directed to develop a National Priorities List of these sites that will come under this legislation. The major criteria for placing a site on the list is based on the severity of the site and the danger it poses to the environment and to public health and welfare. Other factors that impact the priority of site are the probability of contamination of the ambient air or drinking water sources.

From its inception CERCLA has been very controversial environmental legislation. Critics have called it a huge burden on U.S. industry because it negatively impacts corporate competitive advantage by diluting its ability to invest. Many complain that in the past fifteen years most of the funds have gone to pay legal fees rather than to actual cleanup. The funds expended relating to CERCLA have surpassed $5 billion and it is hard to objectively claim any significant success in cleaning up a sizable part of the problem. With all of the projected rumors at the federal level, the prospect for future implementation and successes of this legislation look very bleak.

CONCLUSION

Environmental laws pertaining to land use are a complex web of very complicated legislation at the federal, state, and local levels. It is quite difficult, if not impossible, for most individuals to get a handle on all aspects of these laws. Many of the basic issues of infringements on the rights of states as well as the rights of individuals remain at the center of controversy. It is hard to believe that any breakthrough is in sight. In 1994, Congress started a concerted effort to review or change some of these environmental laws to become less regulatory in nature and more encouraging to business development. The results of these efforts and their subsequent outcome will not be known for decades to come. The balance between environmental and health protection and economic development is delicate and interactively complex in nature. Therefore, careful analysis and thoughtful actions must constitute the core of any decision making process relative to any review of existing environmental laws and regulations.

6
Role of Government in Environmental Protection and Land Use

As legislation is passed and regulations are promulgated, appropriate action does not necessarily follow. Land use, environmental planning, and decision making are usually implemented at the state and local levels of government. Provisions in the U.S. constitution reserve domestic power and authority for the people at the state level. State governments are also subject to state constitutions which establish executive, judicial, and legislative functions very much like those established at the federal level. Except for matters dealing with interstate commerce and issues of clear and unquestionable national interest, the U.S. government limits domestic activity to efforts which support state actions. This usually takes the form of financial and technical assistance, research and training, development of uniform guidelines and standards, and organizational coordination. State governments implement land use and environmental protection programs under constitutionally derived general police powers. More often than not, these powers are delegated to the local units of general or special purpose government.

Land use planning and management is normally performed at the municipal and county (for unincorporated places) levels of government. Environmental protection programs are generally not as well established as land use programs and, as such, may reside in a variety of local or regional agencies. Most local health departments contain an environmental management component, normally with an emphasis on sanitation and hygiene. The national environmental legislation established in the past two decades has been implemented through the organization of areawide or regional units of special purpose government. This phenomenon recognizes the obvious fact that air, water, and soil pollution issues and problems do not respect the usual political boundaries. This chapter addresses the nature and structure of federal, state, and local interrelationships in land use planning, management, and environmental protection. It examines typical state and local efforts to implement land use and environmental protection programs to demonstrate how major areawide or regional efforts coordinate land use and environmental protection.

Halting and reverting the types and volume of pollutants which are hazardous and harmful to health and well-being requires a concerted effort at various levels of government with concomitant cooperative efforts by the private sector. All have a high stake in preserving health and promoting the general welfare of our population. Early efforts in public health and environmental sanitation were local. The works of Lemuel Shuttuck in Massachusetts during the middle 1800s set the stage for development of environmental protection programs, which initiated the public health movement in the United States. However, it was not until the 1930s that significant federal legislation was passed which addressed health and welfare problems at the national level. Even then, federal initiatives were limited to social welfare, unemployment, and labor issues. National concern for health and environmental services is a relatively recent phenomenon which began after World War II and became intensified during the decades of the 1960s and 1970s. By the end of this chapter the reader should hopefully acquire skills in the following areas:

- Identify and discuss primary legal and regulatory activities of state and local governments related to land use and environmental protection
- Define and articulate state, regional, and local efforts designed to coordinate land use and environmental protection activities
- Describe state, regional, and local organizational structures and relationships devised to control land use and promote an improved environment
- Identify and discuss legal and regulatory mechanisms by state and local governments to control land use and enforce environmental health laws.

Today about one-third of the land in the United States—roughly equal in size to India—is owned and managed by the federal government. In order to have a better appreciation of the circumstances concerning federal lands, it behooves us to look at the historical framework of federal land claims. Currently, the entire land area of the United States is about 2.22 billion acres. The main categories of use are divided into forest (29 percent), cropland (20 percent), and grassland/pasture (26 percent).

Some major special land uses, as stated in the 1991 Annual Report of the CEQ are: transportation (173 million acres), wildlife (99 million acres), national defense (25 million acres), and urban (62 million acres).

About 60 percent of the land is in private ownership. The federal government owns about 32 percent of the land, primarily in the western states. The remaining 8 percent represents the land owned by state and local governments and lands reserved for American Indian Nations.

HISTORICAL PERSPECTIVE

After the United States gained independence in 1776, seven of the original thirteen colonies claimed extensive lands outside their current boundaries. When New York joined the Union in 1781, it claimed 200,000 acres of Pennsylvania. Such land claims continued for several decades. The largest United States land purchase occurred in 1803 during Thomas Jefferson's term as president when approximately 523 million acres, which comprised the Louisiana Purchase, were acquired from France at a price of 3 to 4 cents per acre totaling $23 million. This land now hosts thirteen states of the Union, namely, Arkansas, Iowa, Missouri, Louisiana, Minnesota, North Dakota, South Dakota, Montana, Wyoming, Colorado, Nebraska, Kansas, and Oklahoma. In 1819, subsequent to the Louisiana Purchase, Florida was purchased from Spain at a cost of 15 cents per acre totaling $6 million. Twenty years later, in a treaty with Mexico, the United States annexed 320 million acres of the southwest, which included California. The last major land acquisition was the purchase of Alaska (385 million acres) in 1867 from Russia for $7.2 million. There were a number of other land acquisitions adding Hawaii, Puerto Rico, and some of the other territories.

As a result of these purchases, the federal government owned 1,727 million acres consisting of 1,442 million in the contiguous United States and 385 million in Alaska. Today, the U.S. government owns 755 million acres; 700 million acres are from original acquisitions and the balance has been acquired for many other reasons. For example, the Week Act allows purchasing land for national forest, for the military, and so on. From the early days, the U.S. government developed a system of disposition for federal lands as an effective way of reducing the nation's debt. The land ordinance of 1785 and 1787 dealt with disposing of land. Congress chose the New England survey system, which divided the land into a neat and logical rectangular system. So, this very familiar grid system of land division shaped properties and real properties throughout the country. The standard section was 640 acres; each section was broken down into four equal parts for the standard family farm.

For example, in 1802, when Ohio joined the Union, the federal government gave one square mile for every 36-square-mile township. This land was supposed to support schools. The federal land grant programs for higher education and other public common good purposes continued. A large portion of government land was sold to private entities in the nineteenth century, especially along the east coast. After the Homestead Act of 1862, land was given free to settlers; in return they had to live on the land and improve it for cultivation. Every settler received 160 acres at no cost. Roughly 30 percent of federal land changed hands in this manner. Just prior to the Homestead Act, about 40 percent of the federal government was being financed by selling federal lands in subdivisions of 640 acres or larger.

During colonial days, the vast lands and forests in this country appeared to be inexhaustible. Up to this point in time, there was no system in place to manage land the federal government owned. By 1934, the government had 200 million acres of unappropriated land in the contiguous United States and 350 million acres in Alaska. That same year, the Taylor Grazing Act was passed. This law blocked the private acquisition of federal land and regulated the use of land for grazing. So, it should be mentioned, that federal land is used for private businesses, namely, cattle grazing, timber harvesting, and mining. All of these activities are regulated by federal regulations. In addition, most of today's major cities in the United States were built on public land, which the federal government deeded to the states. Unfortunately, many cities did not take the opportunity to use the land in an innovative manner. Instead of investing in the long-range health of cities, as real estate prices escalated, many cities sold their land to private developers. So, they took advantage of short-term profits, foregoing the opportunity to lay the foundation for more efficient cities.

As briefly alluded to earlier, another important federal land disposition—not necessarily because of total acreage but the impact—was the establishment of the land grant colleges. In 1862, the Morril Act provided land grants for at least one college in every state that promotes teaching and research in agriculture and mechanics. The federal government deeded a certain acreage of land to the states where the states had to sell the land to private enterprise and use the funds for financing higher education. Another major federal land use was the land disposed for building the roads and highways. The federal government did not begin to use its influence in this area until a significant amount of the federal interstates were built after World War II.

Today, the federal government owns about 716 million acres in the contiguous United States. About 98 percent of the land is in the 11 western states.

CUSTODIANS OF FEDERAL LANDS

Four agencies serve as the custodians of federal land. These are the National Park Service, the Fish and Wildlife Service, the Bureau of Land Management (BLM), and the Forest Service. The first three agencies are part of the Department of the Interior and the last belongs to the Department of Agriculture. The states own about 62 million acres. Over the years, the amount of land allocated to wildlife, national forests, and parks has steadily increased.

Federal Bureau of Land Management (BLM)

The BLM replaced the General Land Office, whose main role was the distribution of land to settlers under the Homestead Act of 1862. This role was changed to managing the land with the 1938 Taylor Grazing Act. Today, the contemporary role of the BLM is defined in the 1976 Federal Land Policy and Management Act (FLPMA). This entails keeping an inventory of federal land and managing the economic use of these lands for grazing, timber harvesting, mining extraction, as well as resource conservation. In Alaska, the BLM is responsible for transferring the land to Native Americans as mandated by the Alaska National Interest Land Conservation Act. Currently, the BLM manages 266 million acres in 11 western states and Alaska.

Fish and Wildlife Service

The main goal of this agency is to protect and conserve fish and wildlife in all designated refuges. In 1903, President Theodore Roosevelt established the agency after designating the Pelican Islands of Florida as a wildlife refuge. Two years later Congress established another refuge area in Oklahoma. By 1924, funding was initiated for additional fish refuges in Missouri, Minnesota, Iowa, and Illinois, including the Mississippi River. In 1934, the Congress passed the Fish and Wildlife

Coordination Act. Currently, there are 471 national wildlife refuges and 28 wetlands, totaling 91 million acres.

National Park Service

In 1872, two million acres in the northwest corner of Wyoming became our first national park, Yellowstone. Over the next four decades, Congress had established a number of other national parks such as Yosemite and Sequoia in California, Glacier in Montana, the Grand Canyon and the Petrified Forest in Arizona, and Crater Lake in Oregon. Two significant growth periods for national parks came in 1933 and during the 1960s. The last major addition occurred in 1980, when Congress added 43 million acres in Alaska to the national park system. Currently, there are 358 parks totaling 79 million acres.

Forest Service

The Forest Service was established in 1891 when Congress authorized the president to set aside federal land for this purpose. In the first two decades, the size of national forests grew to more than 40 million acres. When President Theodore Roosevelt came into office, he greatly expanded the national forest system close to its present size of 188 million acres. In reaction to this fast expansion, Congress revoked the president's authority to establish additional national forests by passing the Weeks Act in 1911. Today, the Forest Service's role is set forth by the 1974 Resources Planning Act and the 1976 National Forest Management Act to provide assistance to the private entities and different states that manage almost 514 million acres of forest.

STATE LEVEL ENVIRONMENTAL PROTECTION AND LAND USE PROGRAMS

Land use planning and control has traditionally been exercised within the realm of local government, usually by municipal government. County government, being primarily administrative subdivisions of state government, has limited planning and coordinating authority for those areas within county boundaries that remain unincorporated. Statewide land use and control has typically focused on real estate sales transactions and land subdivision. Environmental sanitation has captured the interest of state governments in a more consistent fashion. The state pre-emption of most public health activities has laid the groundwork for initiatives in pollution control efforts at that level of government.

The states can and have established legislation patterned after the NEPA. Although these laws vary from state to state, a significant number of them are comprehensive in scope, requiring impact statements on major decisions of state and local governments, and in many cases, private sector projects. Some state laws are limited in scope and authority to specific classes of projects such as highways, utility plant siting, water projects, and other specialized uses. However, not all states pass legislation, rather, they rely on administrative regulation or link impact reporting to other existing legislation.

Both the CAA and the CWA require state action to implement certain requirements. States are at liberty to establish laws and regulations which exceed federal requirements and many have established programs for pollution source control through the development of land planning and review system procedures and regulations which require land use permits. Under these programs, steps that are refusing or unable to implement federal requirements must defer to the EPA enforcement. Under the CWA, state governments are required to establish water quality standards consistent with federal guidelines, develop and implement antidegradation policies, and administer a program for the issuance of permits to municipal dischargers of pollutants into surface waters. In addition, the states must establish areawide planning agencies and provide guidance and coordination of their activities. Water quality management plans must contain state and local regulatory mechanisms for control of point-and-nonpoint-source pollution. State governments typically regulate water distribution and supply, monitor drinking water, and exercise control over water rights.

Under the CAA, state governments are required to develop air quality maintenance plans consistent with federal ambient air quality standards and establish programs for the prevention of deterioration of air quality in existing clean air areas. Additionally, procedures must be developed to review proposed land uses involving stationary sources of pollution and indirect sources such as highways, airports, shopping centers, and other heavy traffic sites. Solid waste disposal constitutes the major health issue of the next several decades. Individuals and organized groups are vehemently reacting to unchecked, almost random dumping of toxic wastes into the ground and into water supplies, lakes, rivers, and the ocean. Many states have developed plans and standards that establish controls regarding the dumping of certain toxic wastes in particular localities. Enforcement and monitoring programs have been established to deal with this growing problem.

Noise abatement legislation which encourages the development of local ordinances and the use of zoning to control the impact of excessive noise has been introduced in many states. A good deal of planning and zoning is taking place in land areas adjacent to highways and airports, which generate excessive noise levels. This is in addition to the traditional state regulation of noise sources such as muffling devices on motor vehicles, power boats, and motorcycles.

State governments are working with the federal government to implement the National Flood Insurance Program and the Coastal Zone Management Act. All states that qualify for federal assistance under the Coastal Zone Management Act have land use plans and are developing programs for water and land use management. A number of states have stringent zoning legislation for protection of coastal areas. Criteria and standards for land use restrictions have been established in flood prone areas in many states. Technical assistance is being provided by some states to guide development of appropriate municipal plans and ordinances.

A number of states have enacted legislation which regulate land subdivision and sales. Many laws are patterned after the Interstate Land Sales Disclosure Act, which requires a public report and the creation of an official record on certain types of real estate transactions and subdivisions. States may pass laws covering additional subdivision activities that are more stringent than the federal law, but there is traditional reluctance on the part of state government to restrict property rights.

Planning Efforts

There are certain general, or comprehensive, planning and/or coordination activities which provide the framework for the ultimate integration of planning which addresses health aspects of land use. Some states have developed statewide land use planning programs which embrace state planning goals and objectives, and integrate local programs and planning processes. However, the more typical pattern of statewide land use planning involves a variety of planning and operating agencies with overlapping jurisdiction and with no single organization given clear responsibility for comprehensive, coordinated planning.

A number of states have fully developed planning and review processes patterned after NEPA provision for preparation and review of environmental impact statements (see Chapter 5). States have promulgated laws and regulations to safeguard selected areas within their boundaries. For example, the protection of shorelines, wetlands, scenic rivers, and natural wildlife areas are subject to special consideration for comprehensive planning purposes. In similar fashion, some states have established planning and review processes for certain critical areas of concern. Such areas are of general environmental interest because they may be subjected to tremendous pressure for land development or they might be considered ecologically fragile. Typically, a state develops a mechanism for the designation of areas of critical environmental concern and establishes criteria and standards for land use plans which are, in turn, prepared by local planning agencies.

All states are included in the program of comprehensive health planning established under the National Health Planning and Resources Development Act of 1974. States are required to produce health systems plans, based on the areawide plans produced by local health systems agencies and incorporate statewide issues and concerns. These plans are comprehensive in scope and contain provisions for the integration of a wide variety of health perspectives, including environmental health. Unfortunately, these planning efforts are far too ambitious in terms of the resources available to planning agencies and their limited authority to influence decision making. However, there is great potential, since the health planning machinery is in place throughout the nation, and this program has a broad, comprehensive, and almost unlimited mandate.

Organization and Coordination

There is a host of state organizations involved in land use and environmental protection planning and regulation. Perhaps the most significant problem in the field today is the incredible fragmentation of official government efforts. There is no single agency with clear responsibility and authority for land use planning and regulation. Likewise, there is no single agency charged with overall responsibility for environmental protection. It follows that no concerted effort has been attempted to deal uniformly with the health aspects of land use. It is the nature of federal and state legislation to deal with problems individually, in isolation, rather than to develop a systemic approach for dealing with such issues in a comprehensive framework. It is also the nature of government to create administrative organizations to implement laws, usually one organization at a time. Of course, there are some exceptions.

The EPA has a relatively broad mission with respect to land use influence on health status, at least on the federal level. State governments have a tendency to disperse authority and responsibility among many different agencies. In any one state there may be anywhere from ten to twenty separate agencies dealing with land use, for example, public works, air resources, water resources, solid waste management, public health, comprehensive health planning, real estate, transportation department, energy department, as well as commissions, offices, boards, agencies, and so on. However, most states do have a mechanism for coordinating the activities of some of the separate government agencies for reviewing proposed plans and programs.

Provisions for the review of proposed plans and programs by various governmental entities for funding by federal agencies have been incorporated in the Intergovernmental Cooperation Act of 1968. This act intended, among other things, to reduce the proliferation of special limited function district government and to eliminate as much redundancy as possible in project activities funded by the government. In response to this legislation, the Federal Office of Management and Budget issued an administrative circular to comply with the act. This administrative circular established a program that required state and local review of project applications for federal assistance, a review by the governors' state plans required by federal statute, review of plans for funding from several agency sources, and encouraged the coordination of planning at the regional level.

Under this arrangement, states have established clearinghouses at statewide and regional levels for purposes of receiving notification of proposed programs and plans, and reviewing these in terms of their potential impact on overall land use development. These reviews identify duplication of efforts and potential conflicts among agencies. Clearinghouses established at the state level are usually housed within a comprehensive planning agency on an areawide regional level. The clearinghouses and review activities provide a focal point for the assembly and dissemination of much information about plans and programs of various government entities. This is helpful to the extent that public disclosure and awareness can ultimately influence decision making. However, this is not a planning function, and there is no built-in mechanism to ensure consideration of information gained in agency plans and programs. Nevertheless, the potential for comprehensive planning and coordination is enhanced by the existence of a clearinghouse-type repository and review functions at various levels of government.

LOCAL ENVIRONMENTAL PROTECTION AND LAND USE PROGRAMS

Local government in the United States is viewed as the "grass roots" level of government; highly visible, approachable, responsive, and amenable to the desires of the local electorate. Town hall democracy is practiced here, and local elected officials are expected to represent the majority. They are also expected to be accessible and responsive to local voters and taxpayers. Traditionally, all important land decisions have been made by local units of government. The majority of such decisions are still made at the local level. Local governments derive their powers from general state constitutional powers to promote public health, safety, and general welfare. The delegation of such powers does not necessarily imply their exercise in land use and environmental protection management. Many times consideration of individual property rights will prevail over notions of general welfare. More often than not, the exercise of eminent domain by a local jurisdiction becomes a matter of economics, and its expression is more than a simple real estate transaction.

Delegation of State Authority

There are a number of powers that might be delegated by states to local governments. Those related to land use management and environmental protection typically include authority to establish a board or commission to prepare comprehensive land use plans for development of local areas, promulgate and enforce zoning ordinances, adopt subdivision maps and regulations and building codes, and establish plans and programs to protect special areas of environmental or historical significance. Additionally, local jurisdictions normally have authority to pass and enforce ordinances with respect to public health matters such as regulation of drinking water, sewage, solid waste disposal, and disease monitoring and control.

State delegation of power may take a variety of forms. There may be provisions in the state constitution, either in the original or added by amendment, which allow local government the right of home rule. Essentially, this means that local jurisdictions are empowered to adopt ordinances and regulations which are consistent with the general laws of the state. Constitutionality of home rule powers are generally nonspecific in scope and typically require pre-eminence of state law if a conflict presents itself. Home rule powers may be granted through statutes adopted by state legislative bodies. The effect is the same as constitutionally granted powers, except that acts of legislators are more easily changed than constitutional provisions. State legislators may adopt statutes delegating specific functions to localities. For example, the Federal Standard State Zoning Enabling Act of 1920 has been adopted, in one form or another, by all states. This act was developed by the U.S. Department of Commerce to provide a model for states to follow when establishing their own legislation for granting local government authority to regulate land use through zoning. Many public health and environmental protection programs at the local level have been established under powers delegated by specific legislation. The pattern in most environmental, and health-related programs, is the adoption of state legislative acts that enable implementation of federal legislative acts which, in turn, contain provisions for areawide and local functions and responsibilities. This pattern seems to be growing in popularity and tends to dominate many activities in the field.

Municipal Planning and Zoning

Land use or comprehensive planning at the municipal level of government is ultimately carried out by elected officials in cities, towns, counties, and parishes. For incorporated cities, there are elected governing bodies, usually city councils, which are designated in state law as local level land use decision making bodies. Counties or parishes normally perform these functions for unincorporated places. Local agencies are created to perform administrative and technical functions related to land use planning. Since land use planning and zoning are complex and time consuming activities, and decisions made in these functional areas are sensitive in terms of high-level community interest, local municipalities normally establish a planning commission or board to guide plan development implementation. These commissions or boards are responsible for preparation of a comprehensive general plan for orderly development of an area. These planning bodies may have a range of additional duties such as the development and implementation of zoning ordinances, subdivision plans and regulations, and preparation of official maps, studies, and reports on land developments. In some cases, the municipal governing body will delegate zoning enforcement to the planning commission or board.

The general development plan is a basic guiding document, which provides the decision making basis for land use development and management for local areas. The planning agency or department conducts studies, assembles relevant data, and prepares the plan which normally includes a variety of elements such as, housing, recreation, commerce, transportation, noise, and public services. The planning agency reviews and makes recommendations regarding zone variances and changes, subdivisions, and conditional use permits. The planning agency may also be the lead organization reviewing and making recommendations on environmental impact reports. The city or county engineers also play a role in plan development and implementation. Plans for improvement, tract maps, and subdivision proposals are reviewed by the engineer for compliance with applicable state law and local ordinances regarding structural aspects.

The plans developed by local agencies may vary in content and format. Guidelines for uniform development of a comprehensive land plan have been incorporated under section 701 of the Department of HUD and have been incorporated in many local planning efforts. Under these guidelines are seven elements suggested for adoption by local planning agencies. These are:

- Guide for government policies and action with respect to the pattern and intensity of land use, the provision of public facilities, the provision of government services, and the development and use of human and natural resources
- Identify and evaluate area needs (i.e., housing, employment, education, health, and formulation of programs to meet these needs)

- Survey sites that have been officially determined to be of historic or aesthetic value
- Develop long-range physical and financial plans
- Develop capital improvement programs, including priorities and capital financial plans
- Coordinate related plans and programs of state and local governments
- Prepare supportive regulatory and administrative measures

Zoning ordinances and practices also vary from community to community. In the early 1920s, the U.S. Department of Commerce prepared the Standard State Zoning Enabling Act suggesting which areas of zoning authority can be delegated to local governments. This act sets forth rather specific guidelines and standards with respect to zoning procedures, review processes, and regulations. It is recommended that local planning bodies regulate size (height and number of stories) of buildings and other structures; density of population, lot size, and occupancy capacity; size and location of open spaces; and location and use of land for residential, commercial, industrial, and other purposes.

Zoning regulations are to be developed in conformance with comprehensive land use and enforced uniformly within district zoning categories. The Standard State Zoning Enabling Act attempts to relate zoning to health, safety, and welfare concerns within a local community. To this end, localities are recommended to design zones and regulations in such a way as to lessen congestion, ensure public safety from fire and other hazards, provide sufficient air and light, prevent overcrowding, and facilitate adequate provisions for public utilities, schools, parks, and transportation.

Although zoning enforcement may be delegated to a commission or board, the local governing body establishes the zoning regulations and districts, including the zoning ordinance itself. Each major step in the planning and zoning process includes an opportunity for citizens' input and public debate.

Public Health and Environmental Management

A properly administered land use program at the local level will optimize health, safety, and well-being of the community, minimize incompatible land uses, and improve environmental quality. Local environmental health land use planning is concerned with sanitation of the water supply, radiation exposure, noise abatement, vector control, solid, liquid, and toxic waste disposal, and other related activities. Programs conducted by local health and environmental protection agencies have a significant impact on the direction of land use plans and are an integral part of the land use planning and development process. Professional and technical input to the comprehensive general planning process by health and environmental agencies ensures consideration of these factors in land use decision making. Environmental health land use activities can be greatly enhanced and expanded, if formal mechanisms for cooperation and coordination are established among the various agencies.

City and county health departments work closely with local planning agencies in the review of proposed subdivisions, granting of permits, zoning variances, changes, and other land use related activities. Local health jurisdictions also evaluate land development proposals for compliance with statutes and regulations regarding sewage, domestic water supply, solid waste disposal, noise standards, air quality, vector control, and drainage. Additionally, health departments normally review environmental impact reports to ensure adequate consideration for environmental health factors.

In California, evaluation and public health effects for proposed new developments as well as the development of environmental planning guidelines by local governing bodies are authorized and required by the state laws cited in Table 6.1. The local environmental entity is responsible for implementation of these laws to the extent that they have been delegated such authority by the local governing body.

Table 6.1
Designated Responsibility for Implementing Environmental and Planning Regulations in California

Legal Authority	Designated Agency
Environmental Quality Act of 1970, Public Resources Code, Section 21060	Designated state and local lead agencies
Subdivision Map Act of 1975, Business and Professional Code, Section 11525,11549.5	Governing bodies of cities and counties
Local Planning Law, Government Code, Section 65302.66474	Local planning agency
Basic Health Services Community Planning, CAC Title 17, Section 1276 (I)	Local health jurisdiction
Model Cities–Planning, Coordinating, Health and Safety Code, Section 36100 et seq.	Local government
County Ordinance No.	Local government

Source: Amer El-Ahraf et al., *Environmental Health Delivery Within California* (Sacramento, California: State Department of Health Services, 1980).

The goal is to promote and maintain an optimum environment for the protection of the public's health, safety and well-being by minimizing the adverse impacts on and degradation of the environment created by land development activities. The specific objectives include the following:

- To insure that proposed land development projects such as subdivisions, parcels, zone changes, conditional permits, and so forth, will not subject future residents to adverse public health impacts
- To verify that proposed land development projects will not overtax public or private sewage disposal facilities nor result in water pollution or health hazards due to inadequate treatment or disposal of waste water
- To verify that water supplies proposed for all new land development projects are adequate to assure the protection of public health
- To insure that utility plans, such as water and sewage distribution systems, for all proposed land development comply with all public health technical requirements.

The human resources requirement for a land development and use program is based on careful calculation of time required to perform certain functions and time needed to perform them by component of development or activities. These may include major and minor subdivision reviews and number of units in each subdivision, use permits and zoning variances, and land use violation committee and planning commission meetings. Total time calculated should include field time as well as administrative time. The total working-days required are then converted into a position or a fraction of a position needed to perform the work. For example, a combination of field time and administrative time of 230 working days per year is equivalent to approximately one position.

REGIONAL LEVEL ENVIRONMENTAL PROTECTION AND LAND USE PROGRAMS

Most delegated state authority is given to municipal or county units of government. Land use planning and zoning has traditionally been performed at these levels. Unfortunately, there are many land uses and problems which cross over these traditional political boundaries. The spatial distribution of disease and pollution normally follows a pattern which corresponds to natural features of the landscape. These patterns are only roughly approximate to local political boundaries, which are based on "communities of interest" rather than environmental factors.

Pressures for land development and population growth have created problems that transcend municipalities and extend into larger areas, usually referred to as regions. The terms "region" and "areawide" are often used interchangeably and are intended to mean geographic spaces or social, economic, and natural networks which lend themselves to rational planning. These factors, which are considered when defining regions, vary with the purpose in mind. For that reason, many types of regions (i.e., metropolitan, transportation, economic, etc.) seem to be the rule.

Intergovernmental and Regulatory Cooperation

The propensity of state government to retain authority at the state level or delegate to general purpose local units of government has led to the formation of special purpose districts or regions to solve problems which cross over municipal or county lines. School districts are the best-known form of special district government. Other types include housing authorities, sanitation districts, mosquito abatement districts, hospital districts, port authorities, metropolitan transit districts, flood control, park and recreation regions, water and power districts, and sewage districts. These special units of government tend to proliferate because they create the means for accountability for solutions to specific and pressing problems. Also, since they are normally financed by specific bond issues and user charges, their sustenance is in keeping with most citizens' concept of equity and fairness.

Much of the social and health legislation of the 1960s required the establishment of an areawide or regional approach to planning, program development, grant administration, and implementation of federally required standards. Every piece of federal legislation discussed to date contains provisions along this line. The A-95 review process established under the Intergovernmental Cooperation Act and the Housing Act of 1954, which encouraged comprehensive regional planning under Section 701 significantly brought about widespread interest in development of regional planning structures. These grew quite rapidly, taking the shape of regional planning commissions or associations of governments, sometimes referred to as councils of governments (COGs). These intergovernmental organizations are generally voluntary in nature and function to prepare areawide plans, gather and disseminate information and support, and advise local units of general or special purpose government. They typically have no regulatory power or authority to implement the plans they develop. They can only hope to influence decisions made by other governmental agencies. The Intergovernmental Cooperation Act and Section 701 of the Housing Act provide federally assisted impetus to regionalism, mostly in the form of money for planning and technical expertise.

Concerns over the lack of action by regional planning agencies and the fragmentation of effort by various levels of government have led to recent trends in federal legislation to require linkages among programs and interagency agreements to avoid duplication. For instance, use of federal funds to construct highways is limited to those which are in conformance with the state implementation plan under the CAA. The health systems agencies created under the National Health Planning and Resources Development Act are required to develop written agreements of mutual assistance with professional standard review organizations (PSROs) and other appropriate agencies in the areas they serve. In these and other similar programs, federal regulations emphasize that regional or areawide planning agencies must coordinate their activities with each other and with any other governmental comprehensive planning program.

Since voluntary intergovernmental planning efforts have not produced many positive results, it might prove more effective to condition receipt of federal money assistance on evidence of coordinated, linked planning among units of government.

Utilizing federal grant money as leverage many be the only viable alternative at present, given the reluctance of the states to create regional governments with sufficient delegation of police power to effectively deal with issues and problems of land use and environmental protection.

7
Impact of Land Use
on Environmental Health

Growth and decay proceed simultaneously and continuously in our environment. Constant change lies in the dynamic and highly complex nature of the ecosystem. Although many of these processes appear random and devoid of a systematic pattern, in reality, many of these processes are self-regulating, and over the long-run these forces tend to balance. Life on Earth requires the presence and proper balance of four essential elements: nonliving matter, plants, consumers, and decomposers. These elements are briefly defined below:

- Nonliving matter—Oxygen, water, sunlight, organic compounds, carbon dioxide, and a variety of nutrients are required for plant growth.
- Plants—Plants convert water and carbon dioxide into carbohydrates, a process known as photosynthesis, which is necessary for the life-support of organisms in the ecosystem.
- Consumers—Organisms which feed on producers are the consumers. Primary consumers feed on plant life (herbivores), and secondary consumers feed on primary consumers (carnivores).
- Decomposers—These consist of insects, fungi, and bacteria, which serve to break down dead producers and consumers by recycling their chemistry for reuse by plants.

This cycle of biological interactions is absolutely necessary for the production and maintenance of pure air, water, and fertile soil. Destructive influences caused by the seemingly endless variety of technological byproducts can easily upset this essential delicate balance of nature. When this happens, the inevitable result is harm to humankind and other living creatures. This chapter gives the reader an appreciation of the physical and climatic influences on humankind and the effort. This requires an understanding of the public health ramifications of specific land uses, as follows:

- Physical and climatic influences on humans' use of land
- Social and economic factors which impact on land use
- Agricultural land use impact on health
- Industrial land use impact on health
- Transportation systems impact on health
- Public and recreational land uses impact on health

PHYSICAL AND CLIMATIC INFLUENCES

For most of the history of civilization, natural resources including living beings, water, and minerals have been abundant. Since the industrial revolution and the rapid advances of modern technology, however, many of these resources have become limited or endangered. Modern industrialized nations have made heavy demands on natural resources and have contributed to shortages and pollution. Continued heavy use of these resources must be tempered by consideration of the basic characteristics of ecosystems. The tendency of an ecosystem is to recycle its own resources; thus it has been a self-regulating system up to this point. Recycling effectiveness tends to be proportional to the biological diversity of the ecosystem, the greater the diversity of species, the more stable the ecosystem. Given adequate minerals and energy, diversity tends to increase in proportion to water supply, but when any given resource is significantly diminished, species diversity is reduced, and the ecosystem tends to become unstable and vulnerable to damage by use.

Until recently, industrialized nations have had a propensity to exploit resources without giving sufficient care to replenishment and recycling. This has caused instability in many ecosystems, which are highly significant to humankind's well-being and survival. Chronic instability creates vulnerability to outside physical forces and can result in severe damage or collapse of an ecosystem. Continued and unchecked environmental exploitation can lead to dramatic ecological effects. Persistent smog has changed the lifestyles of millions of persons and has forced at least one high technology industry, namely, auto manufacturing, to radically adjust its manufacturing processes. This is not to mention the introduction of governmental regulations, modified fuel requirements, and air pollution alerts which have altered people's behavior. A consistent, severe assault on natural ecosystems may bring about permanent climate changes to the extent that once habitable areas may become uninhabitable. In other words, the societal impacts of irresponsible actions can be very grave.

Once pleasant communities surrounding Love Canal in the Niagara Falls area were rapidly transformed into ghost towns in the 1980s. Popular beaches along the Santa Barbara coast have quickly become nearly deserted. As discussed in Chapter 1, due to consistent lack of care in the former Soviet Union, many towns, cities, and localities were practically uprooted not to mention the suffering of disease of many inhabitants. The displacement of essential life-support systems to accommodate urban-industrial areas most surely has a long-range impact on weather conditions. Large cities, with their enormous asphalt blankets, have a tendency to create their own climate. These cities are highly dependent on other areas for their sustenance, but adversely impact these surrounding areas by their disproportionate creation of pollution of all sorts.

SOCIAL AND ECONOMIC INFLUENCES

The economic development of a community is based on the utilization of resources to produce marketable products or services. Public policy makers try to stimulate the economy by retaining current businesses, encouraging new businesses to move in, and fostering the creation of new economic ventures. The idea is that an increase in the number of jobs improves the standard of living of the community. A strong economy is pivotal for the long-range health and sustenance of any community. To be successful, an accurate projection of future economic trends is critically important, because economic changes affect demographics, traffic levels, environmental conditions, and patterns of land use.

Patterns of human settlement have been experiencing fundamental changes in the past half century. During the 1950s and 1960s, the population shifted as people migrated in substantial numbers out of large cities and settled in smaller cities, towns, suburbs, and rural areas. This trend is a marked contrast to the long-standing shift from rural areas to metropolitan areas. There are some contervailing trends with massive urban redevelopment and rehabilitation programs being carried out by the nation's larger cities under various funding initiatives by the Housing and Urban Redevelopment Department. There is some evidence that revitalization of downtown areas is attracting middle class suburbanites back to the central city. The cultural, entertainment, and commercial attractions of the city coupled with the convenience of job opportunities seems to offer many positive aspects to city dwelling once again. The trend away from cities and metropolitan areas is dominant, however, and the phenomena is dramatic and rapid.

Population increases are occurring in many areas of the country that had lost population in past decades. Growth is still accelerating in the South, Southwest, and the Rocky Mountain regions of the United States. While migration away from metropolitan areas is heavy, the shifting population is no longer relocating to urban fringe areas but occupying rural outposts and planned communities at some distance from urban concentration. The vast network of federal highways has allowed a great deal of flexibility in living and networking spatial relationships. Recent developments in the availability of petroleum and the long-term continual spiraling fuel prices may seriously impact this pattern. This can be further influenced one way or another by further innovation in the energy, transportation, and telecommunication areas or by future changes in the social and economic conditions of the population.

Large central cities, once the magnets of business, employment opportunities, and preferred residential sites, have been steadily declining in attractiveness and economic strength. Deterioration of buildings, lifestyles, and land values have bred poverty, high crime rates, disease, and widespread unemployment in many large cities. Diminished financial resources and the consequent increased need for government services have placed cities in a highly precarious position. All too often government policy has aggravated the situation. Local control over the level of poverty and business taxes indirectly encourages or slows down the growth of community development. Restrictive land annexation policies have created "landlocked" cities, isolated from growth opportunities in surrounding suburbs. Many federal programs have unintentionally encouraged further decline of cities. For example, the process established for obtaining grant funds for hospital construction under the Hill-Burton Act inadvertently favored sophisticated suburban dwellers. Federal financial aid programs for development of water and sewer systems, public works projects, highway construction, and public facilities have generally ignored the plight of the cities.

Emphasis of new systems and facilities at the expense of rehabilitation or modernization will inevitably ignore the needs of large central cities. Certain federal policies and programs such as the Urban Health Initiative and the Urban Development Action Grant Program provided some impetus to reverse the process and aid the cities. A massive and sustained effort to physically recycle the city and preserve the spirit of existing neighborhoods has been the keystone of existing national policy with respect to urban areas. Reduction of urban sprawl, creation of more livable cities, enhancement of urban environment through provision of amenities such as open spaces, parks, and recreation areas, and the inducement of business and other investments in urban properties combined to forge the major features of the urban strategy. Awaiting the successful implementation of this strategy are millions of poor urban dwellers who lack access to basic amenities such as decent housing, clean air and water, medical care, and sanitation.

As one would expect, poverty is not limited to urban areas. Rural poverty is every bit as depressing and humiliating as that found in bit city ghettos. The soil is just as capable as asphalt of depriving humans of their sustenance. Leapfrogging and buckshot urbanization—development of multiuse planned units in nonurban settings—may have an alleviating effect on rural poverty over time. Offsetting this positive feature of planned development units would be the gradual introduction for the very urban problems which give rise to this trend in the first place. In response, many rural communities have established restrictive zoning regulations to prevent overdevelopment in their communities.

ENVIRONMENTAL PROTECTION ECONOMICS

Every action, whether private or governmental, has its costs and benefits. Implied in every decision is the notion that benefits derived from a chosen course of action exceed the cost of undertaking the action. In most situations, it is possible to account and measure these costs and benefits. Studies which attempt to assess potential benefits from environmental protection and pollution control programs typically focus on damage costs as determined by legal action. Because of this approach, and because there is no acceptable methodology for the measurement of such factors as misery and psychic loss, results tend to be quite conservative. Measurement of the cost of pollution abatement programs is straightforward because data on the costs of installing control devices are not overly difficult to obtain.

Today approximately 2 percent of the U.S. gross national product (GNP) is spent on pollution control programs, or an amount nearly equal to $50 billion in annual expense. Roughly half of this amount is spent in response to environmental legislation and the remainder would have been spent on similar areas regardless of legal mandates. These have been gradually increasing for the past several decades with the added legislation and more serious effort to enforce existing laws and regulations. Estimates of financial and social benefits from most control programs are absent and seriously lack scientific analysis. Several studies by the CEQ, American Lung Association, and so on, indicate annual dollar benefits due to cost savings from damages and illnesses, range from less than $10 billion to over $22 billion. Presumably, given sufficient time, the initial investment in pollution abatement technology will result in total compliance with law and regulations, and annual costs will decrease to a considerably less expensive maintenance effort.

It is important to mention that because of environmental laws here are some success stories. For example, in the past few decades, the percentage of air pollutants significantly decreased. According to the EPA, between 1970 and 1988, the level of particulates dropped to one-third the original value and the lead level dropped more than a factor of twenty. Similarly, other priority pollutants such as sulfur dioxide, nitrogen oxides, carbon monoxide, and volatile organic compounds experienced significant reductions. During the same time frame, the amount of municipal and industrial water discharges also dropped. Based on EPA sources, the level of TSS and BOD concentrations of municipal and industrial discharge experienced sizable drops.

Thoughtful individuals and groups do not argue against the necessary enforcement of control measures or the efficacy of abatement methods and techniques. However, individuals and groups express great concern over the economic impact of environmental protection costs and wonder if benefits do in fact outweigh the costs. Increased fuel costs, in times of energy resource scarcity, cause very legitimate challenges to the overall utility of pollution control methods such as auto emission devices. The higher inflation figures also cause serious rethinking of the ability of business and industry to bear the costs of abatement. Recent studies, however, indicate minimal impact. About fifteen years ago, the Department of Commerce conducted a survey of industrial plant closings associated with pollution control requirements and found that only one-half of one percent of the plants closed because of control burdens.

Although this is not a large percentage, many of the closings have occurred in economically depressed areas which could least afford such events. Targeted programs are now being developed by the federal government to provide economic assistance in such cases to allay further economic displacement and avoid exacerbating unemployment rates. Overall, pollution control expenditure appears to have little impact on employment or inflation. Over the past several years, the pass-through costs of pollution control have resulted in less than four-tenths of one percent increase in general inflation rates. These results notwithstanding, there is justifiable concern over the immediate and future economic impact of environmental protection and other governmental regulatory activities. In response to these concerns, about two decades ago President Carter established the Regulatory Analysis Review Group, composed of representatives from the Office of Management and Budget, the Treasury Department, the EPA, and others, to review new government regulations and comment on their economic consequences. In 1994, with the landslide victory and gaining a majority in both House and Senate, the conservative Republicans have taken a very forceful crusade in rolling back most environmental legislation that had been enacted in the past four decades. Based on the current mood of the public at large, this appears to be a very popular topic. It is very evident that there will be some rollback. However, the true outcome of these actions and political postures are not yet known.

AGRICULTURAL USES

Agriculture pertains to cultivation of the soil for purposes of food and plant production. Many different types of land are used for agriculture, depending on soil quality and characteristics. Through the use of fertilizer, herbicides, insecticides, water and land management practices, humans have been able to adapt land to meet a variety of agricultural needs. Since nearly 90 percent of the land in the United States is used for nonmetropolitan purposes, there are many alternatives available for agriculture. The concept of mixed agricultural land use seems to be gaining favor. Unlike rotation of sites for the production of crops only, mixed agricultural use involves combining field crops, orchards, pastures, hay production, and other products, all rotated in accordance to a planned sequence designed to preserve the land and optimize productive capacity.

Thought is being given to the use of urban land for agricultural purposes in a planned pattern of mixed land use. The revitalization of natural ecosystems is very badly needed in urban areas. Economists would argue against this practice, naturally, therefore other incentives and economic assistance have to be devised to encourage such use of high-priced land. The incorporation of open spaces and tree lines in urban land use plans also enhance environmental stability.

From the early days, as the number of settlers increased so did the need for cultivated land. This trend continued until the 1930s when the total area approached about 400 million acres. The agricultural land used for crop production primarily expanded in the Midwest and Northwest, while grasslands in the West were used for raising cattle and sheep. Until 1934, cattle and sheep herds could graze freely throughout federal lands, which resulted in significant damage to them. Since this time, federal lands have been managed to reduce further damage. Today about one-fifth of the land in the United States is dedicated to agriculture, and less than 10 percent of all livestock raised in this country is raised on federally owned land.

The population of the United States, now estimated at 240 million inhabitants, demands growth of agriculture and consequent efficient use of prime crop and pasture land. It is estimated that approximately one million acres of prime farmland is being converted, chiefly for urban and suburban uses. The loss of farmland not only influences the production of agricultural products, but also has environmental effects. Open land areas serve to maintain and replenish natural ecosystems, including local water supplies, and protects the hydrogenic integrity of wetlands. These areas are also instrumental in purifying air, thus reducing levels of air pollution.

High winds, floods, drought, and dust storms have wrought damage to the nation's farmlands throughout history. The Department of Agriculture has estimated that nearly one-third of the topsoil in the United States has been lost in the past 200 years; approximately 100 million acres have suffered degradation to the point of uselessness for agriculture, and another 100 million acres have been subjected to at least 50 percent topsoil loss. Most of this loss is through removal of sedimentation by water movement. About four billion tons of sediment are deposited in the nation's waterways every year.

Control of insects has always been a major concern to farmers and others interested in agricultural production. To protect the crops from pests, there has been a growing dependence on numerous chemical pesticides. These have been highly effective in controlling infestation of insects, but there is growing evidence that many species of insects are developing resistance to commonly used pesticides. This phenomenon will naturally destroy the effectiveness of chemical approaches to pest control. One has to doubt the efficacy of chemical pesticides in view of this and other problems which have surfaced associated with their use. For instance, it is known that the destruction of natural enemies will have countereffects and lead to outbreaks of secondary pests. Reduction of pollinators and other beneficial species, environmental contamination, and potentially severe health hazards have been associated with the use of chemical pesticides. Integrated pest management, which places considerable emphasis on natural controls over populations of harmful pests in concert with organic farming methods, holds promise as an alternative to the unrestrained use of pesticides. Chemical pesticide use is not totally abandoned in the approach, but is judiciously applied to the extent necessary in view of assessment of the costs and benefits involved in each situation.

From the early 1920s, soil erosion became a problem for a sizable portion of agricultural land because of two primary reasons. These were due to farm abandonment by many farmers during the Depression and the introduction of more mechanized farming practices. To address soil erosion, Congress passed the Soil Conservation and Allotment Act in 1935, which gave the USDA responsibility for soil conservation. The continual efforts in fighting soil erosion have to some extent been successful, but the problem persists in some areas. With improvements in technology, the productivity of agricultural lands steadily increased faster than domestic consumption. Over the past fifty years, the crop yield increased by a factor of 2.5, which enabled the United States to become a major exporter of grains and other agricultural products.

The rise in productivity was partly due to increased use of chemical fertilizers, machinery, and pesticides. Between the 1960s to early 1980s, the amount of fertilizers increased from less than 8 million short tons to over 23 million short tons. During the same time frame, the use of pesticides increased from 316 million pounds to 870 million pounds. The combination of the increased use of chemical fertilizers, machinery, and pesticides resulted in exacerbating soil erosion and creating other environmental problems. As discussed in earlier chapters, several environmental laws impacted agricultural land use, such as the CWA and FIFRA. For example, the EPA classified large animal-feeding operations as point-sources for waste water discharge and issued procedures for NPDES permits for such facilities under the CWA. Similarly, EPA and USDA joint efforts informed farmers about the harmful effects of the overuse of pesticides and explained the responsible use of these chemicals as well as the environmental hazards associated with them. This was done through the Integrated Pest Management (IPM) program.

Conversion of wetlands to agricultural use has been given serious consideration lately In such cases, as long as the hydrologic regimen remains intact and the extinction of species is not extensive, restoration of such lands can be achieved through natural succession. For example, approximately five million acres of Mississippi Delta have been converted to soybean cultivation and nontimber uses since 1930. Unfortunately, this type of land restoration takes considerable time and is somewhat costly. Also, some wetlands are not renewable because of the devastating effects of constant erosion which leaves the land barren and unproductive. Additionally, since many of the wetlands border urban areas and serve the purpose of revitalization of the ecosystem, it may not always be in the best interest of society to alter this land use.

Congress, concerned with long-term conservation of agricultural soil passed the Soil and Water Resource Conservation Act (RCA) in 1977. This law required the USDA to conduct periodic examination of soil and water as well as other related resources as a national priority. In the early 1980s, USDA reports showed problems with water shortage and soil erosion that needed immediate attention. So by 1985, Congress enacted the Food Security Act (FSA) which required that any farmer who wanted to benefit from federal subsidies had to participate in land conservation programs. Moreover, any conversion of wetlands to agricultural land would terminate federal subsidies for a farmer. These efforts increased with the passage of the Food, Agriculture, Conservation and Trade Act (FACT) in 1990. According to this act, the Environmental Conservation Acreage Reserve Program (ECARP) expanded the eligibility of environmentally sensitive land. But despite all of these laws the lack of proper and adequate drainage has polluted the ground water and leached into the drinking water. Many water wells close to agricultural land have experienced high levels of nitrate, animal waste, and phosphate. In addition, many lakes and rivers have been polluted with animal waste and other chemicals associated with fertilizers and pesticides. In fact close to one-fifth of the estuarine waters have been negatively impacted by agricultural sources.

INDUSTRIAL USES

Industry produces the artifacts of modern civilization. A host of consumer products, appliances, and convenience devices are manufactured by the machinery of industry on a daily basis. Both the productive results and processes of industry have environmental consequences. Process wastes contain hazardous substances, the means of production are often harmful to health, and the products themselves may pollute the environment or cause sickness and injury to the consumers and workers.

The American Chemical Society lists over 4,000,000 chemical compounds in their registry of chemicals. Approximately 6,000 new compounds are added to the list every week. Nearly 70,000 of these are used for commercial production in the United States. This barely scratches the surface with respect to the need for knowledge about the possible health and environmental impacts of these substances. Research efforts have been minimal, information has been fragmented and inadequate, and study results in many instances have been sparse and inconclusive. A lot of work remains to be done.

Several years ago, on the campus of University of Southern California School of Medicine in Los Angeles, a vial containing a gaseous substance resembling nerve gas was discovered in a cancer research laboratory. Although used in a controlled environment under professional supervision, it was later reported that a fire or explosion within the laboratory could have unleased this deadly gas into a densely populated area, possibly causing thousands of deaths and untold injuries. Paradoxically, the laboratory was situated across the street from the 2,000-bed Los Angeles County–U.S.C. Medical Center.

PCBs have been discovered in the sediments of lakes, streams, and coastal waters and have found their way into the human food chain through fish. PCBs are industrial chemical compounds similar in nature to DDT and highly toxic to humans. Epidemiological surveys indicate a highly significant correlation between cancer and polycyclic aromatic hydrocarbons, which are emitted by motor vehicles. This no doubt has implications for persons residing near highways and major streets and certainly spells trouble among those whose work requires intimate exposure to the internal combustion engine. The marine food chain requires the presence of algae and phytoplankton, which are sensitive to ultraviolet light. The large scale, continued emission of ozone-depleting substances may eventually endanger these essential ingredients of life and produce dire effects on major ecosystems.

The National Institute of Occupational Safety and Health (NIOSH) surveyed over 4,500 industrial plants employing nearly one million workers in 1977. The study concluded that potentially hazardous chemicals were in such abundance that one out of every four workers is exposed to at least one substance capable of causing disease and possibly death. According to studies performed by the Environmental Defense Fund, the Hudson River in New York is polluted with a variety of contaminants including PCBs, benzene, chloroform, and a host of other substances potentially harmful to health. The University of Chicago conducted research which concluded that asbestos fibers can be found in the lungs of practically all Americans. As research continues, more and more unsuspected hazards from industrial chemical use are discovered. The National Cancer Institute has an ongoing program to evaluate relationships between cancer and various chemical compounds. Long-term animal studies have shown that a large number of commonly used chemicals, drugs, and pesticides are carcinogenic.

The above discussion is very alarming and it should be, but the fact of the matter is that most chemicals in use are not considered harmful to health in the concentrations normally found in the environment. Those which are considered hazardous are subject to regulation under several congressional actions, including the TSCA, CAA, CWA, and the RCRA which calls for government control over hazardous solid waste from point of origin to disposal sites and requires development practices which encourage resource recovery and recycling.

Herein lies much of the problem. There are many acts of Congress dealing with toxic substances. This has led to a multiplicity of government agencies at the federal, state, and local levels attempting to regulate activities in this area. Uncertainty over jurisdiction, bureaucratic entrenchment, industry resistance, and legal obstacles have resulted in fragmentation of the efforts or procedures that work at cross-purposes with each other. Some uniformity in approach and a great amount of coordination is necessary for significant progress to be made in reducing harmful effects of toxic substances.

However, progress has been made in certain areas which should be noted. For instance, lead poisoning in children throughout the United States has been reduced through early screening and detection efforts. Concerted efforts by the EPA, Occupational Safety and Health Administration (OSHA), FDA, and the Consumer Product Safety Commission have been aggressively directed at consumer, environmental, and occupational exposure issues.

TRANSPORTATION USES

The scope and direction of transportation imposes land use patterns on humans. More often than not, the flow of civilization follows highways as it once followed rivers and waterways in this country. Industry, commerce, and residential areas seem to emerge in the wake of highway development. Since the initiation of the federally aided interstate highway system in the mid 1950s, the pace has quickened dramatically. Population shifts away from metropolitan areas would not be possible without this massive interconnecting system of highways. The nation and its leaders have taken great pride in this system and rightly so. It is not without its drawbacks, however. A pattern of development which includes residential sprawl, commercial strips, and outlying industrial parks has produced some adverse social, economic, and environmental effects.

Unchecked growth essentially in rural areas has disrupted the natural ecosystems and patterns of social relationships in many small communities. Widely dispersed land development causes strain on energy resources and pulls employment opportunities and public service away from inner cities, where they are desperately needed. If rapid transit systems are developed to forge linkages between those in need of jobs and services, in all likelihood the costs will be prohibitive; it will certainly be beyond the reach of the aged, poor, and those otherwise disadvantaged. Obviously, a more balanced approach is required, namely, one which bridges between urban needs and the natural desires for open spaces.

Today, transportation is consuming slightly less than one-quarter of our GNP and roughly one-third of the total energy consumed. In addition, an appreciable percentage of the land in this country is used for transportation infrastructure. The main transportation systems in the United States include canals and waterways, railroads, trucks, automobiles, and aircraft. The role and importance of each one of these modes of transportation has continuously changed over time. The construction of canals and waterways in this country began in the early 1800s. By the 1860s, the total length of canals peaked at 4,000 miles. This coincides with the increased use of railways. As time went by, the importance and role of canals declined.

Commercial railroads started around 1830. In a hundred years, the total track length increased to more than 300,000 miles. This was the maximum growth of railroad infrastructure. Starting in the 1930s, the railways declined steadily and by the 1980s, the total track length was reduced by one-third. This was mainly due to the increased popularity of the automobile for transportation and trucks for hauling merchandise. The total number of automobiles in 1894 was only four, but by 1900 the number had increased to 8,000, and more than a million in just a decade after that. The number of automobiles increased to about 23 million by 1930 and for all practical purposes took over the roads from the horse and buggy. Parallel to this increase in the number of automobiles was the increase in the total number and mileage of roads. The total mileage of surface roads by this period had surpassed three million miles.

Highways require large land areas for development. A mile of highway consumes nearly 50 acres of land. It is estimated that over 25 million acres of land is devoted to highway use in the United States. For all intent and purposes, this land use is irreversible and it displaces neighborhoods, businesses, natural areas, and farms. In large cities, most land use is dedicated to streets and other transportation facilities.

The flow and concentration of air pollution correlates directly with the presence of transportation arteries. It is no wonder that our major cities are plagued by chronic air contamination. When air pollution is coupled with noise pollution from highways and streets, the misery is compounded. The EPA attributes most of the air pollution problem to transportation. Today, over 73 percent of carbon monoxide, 52 percent of all hydrocarbons, and nearly one-half of all nitrogen oxides found in ambient air comes from transportation sources. One need not stretch the imagination too far to deduce the contribution of transportation to air pollution in urban areas. Additionally, the EPA has concluded that traffic noise is the most significant noise pollutant found in both rural and urban environments.

Every year highway accidents inflict a major toll on the population in terms of injury and loss of life. Currently, the number of highway fatalities exceeds 40,000 annually. Most of this is due to carelessness, alcohol and other substance abuse, and mechanical failures rather than the mere existence of highways. Our well-designed highways, if anything, should reduce the number and severity of motor vehicle accidents. However, there is no doubt that our extensive system of roads and highways along with our penchant for automobiles have served to foster widespread highway usage, which inevitably leads to increased levels of risk. The heavy use of highways for commercial trucking purposes adds to this peril.

Furthermore, land displacement associated with highway construction contributes to soil erosion and pollution. Constant, heavy traffic leaves a residue of oil wastes and other contaminants on the surface of streets and highways. These pollutants eventually find their way into ground waters, streams and rivers, and pollute water supply sources. Concern over the environmental implication of highway planning and construction has prompted the EPA to require transportation control plans in areas which have large population concentrations. This program was initiated with the ambient air quality standards established under the CAA. Under the Federal Highway Act, urban transportation development must be preceded by a comprehensive transportation plan prepared in concert with the state, regional, and local planning agencies. This plan is also subject to environmental assessment requirements under the NEPA. Air quality must be given appropriate consideration in highway planning, and the EIS must include the following elements:

- Clear identification of the impact of highway construction on air quality
- Design of the methods used for environmental analysis
- Summary and review of consultations with the local air pollution control agency
- Determination of consistency of highway construction plans with the approved state plan

The personal automobile is the least efficient form of mass transportation and produces the highest amount of environmental pollution. Continued emphasis on highway construction will only encourage more vehicle usage. Transportation alternatives such as urban mass transit and light rail need to be explored thoroughly for major metropolitan areas. Mass transit systems are highly energy efficient and require minimal land displacement. Moreover, they can significantly reduce traffic congestion. For instance, studies have shown that a bus will travel the equivalent of eighty passenger miles per gallon of gasoline in comparison to fourteen passenger miles per gallon for an automobile on urban streets, which is a six-fold increase in efficiency. Therefore, less pollution, less noise, and fewer personal irritations are produced when urban areas are served by modern, well-planned rapid transit systems. To be successful, however, such systems must be economically competitive with private auto use in terms of cost and convenience. Energy shortages of the 1970s sparked renewed interest in the development of rapid bus and light rail transit facilities in large urban areas; unfortunately, only a handful of cities were able to implement a financially sustainable mass transit system.

Another mode of transportation that has major land use implications is air travel. Commercial air carriers went into operation in the 1920s. In less than a half century, the use of aircraft as a means of transportation increased more than a hundred times. Today, worldwide air travel is approaching one trillion passenger miles per year. The number of commercial aircraft, in the meantime, has increased to more than 10,000. As the size and number of aircraft increased, it resulted in dedicating larger and larger parcels of land for airports. The airport expansions in all cases meant an increase in traffic, noise level, and congestion for neighboring communities. That is why airport expansion proposals normally face stiff opposition from their surrounding communities. It is well-known that the presence of airports create significant environmental problems—air pollution, large land displacement, and traffic congestion. The most serious issue, however, is noise from ascending and descending aircraft.

In addition, airports require large contiguous parcels of land to sustain the wide variety of operations associated with aviation. Community pressure is forcing the aviation industry to develop airport facilities in outlying areas. This in theory makes a great deal of sense in terms of pollution control, but generates other problems from a cost and convenience point of view. For these reasons airport planners have been searching for relatively accessible land sites such as marshlands, vacant areas near waterways and beaches, and other open spaces near population centers. The problems with many airports in large metropolitan areas are complex. When most airports were first established fifty to sixty years ago, they were located a good distance from metropolitan areas. However, cities expanded and, in many instances, encircled the airport. Now when these airports want to expand the community opposition is fierce.

Moving airports to new locations can cost billions of dollars. For instance, in Hong Kong the city is moving the airport to a new location which will abate many of the concerns. The total cost of this project is over $44 billion. The only factor that makes such a project feasible is the high real estate value and demand for the current airport site. In response to the widespread opposition of airport expansion plans, the FAA de-emphasizes planning large airports and stresses the development of smaller facilities and modernization of existing terminals.

Creating open buffer zones around airports and routing air traffic over less populated areas are highly effective strategies for noise control. Buffer zones are expensive to create because they involve the purchase of large parcels of valuable land. These techniques combined with aircraft source control and architectural standards requiring sound mitigation in surrounding communities, comprise the most viable approach at present. Architectural standards designed to improve safety in the flight pathways apply to buildings surrounding the airport including height limitations and other measures to prevent accidents during flight landing and take-off. Future airport development must be based on comprehensive, integrated planning approaches and must fully utilize a variety of zoning applications. In fact, the Airport and Airway Development Act of 1970 required the secretary of transportation to prepare a national airport system plan to consider environmental and health impacts, with public input and consultation from the administrators of the EPA. The act required the following:

- Consideration of economic, social, and environmental effects of airport location, and the objectives of urban planning efforts of local communities.
- Assure airport projects will be in compliance with the appropriate air and water quality standards.
- Assure that airport projects are consistent with national policy with respect to the protection and enhancement of natural resources and environmental quality. Moreover, all airports must conform to federal standards related to site location and layout, grading, drainage, paving, lighting, and safety of approaches.

The role of planners is to respond to the increase in transportation and supply the needed infrastructure to serve the demand. The 1934 Federal Highway Act allowed the states to use up to 1.5 percent of construction for planning. After the end of World War II and the increase in population, the need for more highways was evident. In response to this need, the 1956 Federal Highway Act initiated the most ambitious public works project ever launched in its plan to extend the federal highway system by 41,000 miles. Up to this point, there was not very strong support for major public transportation projects. The Urban Mass Transportation Act of 1964 began a process of coordinating public transportation with regional highway planning. This initiative was reinforced by the 1973 Highway Act. Two years later, another positive move in this direction was made when the Federal Highway Administration (FHWA) and the Urban Mass Transportation Administration (UMTA) developed joint regulations to give the responsibility of the coordination effort to one entity, namely, Metropolitan Planning Organization (MPO). The energy crunch of 1973 caused a strong interest in energy conservation and the National Transportation Policy Study Commission recommended a 20 percent reduction in the amount of energy used by transportation.

PUBLIC AND RECREATIONAL LAND USE

The use of land for recreation is not something new. During ancient Roman days, the rich and powerful escaped the summer heat of Rome by retreating to the countryside. Later, European royalty built very elaborate summer castles and gardens in the countryside for their own use. In the early days of this country, similar vacation homes were built by rich and influential individuals. The first major public recreational facility in the United States was the opening of Coney Island in the 1860s. Over time, the number of public parks and other commercial recreational facilities steadily grew. For instance, by 1919 the number of amusement parks approached 1,500. In the next two decades with the economic hardship of the Depression, the number dwindled to only one-third this number.

With the creation of the Civilian Conservation Corps and the Public Works Project by President Roosevelt, the number of national parks grew rapidly. After World War II and the growing affluence of Americans, more and more individuals and families could afford to go on vacation. This resulted in a significant boom for the tourist industry. In time, leisure sports such as boating, skiing, golfing, and so on, gained ever increasing popularity, which in turn increased the demand for such facilities. Many vacation resorts emerged in places such as Florida, South Carolina, Nevada, California, and many other states. With the opening of Disneyland in 1955, the concept of theme parks rose to new heights. As time went on, more federal highways were built and air travel became more affordable making many of these locations accessible to a steadily increasing percentage of the population.

Since recreational land use is determined by government action and in the public domain, it makes sense to jointly consider the health and environmental aspects of land use. The federal government is the single largest landowner in the United States. Over one-third of the nation's land is owned and operated by the U.S. government. Most of this land is dedicated to recreational purposes and nature appreciation. It is national policy to manage these lands in such a manner as to protect the natural resources, prevent exploitation, and generally provide maximum benefit for the general public. These public lands have a variety of uses such as recreation, parks, wildlife preserves and refuges, forests, watersheds, forage, commercial use (i.e., timber, minerals, etc.), and residential. Most public lands are administered by the U.S. Department of the Interior. Approximately three-fourths of the nation's public lands fall under the jurisdiction of three Interior Department agencies—the BLM, the Fish and Wildlife Service, and the National Park Service. The remaining lands are administered by the Forest Service in the USDA, various military departments, the Bureau of Reclamation, and the Energy and Development Administration.

Public lands can simultaneously serve both commercial and private uses. For example, the Forest Service sets aside segments of timberland for access by commercial logging interests. Obviously, care must be taken to ensure judicious, well-planned allowances on the location and the volume of timber cutting. Failure of proper timber management will have dire results upon the ecological balance of these natural resources. Logging operations, including necessary access road construction, result in landslide possibilities, increased soil erosion, and water pollution. Wildlife, fisheries, and recreational elements are also disturbed by major logging operations. Timber cutting reduces shade, logs clog rivers, and debris clutters the environment. All of these activities certainly have an adverse effect on the ecosystem if carried out to any extensive degree. These and other facts illustrate that clear-cutting is a damaging environmental practice as it increases soil erosion and diminishes chances of forest regeneration. It is also economically unsound because it results in eventual disappearance or severe reduction of a renewable resource and loss of job opportunities for a segment of the population.

Mining and extraction of mineral resources may also have deleterious environmental consequences. Oil drilling on the Outer Continental Shelf, for instance, has produced seepage and spillage, which damages sea life and birds. Moreover, it reduces the aesthetic value of shorelines. Strip mining leaves land barren and subject to erosion and is prone to cause water pollution through filtration of residues. It is rarely possible to reclaim such lands. Unchecked grazing on public lands can lead to negative changes in plant ecology, water quality deterioration, diminished wildlife, and severe erosion. Overgrazing by sheep and cattle, for example, has led to stunted plant growth because of trampling and overforaging. This leads to fundamental changes in the nature and characteristics of the land.

Humankind is capable of wreaking havoc on public lands. To be sure, people need recreational space to repose and draw close to nature. This type of land use is not only proper, but in this complex, congested, and mechanized society, it is absolutely essential and therefore must be preserved at all costs. However, popular national parks are attracting more and more visitors every year; sometimes those who are seeking escape from overcrowded metropolitan areas encounter crowded national parks. Overuse of recreational spaces produces many of the same environmental problems found in cities, that is, noise pollution, air pollution, toxic waste debris, and water pollution. The extensive use of off-road vehicles has extended human's ability to pollute the nation's parks, deserts, beaches, and wilderness areas. Off-road vehicles damage soil, destroy vegetation, disrupt wildlife habitats, and deface artifacts of historical significance. In addition, litter is ever present in the wake of off-road vehicles.

Among the efforts to counter increasing encroachment on recreational spaces and public land is the development of the master plan for public land management. This has been a most promising effort which includes plans for the national parks. NEPA requires the preparation of environmental impact reports on major decisions regarding public land use management. These reports, along with the public input process accompanying them, are essential elements of the master plan alluded to in the earlier paragraph. Plans and environmental impact reports are required for the many activities of the Forest Service, National Park Service, Bureau of Reclamation, the Army Corps of Engineers, and the BLM. These activities involve diverse land uses such as wilderness, mining, oil and gas extraction, forestry, national parks, grazing, vegetation, and water resources projects.

8
Process of Land Use Planning

Planning is defined as preconceived, deliberate, and purposeful intervention to bring about change in a situation or event. It is forward thinking in a structured fashion, which involves designing activities with due consideration for the practicalities of implementation. Planning involves a process which is cognitive, articulative, and political in nature. Obviously, planning is a generic process, applied by individuals and organized groups for a variety of purposes. It is absolutely essential for an individual or group to engage in planning. Failure to think ahead will eventually lead to an individual's demise and an organization's stagnation. Growth is mandatory for healthy subsistence of all living things, and the primary ingredient of growth is change. Our environment is dynamic and constantly adapting to change. If humankind is to live harmoniously with the environment, we too much adapt and develop strategies consistent with the common needs of nature, the land, and human welfare.

There is no single, integrative planning process that comprehensively considers the social, economic, public health, and environmental aspects of land use. Instead, there are a multitude of such processes. Private individuals, business organizations, citizens' groups, and government agencies at all levels are involved to some extent in land use planning. The diffusion of power is a notion deeply ingrained in the American character. It normally takes a crisis of major proportions (i.e., war, epidemic, natural disaster, etc.) to rally the American spirit to engage in concerted action. Lacking such motivation, the norm is incremental and fragmented. Planning designed in such a way maximizes individual rights without much regard to social costs.

Historically, planning in the United States can be divided into several distinct eras. During the early colonial days, planning was totally centralized. Many townships were designed in Europe or by land surveyors following grid patterns for cities . With very few exceptions, there were no specialized land uses; the emphasis was on providing havens for settlers. This pattern persisted until the emergence of the industrial era during the Civil War, when cities grew appreciably and became very crowded. Sanitary conditions were poor and many recent immigrants were living in very tight spaces under difficult conditions. During the early part of the twentieth century, many cities enacted ordinances to improve the situation. Cities such as Los Angeles, Cincinnati, Chicago, and Hartford enacted ordinances concerning land use. Up to this time, land use planning concentrated primarily on urban planning. In the 1930s, President Franklin D. Roosevelt created the National Resources Planning Board (NRPB). This was the first time planning expanded beyond the cities and incorporated areawide living concepts. After the end of World War II and the unprecedented rise in the standard of living and the increase in population, concerns for the environment grew, and in the 1970s a large amount of environmental legislation was passed by Congress; this constitutes the current planning era.

This chapter discusses the fundamentals of planning processes and data requirements, addresses the social and political framework within which planning needs to occur, and articulates organizational and structural characteristics of planning efforts within the public health aspect of land use. Gathering appropriate data is of paramount importance in assessing the environmental impacts of land use.

There are three essential phases in any well-conceived planning process, namely, predesign, design, and postdesign. These activities are defined below:

- Predesign—Organization and development of databases, a conceptual framework, and procedures for review, approval, and appeal of planning decisions.
- Design—Identification and assessment of needs and problems, establishment of goals and objectives, and development of specific plans and plan documents.
- Postdesign—Development of strategies for intervention and implementation, and systems for evaluating and monitoring results.

Unless planning is the activity of one individual, some type of planning body normally convenes. This might take the form of a small group of interested persons or the establishment of a formal governing organization with committees, task forces, and full-time staff.

ORGANIZATION AND STRUCTURE

Environmental and land use planning is a proper concern of government. Formal planning activities in the field are either carried out by government agencies or are somehow subsidized by the government. The purpose and structure of planning organizations are similar in nature and characteristics. The three phases of planning activity mentioned above are usually engaged. There is always a group of individuals providing guidance and direction (governance) to planning efforts. There is usually a professional staff of varying size associated with the program. There is constituent interest supporting or blocking initiatives. Those individuals or groups affected positively or negatively by plans might be specifically interested in environmental and land use matters, or in general issues such as government intervention, consumer rights, and so on.

The organizational structure for planning in the United States is based on three fundamental notions, namely, (1) government by constitutionally based laws, (2) open public participation in the decision making process, and (3) the undeniable right to legally appeal adverse decisions. It is therefore important that planning processes allow access to those interested in the proceedings. It is equally important that planning proceed within a sound legal framework. Many useful and desirable plans have met their demise by running afoul of legal technical requirements.

Basic planning structure involves the following basic elements:

- A legal framework in the form of federal or state enabling legislation and regulations, or a local ordinance based on delegation of state powers.
- An organizational structure, in the form of federal, state, or local government agencies, or private entities empowered with governmental authority to plan.
- A decision making group empowered to approve plans and related policies. This group may be an integral part of a planning agency or it may be one step removed.
- One or more advisory panels established to provide technical input to planning activities.
- A communication apparatus designed to ensure information flow throughout the planning process. Communication is essential to maintain the integrity of planning and avoid legal violations.

A great deal of time and effort is invested in the production of plans and the maintenance of the legal framework of the legal process. This is of paramount importance in the tail wagging the dog scenario. The main purpose of planning is not to produce plan documents in adherence with rigid legal procedures. They should be viewed only as a means to an end, where the end is progressively improving humankind's environment. Plan documents are recorded evidence that planning has taken place, and are continually modified as change occurs, either for better or for worse. The final test of planning validity is acceptance by concerned individuals and groups. When these individuals and groups are intimately and legitimately involved in a meaningful fashion, planning is more likely to be successful. Therefore, sound planning organization provides for and encourages participation.

SOCIAL AND POLITICAL ENVIRONMENT

All planning dealing with environmental and land use issues occurs inevitably in a milieu saturated with political machinations and social interactions. The pluralistic nature of politics in the United States is an expression of the diversity of values held by its citizens. In a multicultural society, a divergence of views is to be expected. It is important to remember that not all individuals feel strongly about well-balanced, environmentally sensitive land use. There are legitimate economic concerns which much be accommodated in any open planning process.

A planning process lacking power, influence, and authority is not likely to be fruitful, and competing interests may lead to deterioration of the entire process. Diplomacy in leadership is obviously essential for resolving differences and paving the way to positive outcomes. Politics molds diverse perspectives through the use of power, influence, and authority in order to accomplish change. Power is the ability to command others to abide by one's will. It can be inherent in a person by the virtue of charismatic qualities, knowledge, or expertise, or it may be conferred on a person by the community. Inherent power is referred to as influence; conferred power is referred to as authority. Power can be exercised individually or collectively. Thus, organizations and groups as well as individuals use power to achieve their purposes.

In any given planning organization, power may be concentrated in a few individuals or certain units, or it may be widely dispersed throughout the group. It may flow from the top of an organization down to subordinate units, or it may move up from the bottom of the organization. In some instances, it may move sideways across parallel units of an organization. The culmination of power is decision making which determines the direction and fundamental purpose of planning activities.

Individual behavior is highly complex and easily misunderstood. We all tend to perceive others' behavior in terms of stereotyped notions and expectations. For instance, physicians are "supposed" to defend the medical establishment, environmentalists are "supposed" to argue forcefully in favor of environmental protection, and minorities are "supposed" to push affirmative action. Similarly, oil company executives are expected to present economic arguments and government officials are "bureaucratic" by definition. The list is not necessarily accurate. After all, physicians are also patients, oil company executives must also breathe polluted air, environmentalists need gasoline at a reasonable price for transportation, and government officials also grow impatient with the excessive red tape.

In many circumstances, personal factors make the difference between success and failure. People must be recognized for what they are. It would be naive and highly inappropriate to assume altruistic motives when such is rarely the case. Individuals expect rewards for their participation in planning activities. These rewards may include, but are not limited to, the following:

- Belonging to a group
- Being part of a worthwhile cause
- Receiving financial or other economic return
- Gaining status in the community
- Satisfying ambition
- Protecting vested personal interests
- Gratifying the need for power
- Achieving professional growth and development
- Deriving spiritual or moral satisfaction

The essential characteristics of leadership in a successful planning process requires a genuine willingness to study a situation, assess the various personal agendas present, and the ability to skillfully direct diverse interests into common goals and objectives in a nonthreatening manner.

MEASUREMENT, VALUE, AND DATA

Value refers to relative worth, importance, desirability, or usefulness. It may be intrinsic or a matter of preference. Intrinsic values are difficult to assess and are usually not amenable to quantification, however, they are real and have to be considered. Whereas the intrinsic value of minerals found underground may be assessed in monetary terms, the value of land for its own sake is difficult to perceive. So, it makes infinitely more sense to think in terms of the use value or exchange value of land. In this way, measures of preference can be applied, which allows comparison of relative worth, importance, desirability, or usefulness.

The exchange value of land is normally measured in monetary units, although in some instances land is swapped or traded for goods or services. Land and improvements upon the land are bought and sold on the market. The price is determined by what a seller and buyer agree upon. Exchange values may be based on figures such as return on investment and potential appreciation, or they may be based on intangible factors such as sentimental attachments, status address, response, and the perception that "it is a nice place to live."

The use value of land relates to its utility for meeting a variety of human needs. It is a higher order of value that addresses public health and welfare in the broadest sense. Land which has a high degree of exchange value does not necessarily have a correspondingly high degree of use value, and vice versa. For instance, deserts and wetlands normally do not command high market prices, but their value in sustaining natural ecosystems is priceless. This is why attempts to convert such lands to commercial and residential uses are often met with open hostility.

There are a variety of methods and techniques available to appraise the value of land in terms of ownership and environmental factors. Real estate appraisal is relatively straightforward. Appraised land value is established according to generally accepted accounting principles which consider such factors as cost, comparable property sales prices, depreciation, and physical and locational characteristics of the land. Environmental factors also affect land appraisals. For example, residential areas in heavy smog belts have lower values than comparable areas where little or no smog exists. Mountain or seacoast views increase the appraised value of residential property. Proximity to an open dump site adversely impacts land value, as would be expected.

Valuation of land in terms of environmental factors is approached from a perspective entirely at variance from that of a buyer or seller of real estate. It is extremely difficult, but not entirely impossible, to assign measurements or weighting factors to open space, preservation of our natural resources, cultural and historical enhancements, air and water, and overall social costs. For instance, we can measure clean air and water in terms of the levels and concentrations of pollutants. We can measure preservation of natural resources in terms of timber cuts, acres under development, and the extent of damage to plants and wildlife. It is possible to measure cultural deterioration in terms of encroachment or downright extinction of artifacts and locations known to be culturally significant. The absence of open space in an urban area is not difficult to document.

The problem is not really in the ability to measure these values, but in the ability to reconcile them in order to derive just and reasonable solutions. The derivation of good solutions depends to a large extent on the collection and analysis of valid and meaningful data. Vigorous debate over inadequacies of information and the decision making process can follow its normal course to a solution. This solution may not and probably will not please everyone concerned, but it is understood by all that the process which produced the solution is valid and acceptable. It is naturally assumed that such a rational decision making process is open to unrestrained participation by all interested parties.

The validity of meaningful data depends upon its utility in terms of decisions which must be made. The tendency is for experts to present literally "tons" of hard facts to either support their view or discredit an opponent's view. The decision making body is required to sift through all this material and select that which is relevant to the problem. The key to data selectivity is a clear understanding of the problem or set of critical problems involved. A well-defined problem statement will contain within it, the exact specifications for data collection and analysis. It is also helpful to define problems as questions which need to be answered before solutions can be found. From this perspective, information requirements will be selective and it will be much easier to separate the data wheat from the data chaff.

ENVIRONMENTAL ASSESSMENT AND IMPACT REPORTING

The idea of examining the impacts of projects is not new. However, traditionally, impact reporting concentrated on the economic and political impacts of land use, which resulted in land degradation and environmental carnage in addition to substantial adverse social impact. Lack of regard to the environmental effects of projects caused soil erosion, destruction of wetlands, polluted rivers, and the deterioration of air quality. All of these factors negatively affected the environment and impacted public health in a significant way. Environmental impact analysis is a proactive approach that examines all aspects of a project including the economic, social, physical, and environmental dimensions, that is, climate, air and water quality, noise, vibration, income, employment, health care, aesthetics, community displacement, and so on.

One of the earlier attempts in illustrating the environmental impacts of development was in 1864 by George Parkins Marsh. In his book titled *Man and Nature*, he examined the anthropogenistic changes that have affected the physical geography of the land. He based the book on his studies of environmental devastation Europe was experiencing in the emergence of the industrial era. He discussed problems relating to deforestation, soil erosion, flooding, and so on. It remains a classic on the beginning of a sizable movement of later writers to heighten the sensitivity of the general public toward these issues. One can clearly see the formidable tasks these early environmentalists pioneered at a time when all of this young nation's resources looked literally inexhaustible. In 1878, Major John Powell sent his report of the Rocky Mountain Region survey to Congress in which he proposed to change the lot size allocation based on the capability of the land rather than fixed sizes. As described earlier, the Homestead Act gave individuals lot sizes of 160 acres without any regard as to whether the land was suitable for agriculture, grazing, or timber harvest. In 1898, Ebenezer Howard published his book titled *Garden Cities of To-Morrow*, in which he emphasized protection of agricultural lands. He was very much against standard rectangle lot divisions and emphasized land uses that would be close to the natural contours of the land. His ideal city was surrounded by a green belt which eliminated the possibility of two adjoining towns meshing together to form a large metropolis.

At the beginning of this century, environmental concerns and their impacts grew out of President Theodore Roosevelt's Commission on Country Life, which addressed topics concerning soil erosion, deforestation, landscape preservation, and so on. During the 1910s and 1920s, Thomas Adams and Frank Waugh emphasized the need for better management of natural resources such as soil, landscape, contours, and forests. During the Depression, President Franklin D. Roosevelt created the Soil Conservation Service with the USDA to address the problem of soil erosion and to propose legislation to protect the environment. It established planning groups in more than 2,400 countries to address flood plains, agricultural runoffs, deforestation, soil erosion, water quality, and a plethora of other related issues.

Earth Day, established in 1970, grew out of concerns for the environment. During the 1970s, landmark environmental legislation was passed, beginning with the passage of NEPA which established the EIS framework. Other bills focused on related aspects of land use (see Chapter 2).

There are two different elements that constitute environmental land use planning, namely, environmental impact assessment (EIA) and land suitability analysis (LSA). LSA emphasizes the fitness of land for a particular use while EIA looks at a number of possible uses for a specific piece of land. Furthermore, EIA investigates any impacts and measures that can be taken to mitigate impacts as well as determine impacts that cannot be mitigated and are irreversible. The typical issues that LSA examines are whether a site is best suited for residential, agricultural, or leisure use. That is to say dry land is better suited for residential use than agricultural use and flat land is better suited for agricultural use than steep slopes.

The first step in land suitability analysis consists of collecting soil samples and other relevant data from the area under study and break them down into a number of different classifications for different uses. The classification of land can become very complex because of the different disciplines employed in the process, such as geology, hydrology, botany, history, geography, and land survey. With the availability of computer programs, these concerns are more easily addressed.

Agencies which are subject to provisions of NEPA must prepare a detailed statement which presents information relevant to the impacts of plans and projects on the environment. There are five general areas of concern which must be addressed.

1.   Overall environmental impact of proposed actions, plans, or policies.
2.   Unavoidable adverse environmental impacts.
3.   Feasible alternatives, including no action.

4. Relationship between the short-range and long-range ramifications of various land use alternatives.
5. Irreversible commitments of resources, should the action be taken.

An environmental impact analysis contains a clear statement of the project and its specific goals, analyzes all the natural resources around the project that would be affected by the project, evaluates different alternatives for the project, selects a plan, and implements the most appropriate plan that optimizes all issues in question. Therefore, in principle the process is very similar to any other management decision. However, what makes this process more complicated and difficult compared to any typical management decision is determining the scope of the impact analysis. This is due to a myriad of issues that might have to be addressed, and the challenge is to choose appropriate issues for examination and eliminate the rest in an effort to keep the cost of such studies within reason. One of the important elements of these studies is looking at the cumulative effect of impact interaction between the project at hand and other approved projects.

Impacts are categorized as primary or secondary. Primary impacts are more direct. For instance, a housing district will accommodate so many families, generate so many jobs, increase the tax base for the community, increase traffic congestion, noise, and so on. Secondary impacts include affects on air quality, population growth, and so on. Some agencies have developed checklists to identify impacts. Other agencies utilize matrices to investigate the causal relationships between specific elements of the project and their effects on the environment. In more complicated projects, more sophisticated quantitative techniques such as network analysis, Delphi techniques, statistical correlations, and computer-based simulation techniques are used.

Once the impacts have been determined, the next step is to display the information. One approach groups the impacts based on taking no action, postponing the action, and further studies are needed prior to taking any action. This enables one to evaluate different options and the tradeoffs among various options. In this approach the impacts and proposed mitigation measures can be seen side by side. The impact can range from having no significant impact to irreversible impact. One of the important issues concerning environmental impact studies are finding ways to reduce the duplication of effort and have a mechanism to use the studies of past studies. To address this, Section 204 of the Demonstration Cities and Metropolitan Development Act of 1966, the Intergovernmental Act of 1968, and the Office of Management and Budget Circular A-95 of 1969 created certain requirements for projects. A later revision of Circular A-95 in 1971 required the involvement of local and state agencies as well. Therefore, Circular A-95 became the clearinghouse model for all states and local government. In 1980, the National Urban Policy report wanted to increase the role of Circular A-95 but President Reagan delegated the processes of establishing their own review process in an executive order that year.

Consideration of the above will at least ensure that environmental concerns are made an integral part of the decision making process. The real effect of environmental impact reporting is to bring factors to mind which might otherwise be ignored, thereby forcing dialogue about the potential environmental implications of actions, plans, and policies. An environmental impact report (EIR) will contain an environmental inventory, an environmental assessment, and an EIS. The report must contain a thorough description of the existing conditions concerning the environment of the area involved in the proposed action. This inventory is essentially a composition of descriptive data regarding physical, biological, and cultural aspects of the environment. It includes information relevant to geology, topography, climate, air and water quality, flora, wildlife, biological species diversity, human population characteristics, economic indicators, and similar elements. This serves as the informational basis for assessment of potential environmental effects.

Environmental assessment involves (1) prediction of environmental change over time, (2) specification of the possible magnitude of such change, and (3) assignment of appropriate weights to each type of environmental change. Proper and valid assessment requires sophistication, application of scientific methods, and expert input from a variety of disciplines. The individual performing the overall environmental assessment must be firmly established in the principles of planning and analysis, and articulate in the communication of evaluative information.

The EIS essentially restates the environmental inventory and assessment in summary form. Several approaches are in use to develop comprehensive environmental inventories, and space does not permit a complete survey. Although the nature of an inventory and the inclusion of factors will vary according to the type of project, a very comprehensive listing prepared by the U.S. Geological Survey provides guidance for the collection of required technical information to be utilized in the assessment stage of environmental impact reporting (see Appendix A). Each alternative proposal must be reviewed in terms of appropriate environmental factors.

Forecasting is necessary since many environmental impacts unfurl over time. Commonly used forecasting techniques such as regression analysis, straight-line projections, and future scenario development are employed in this process. Although a wide variety of methodologies are used in assessment of environmental impact, most of them employ a scale of values which include weighting for significance. Scales may be devised in terms of deviations from established environmental quality standards such as those promulgated for air, water, and noise quality. Some rely on normative or authoritative approaches in the absence of clearly identified quantitative values. The selection of a method for assessment necessarily depends on the situation. In order to see how EISs are handled, let us look at California because it has one of the most comprehensive programs.

California Environmental Quality Act (CEQA)

The last amendments to the CEQA were passed on October 10, 1993. In accordance to CEQA, a lead agency is required to prepare and certify an EIR on a project that may have a significant effect on the environment. Otherwise the agency should file a negative declaration stating that the project will have no affect because of the way it is proposed or the manner in which it is mitigated. The EIR should limit the discussions to measures that are feasible and avoid lengthy, unnecessary, irrelevant descriptions. Furthermore, it is the responsibility of the lead agency to determine what type and level of EIR is needed for a particular project. All counties which have a population of more than 200,000 are required to designate at least one judge who will be versed in environmental laws and land use. Appendix B represents a good example of an EIR prepared for a proposed major project within the California State University system. At this point let us define the various different types of EIRs, namely, master EIR, focused EIR, negative declaration, and a mitigated negative declaration.

Master EIR. A master plan report is prepared if a project is part of a general plan or its amendment, involves a number of individual projects, will lead into subsequent development projects, a mass transit or a highway project which will have various stages of review, and any regulation that will lead to future projects. Such an EIR includes the description of future projects, beginning with reference to their type, size, and density as well as probable locations, for example, the maximum and minimum number of single-family houses in a block or the number and sizes of industries that occupy an area. This information helps determine infrastructure such as utility requirements. In addition, the EIR includes anticipated schedules for implementing the individual projects.

Focused EIR. Following a master EIR, any subsequent EIR pertaining to individual projects is called focused EIR. As would be expected, this EIR examines the project in more detail and studies the cumulative effects, growth-inducing impacts, and notable irreversible effects for this and subsequent projects. Moreover, the report addresses any other relevant significant environmental changes since the master EIR was filed. The report examines the adverse environmental impacts in detail including mitigation measures identified in the master EIR which might have been infeasible then and may be feasible now. Additional significant impacts that were not addressed in the EIR but identified now have to be examined in more detail.

Negative declaration. Negative declaration is a report examining and subsequently stating that a particular project has no substantial evidence of significant impact. This definition implies that, based on objective and reasonable facts, there is no known impact. In other words, the decision cannot be based on unsubstantiated speculations, opinions, or conjecture. Prior to filing a negative declaration, the lead agency is required to contact all other public agencies that have jurisdiction to determine that no other agency will be challenging the decision for the action.

Mitigated negative declaration. Sometimes after a negative declaration has been filed on a project, potentially negative impacts may be identified during the initial study. If the project is modified or revisions are agreed upon by the applicant before the negative declaration is released for public review. In such a case the EIR is referred to as a mitigated negative declaration.

According to CEQA, every draft EIR must be filed with the California State Clearinghouse and made available for public review for a period of thirty days and twenty days for a negative declaration. The notice of the project must be published by the public agency in the newspaper which has the highest general circulation in the affected area. The lead agency should post the notice on site of the project as well as off site. Also, there must be a direct mailing of the notice to owners of all contiguous properties. All documents pertaining to the draft EIR must be available for review and comment. An EIR must include the following information:

- Significant environmental impacts of the project
- Any significant environmental impact that cannot be avoided
- Any significant environmental impact that will be irreversible
- Mitigation measures that will minimize the significance of the environmental impact
- Alternatives to the proposed project
- Discussion of the short-term human use and enhancement of productivity
- Mention other effects that will not impact the environment and thus were not discussed

To minimize the effort, time, and cost of environmental impact reports, CEQA created a means to incorporate results of prior EIRs, general plans, specific plans, and coastal plans into any future report, thus reducing redundancy. Another area that CEQA specifically addressed was the preservation of archaeological resources. The lead agency is required to determine if the proposed project may have a significant effect upon archaeological resources. If the project is having such an impact, the report must address the issue, otherwise a negative declaration of nonunique archeological resources needs to be filed. If there is an archaeological impact, one of the following courses of action can be taken:

- Arrange construction site in order to avoid the archaeological site
- Deed the archaeological area for permanent conservation easement
- Cap the archaeological site with a layer of soil before starting construction
- Plan to build a green space, park, or other open spaces
- Present any other option that would preserve the archaeological resources

If the archaeological resources cannot be preserved in place and the site cannot remain undisturbed, then the applicant must provide a financial guarantee for half of the mitigation measure to the lead agency. Excavation must be limited to objects that will be damaged by the project. Finally, CEQA exempted many types of projects from filing an EIR, including the following:

- The burning of municipal waste, hazardous waste, and refuse-derived fuel
- The exclusive burning of agricultural, wood, and other biomass waste
- Exclusive burning of flare-methane-gas at municipal sewage treatment plants. This includes partial or total burning of gas during the waste treatment process.
- Exclusive burning of less than 1,200 pounds per day of medical waste

This section has paraphrased the CEQA to give the readers a better appreciation of the specific elements in the EISs. For a better understanding and examination of the topic, the reader is strongly encouraged to refer to California Assembly and Senate bills AB 1888 and SB 919, respectively.

Increased sensitivity to environmental issues and concerns will certainly result in a greater reliance upon impact assessment and reporting to guide governmental and private decision making in the future. It is anticipated that more and more land use proposals will be subject to the type of in-depth analysis required under the NEPA and other environment-related legislation. There is no apparent need for additional planning or reporting requirements. On the contrary, the problem is that there might be too many laws and regulations. There is a tendency for agencies responsible for the administration of these laws and regulations to compete with each other for jurisdictional privilege. The result is an inevitable duplication and fragmentation of effort, with no single agency taking a broad view. An integrated approach which considers the relationship of land use to environmental quality is highly desirable and certainly would be more efficient. An integrated land use plan which considers health aspects of use must be formed on the basis of the following criteria:

- Maintenance of individual legal rights to property ownership and use.
- Emphasis on individual responsibility for protection and enhancement of the environment.
- Economy and efficiency in governmental operations.
- Respect for traditional authority relationships among federal, state, and local governments.
- Maximum citizen participation in decision making and planning.
- Enhancement of public health, welfare, and safety.
- Consideration of the relative costs and benefits of alternative land uses with respect to economic, social, and environmental values.
- Use of scientifically based analytic approaches for assessment wherever possible.

These criteria would argue against the proliferation of government programs and rely more on the well-intentioned actions of individuals at the local level. Planning integration must also occur at the local level of government. Rather than create new sense to simplify planning procedures by shifting existing resources to local agencies which are concerned with comprehensive land use planning in all respects, state governments could function as coordinating bodies and suppliers of necessary legal authority to enable local agencies to carry out planning, monitoring, and enforcement activities. The federal government could serve as a repository of information and expertise, a role it is well suited for, given the scope of its influence and its ability to muster a diversity of resources.

The integration of land use and environmental planning must occur if significant long-range enhancement of the quality of life is to be expected. To be sure, there is the need for additional data and further research on the health aspect of land use, but this is not a valid excuse for allowing an unwieldy, inefficient process to continue unchallenged.

USE OF CENSUS DATA

A significant amount of information relevant to land use planning and environmental assessment can be obtained through a variety of data products supplied by the U.S. Bureau of the Census. Although the bureau conducts many surveys, the most comprehensive source of demographic and socioeconomic data is the population census taken at ten-year intervals. Through complete count enumeration and sampling, the census includes data aggregated at various geographic levels. The extent of data provided depends upon size of the geographic area, that is, the larger the area, the greater the coverage. Definitions of these areas are included in the *Census User's Guide* produced by the Bureau of the Census.

Regions and Divisions

The survey is divided into contiguous states according to points on the compass as shown:

Northeast Region
    New England Division
    Middle Atlantic Division
South Region
    South Atlantic Division
    East South Central Division
    West South Central Division
North Central Region
    East North Central Division
    West North Central Division
West Region
    Mountain Division
    Pacific Division

Standard Metropolitan Statistical Areas (SMSAs)

These areas are comprised of either a single county or a grouping of contiguous counties, which include at least one city with a minimum population of 50,000. An SMSA contains counties adjacent to the central city which are metropolitan in character and socially and economically integrated within it as well as rural counties. State lines may be crossed, and there is no limit to the number of counties which may be included.

Urbanized Areas

These are areas which consist of a central city with a population of at least 50,000 inhabitants and surrounding densely settled communities. Urbanized areas can be distinguished from SMSAs in that rural places and communities are not included.

Places

Geographic areas in the United States can be classified into incorporated or unincorporated places. Population concentrations are normally found in incorporated cities and towns but some areas remain politically unincorporated. The Census

Bureau reports data on all places except unincorporated areas with fewer than 1,000 inhabitants.

Minor Civil Divisions (MCDs)

These areas are the basic political and administrative subdivisions of county government. These vary significantly in number of inhabitants and geographic size. Precincts, magisterial districts, townships, and other such entities are considered in this group.

Census Tracts

Since trend analysis requires consistency over time, and because geographic areas based on political jurisdiction are subject to change, census tracts were designed to provide a common area unit for analysis. Census tracts are relatively small areas, of approximately 4,000 inhabitants, which are relatively homogenous with respect to population characteristics, social and economic status, and living conditions. These areas provide very useful data for planning and analytical purposes.

Block Group

These areas are comprised of contiguous city blocks which contain between 200 to 600 households, with an average population of approximately 1,000 persons. Block groups are used for administrative and sampling purposes. They are subdivisions of census; with an average of four groups per tract.

Blocks

Blocks are precisely defined land areas, bounded by streets and roads and contain a population of approximately 100 persons. Blocks do not cross census tract boundaries, but they may cross city, town, and other boundaries. There are approximately forty blocks per census tract, and ten blocks per block group.

The inhabitants of the United States are further designated into "urban" and "rural" groupings. Urban populations consist of those persons residing in a place with a population of more than 2,500 people or densely settled urban fringe of urbanized areas. Rural areas are those which do not fall into the above categories.

Census data is available in printed reports, computer disks, microfilms, and microfiches. The magnetic forms of data storage include considerably more detailed information than the printed reports and other data storage formats. In addition, magnetic formats can be manipulated for a variety of geographic areas. The Census Bureau operates an office—the Central User's Service—to provide information and to act as liaison for census users. Population counts are but one dimension found in the census results. Examples of additional information important to land use planning and environmental assessment are age, sex, race/ethnicity, and marital status; education level and the number of children in the family; employment status, occupation, and income; length of residence, place of work, and means of transportation to work; presence and duration of disability; housing characteristics and property values; use of land for farming, and source of water for residential use and sewage disposal method. This information is key to intelligent planning and decision making relative to the environmental health aspects of land use.

Demographic Analysis

The use of census data for direct analysis of the size and composition of the population for a variety of geographic areas is obvious and, of course, absolutely essential for health, environmental, and land use planning, development, and assessment. Another very important use of census data is the provision of denominator data in the compilation of ratios for demographic analysis. It is generally not sufficient to draw conclusions regarding health effects solely from the analysis of census data. The relationship among health, environment, and demographic characteristics require data from other sources which can be linked to demographic data.

Linkages may be forged with national, state, and local health and environmental data sources. This can be accomplished either manually or by merging and manipulating computerized data files. For example, at the national and state levels, census reports can be compared to reports on vital events and reports on air pollution levels to provide insights into relationships among important variables. At the local level, printed reports are normally useful at the city and county levels. Community and neighborhood data normally lack consistency in geographic configuration and definition. However, many data items are aggregated at the census tract level especially in the urban areas of the United States. Census tracts can further be configured into small areas which correspond to community and neighborhood areas of concern. Some prime examples of ratios constructed from linked data sets are shown in Tables 8.1–8.3.

Table 8.1
Mortality Ratios

Numerator Data	Denominator Data
Total Death	Total Population
Cause by age, sex, and race/ethnicity	Age, sex, and race/ethnicity
Geography	Geography
Occupation	Occupation
Infant deaths	Children less than one-year old
Maternal deaths	Women of child bearing age

Table 8.2
Morbidity Ratios

Numerator Data	Denominator Data
Reportable Diseases	Total Population
Acute diseases	Age groups, sex,
Chronic diseases	Race/ethnicity,
Contagious diseases	Occupation

Many ratios can be calculated from linked data sets which shed light on the relationships among demographics, health status, and environmental factors. Further linkage between geographic factors and land use patterns greatly assist in a better understanding of health and environmental aspects of land use.

State and federal involvement in land use planning has significantly increased during the last fifteen years as a result of the failure of local government to implement effective land use controls and to mitigate the resulting adverse impact of poor local land use decisions which impact other jurisdictions and the public. These types of problems eventually require the involvement of state and federal agencies for effective resolution. A land use program must have strong local input. Such programs should secure and promote the health, safety, and well-being of the public and prevent environmental degradation through environmental health and administrative measures.

Table 8.3
Nationality Ratios

Numerator Data	Denominator Data
Total Births	Total Population
Age of mother	Age by sex
Plurality	Age, race/ethnicity, income
Place of birth	Place of residence
Legitimacy	Marital status

9
Toward a Sustainable Land Use Model

A comprehensive land use plan considers implications for the environment and public health as an integral part of the overall framework. The science of ecology has given valuable information concerning the relationship of organisms and their environment. Therefore, land use planning that incorporates these dimensions is a complex, multidisciplinary activity that impacts many aspects of the legal, social, and economic fabric of a nation and is a multidimensional problem with apparently conflicting interests. This apparent conflict can be resolved by shifting our paradigms from exclusively considering immediate impacts to addressing long-term implications in a comprehensive manner. Before discussing possible models it behooves us to concentrate on the status of public health issues resulting from public policy decisions affecting the environment.

Since the turn of the century, changes in the public health field have been gradual, but profound. As we move to the next millennium, public health challenges may be categorized as philosophical, technical, and political. To have a better appreciation of these issues, we must first examine changes that have occurred in the corresponding spheres of influence.

In the first sphere of influence, the philosophical, we have witnessed changes in the definition of health. These changes reflect prevailing ideologies as well as political and professional forces of the times. In early 1900, health was negatively and narrowly defined as the absence of disease. However, more than four decades ago, a broader definition of health, developed by the World Health Organization (WHO), expanded personal health concerns beyond that of the physical into social and mental well-being.

In 1972, working with the President's Committee on Health Education, El-Ahraf and Hanson developed an ecological definition of health. The new definition of health was based on that of WHO and then expanded in recognition of the reciprocal relationship and interdependence between personal and environmental health as follows: "Health is a complete state of physical, mental, social and environmental well-being and not merely the absence of disease, infirmity or eco-pathological conditions" (El-Ahraf and Hanson 1972: 1, El-Ahraf 1986: 3). The El-Ahraf and Hanson definition was recognized by the 1986 World Conservation Strategy Conference held in Ottawa, Canada. In such a model, environmental and eco-pathological parameters are recognized to have substantial impact on the health of society and its sustained development.

In the second sphere of influence, the technological, changes have brought about these startling events:

- the first public health revolution against most communicable diseases
- reduction of disability and death rates among patients suffering from chronic diseases
- recognition of health-threatening impacts of a chemically sophisticated second industrial revolution
- recognition of the enormous cost and shortcomings of the latest medical and industrial revolutions

The changes in the third sphere of influence, namely political, are signified by the environmental revolution of the 1960s, followed by landmark legislative action. The creation of environmental protection institutions such as the EPA and the Occupational Safety and Health Administration (OSHA) increased the nation's emphasis in evaluating and controlling toxic substances in the air, water, and land. Unfortunately, the flourishing of the environmental protection agencies has resulted in a false dichotomy in the administration of personal health services and environmental protection programs. Personal health services goals cannot be achieved in a vacuum that ignores the interdependency of personal and environmental health. Several departments of health have exacerbated the dichotomy of relegating environmental health services to a lower position than personal health services and stressing tradition over innovation, in other cases, environmental matters were administered within organizations completely separate from health agencies. This is despite the growing recognition of the importance of the relationship evident in the amount of research conducted on local and national levels and the use of health data to justify enactment of some environmental legislation and vice versa. Yet, environmental movement has matured and has established the environment as an important constant in national and international political arenas.

INTEGRATIVE MODEL FOR ENVIRONMENTAL MANAGEMENT

One must take a historical view on environmental management and the underlying factors that affect its contemporary development. Environmental management differs from other kinds of management in one basic respect: it represents a sense of mission, a commitment to the quality of life, survival, and well-being of human, animal, and plant species and the preservation of their ecological system. This supports the idea of ecologically sustainable development and understanding of the health implications of environmental factors.

There is no doubt that environmental management is socially important. The scope and magnitude of environmental management straddles both the synthetic and natural environments. For example, in the area of pollution abatement alone, control measures must represent the full spectrum from man-made pollution of industrial nature (such as water pollution, one of the most pervasive threats to the economies and health of modern society) to naturally occurring contaminants of microbial origin (such as aflatoxin, one of the most potent hepatocarcinogens ever discovered). The balance between industrial development and protection of natural systems is another example. These and other factors have resulted in significant public and governmental commitments at national and international levels, to alleviate these problems and to establish a new rational order of environmental management. Social concerns about the quality of housing and the residential environment added to the significance of an emerging commitment to a quality environment for all. A commitment toward appropriate environmental management requires application of natural and social sciences as well as a high degree of imagination and creativity. The success of modern environmental management depends on how well it faces challenges and to what extent it can utilize opportunities. The major ones are noted here.

The Broadened Scope of Environmental Management

There is evidence that governmental units and the public tend to define "environment" in a broad, if not vague, sense. However, environmental priorities tend to be defined more specifically. For example, U.S. cities identify land use as a primary concern, followed by general growth problems, solid waste, and waste water. On the other hand, counties define solid waste and land use as their primary problem with waste water and growth problems following. In both cases, environmental health concerns are self-evident. A survey of local environmental management problems conducted by the International City Management Association for the EPA asked local governments to select the most applicable definition of four alternative definitions of "environment" these were as follows:

1. Considered aspects such as air, noise, sewage, solid wastes, toxic substances, and water.
2. Included the additional elements of energy, historical preservation, land use, open space, radiation, population, and wildlife preservation.
3. Added aesthetics, health, housing, mass transportation, recreation, streets, and highways.
4. Considered all of the above and economic development, education, employment, public safety, and welfare.

Results indicated that cities and counties favored one of the two broad definitions (3 and 4). The acceptance of these broad definitions illustrates the basic elements of the modern concept of environmental management as both intersegmental and interdisciplinary in nature. It is clear that healthy economic development depends on healthy individuals and vice versa. Such an understanding is essential to achieving a sustainable ecological development.

Broadened Scope and Philosophy of Health

The important step taken by WHO to broaden the definition of personal health to a significant degree set the stage for progress. There is no doubt that the acceptance and proposals of broader health definitions stem from past successes of the public health and environmental measures in controlling communicable diseases. Also, broader definitions reflect the advances made in the biomedical and behavioral sciences that brought new dimensions to health and enhanced awareness of ecological systems. In turn, that awareness brought new understanding of the interacting relationship between health and the environment and consequently the health implications of environmental factors.

Environment as the New Frontier in Health Research

WHO and the U.S. National Cancer Institute statistics indicate that 60 to 90 percent of cancer causes are environmentally related. Thousands of new chemicals are introduced annually with only a fraction tested for carcinogenic effect.

The role of environmental management has been emphasized as a practical consideration in improving public health. It is now generally recognized that impressive improvement in human health can be achieved not through specific therapy but through an improved environment.

Environment in Public Policy

The environment has been an issue in public policy making for the past forty years, and it seems that it will stay with us for some time to come. Illustrated by NEPA, three factors contributed to this trend: (1) environment is a social issue; (2) the environmental movement has matured; and (3) the environment has become an essential ingredient in the public policy decision making process.

Today environmental management must deal with the fact that the environment is a social issue as well as a scientific endeavor. Caldwell has noted that "A social issue is a question or problem that has aroused concern within society and that requires social or public decision for its resolution. Such issues are social because they require collective action and cannot be resolved solely by individual choice. They inevitably become political and governmental, because politics in the broad sense is the principle process of social decision, and the principle instrument of politics is government" (Caldwell 1971: 24). The maturity of the environment as a social and public issue has been expressed in the enactment of legislation and the establishment of governmental agencies to enforce it.

The CAA, CWA, EPA OSHA, NIOSH, Occupational Health and Safety Act and the Consumer Product Safety Commission (CPSC) represent examples of legislation and agencies created because of public pressures. Additionally, the Metropolitan Development Act and the Model Cities and Model Neighborhood Programs were developed in the 1960s to respond to growing professional and public concerns about deteriorating health and social conditions in the inner cities and the need to provide innovative and imaginative solutions to old problems. Similarly, the concept of zero tolerance of carcinogens in food came as a result of public and political pressures and continues to be effective because cancer is a social issue as well as an environmental health problem.

The emergence of the environment as a social issue and a factor in public policy is reflected not only in the complexity of environmental laws within nations and across international boundaries, but also in the broad human-rights-type declarations in some of these laws. For example, NEPA asserted the right of U.S. citizens to an aesthetically pleasing and healthy environment.

Broader Scope of Environmental Health

While environmental health can be viewed as an ecological balance between humans and their environment, it is also a representation of a complex relationship between the environment and human health. It can also be described in terms of levels of concern that include human survival, freedom from illness, health maintenance, human efficiency, comfort, enjoyment of life, environmental aesthetics and preservation of natural beauty.

One level of environmental health concern is not necessarily separated from another. Together they represent a gradient of important aspects of the human condition and how it can be influenced by the surrounding environment. Furthermore, environmental health can be defined as the "interface between environment and health as well as between scientific endeavors and social issues. It revolves around human daily needs for safe food, clean air and water and healthy residential, occupational and work environments" (El-Ahraf 1986: 4).

Environmental health has unique features. It interfaces between environment and health and between scientific knowledge and social awareness. It revolves around human daily needs and requirements for safe water and food, healthy work environment, housing maintenance and occupancy, and proper land use and management. These features provide the basis for the emergence of environmental health as an organizing concept of significant issues in global environmental management with its emphasis on ecologically sustainable development and an understanding of the health implications of environmental factors.

INTEGRATIVE APPROACH TO INTERNATIONAL ENVIRONMENTAL MANAGEMENT

Several efforts have been made and currently are being made to formulate contemporary environmental management concepts and comprehensive environmental policy. Since 1969, more than 300 multilateral environmental treaties have been adopted. These involve issues that require international cooperation to adequately address the problem. Some of the important international treaties are listed below:

- 1989 Basel Convention addressed the trade and transfrontier movement of hazardous substances.
- 1985 Vienna Convention for the Protection of the Ozone Layer led to the 1986 Montreal Protocol where the production of ozone-depleting substances were phased out.
- 1975 Convention on International Trade in Wild Flora and Fauna concerning the trade of wildlife.
- 1971 Ramsar Convention addressed national wetlands that have international significance.

Such agreements are of paramount importance to protect the ecosystem and conserve the biological diversity of the Earth. Scientists estimated that of the 10 to 30 million plant and animal species known to exist in 1980, roughly 1.5 to 6 million will be extinct by the next decade. This is three to four orders of magnitude faster than during any other time in the earth's history. This avalanche of rapid extinction can exclusively be attributed to anthropogenic impacts. Preservation of the environment does not recognize political boundaries, and ecological challenges ignore national maps. Today no one country can solve environmental problems alone. The key for success in current and future challenges is cooperation among neighboring countries, regional treaties, and global agreements. The first effort toward the formulation of comprehensive environmental policy has been planning. But, planning, at least in the United States, generally lacks the authority to execute. Because of this and other factors, planning remains a technical process that has not succeeded fully in becoming policy.

A comprehensive environmental management approach must reject segmental thinking and segmental decision making. Some of today's environmental problems are blamed on the limitation of segmental thinking and segmental decision making in the past. Some problems of housing, urban renewal, water quality, transportation, sewage, solid waste, and others were made more difficult than necessary by failure of the community or its decision makers to think in an integrative fashion. For example, public housing, particularly in urban renewal areas, has substituted a new set of socioenvironmental problems for those presumed to have been solved. Despite success on many fronts and general improvement, examples of failure to think in environmental terms can be found in many other areas. For example, in a number of developing countries, advances in clean water projects progress far ahead of sewage disposal projects. Yet, it is clear that piped water in villages means greater utilization thus aggravating the sewage disposal situations. This, added to poor land use decisions, has resulted in pools of stagnant water breeding disease-carrying mosquitoes and causing a foul odor in many neighborhoods. In the international arena, the tendency to separate water quantity from water quality considerations among countries with common water resources still prevails.

However, in the past few years, a number of regional agreements and models have addressed environmental issues successfully through innovative approaches and mutual cooperation. Three examples are briefly discussed below that demonstrate what is possible when a serious attempt is made to tackle environmental challenges in a comprehensive manner.

Bahrain Environmental Code of Conduct

This accord was proposed by Japan and ratified in 1994 by delegations from forty-one countries including Algeria, Bahrain, Egypt, Israel, Jordan, Kuwait, Morocco, Oman, Palestine, Saudi Arabia, and others. The accord created a framework for environmental issues that will govern national development policies. In addition, the countries will cooperate in finding solutions for common regional threats such as desertification, pollution, rapid urbanization, and so forth and will work to protect the unique ecological features of the area.

Metropolitan Environmental Improvement Program

The Metropolitan Environmental Improvement Program addresses the growing environmental concerns surrounding major metropolitan regions in developing countries. In 1989, the United Nations Development Program, the World Bank, and the Metropolitan Environmental Improvement Program (MEIP) assisted several major metropolitan regions in developing countries to find practical solutions to growing environmental challenges facing these countries. According to a World Bank report, by 1993 programs were underway in six Asian nations and work had begun in Beijing, Bombay, Colombo, Jakarta, Kathmandu, and Manila. The overall framework of MEIP insures that impacts are studied across all relevant sectors to insure the involvement of all stakeholders of the urban community and its natural support system.

The Natural Step

The Natural Step (*Det Naturliga Stegett*) was founded as a nonprofit organization in 1989 by Karl-Henrik Robert, a Swedish physicist and cancer researcher. The organization has tried to attract attention to environmental concerns and seek solutions to preserve the prerequisite for the existence of life. The fundamental principle behind Robert's thinking is both simple and elegant. He asserts the basic prerequisite of life on Earth is the cell and in order to preserve life on the planet, we must all join forces to protect it. With this basic philosophy, Natural Step has focused on being an educational resource for companies and municipalities in Sweden. A program based on the following four basic questions relevant to the ecological impacts of a given development project:

1. How does a particular project impact the consumption of finite material resources?
2. Is the use of long-lived synthetic materials reduced or increased as a result of the project?
3. What is the impact on natural diversity and ecocycle? Is it increased, decreased, or does it remain the same?
4. What type of an impact does the project have on energy consumption? Will it increase, decrease, or remain the same?

Based on these efforts and the Natural Step, by the end of 1996, all Swedish municipalities were expected to complete a plan based on ecocycle principles. This movement has expanded into almost all spheres of Swedish society and is now attracting a fair amount of attention worldwide. It is likely that many other countries will emulate their success story.

HEALTHY COMMUNITIES MOVEMENT

A healthy community is one that supports its people in achieving a complete sense of physical, mental, and social well-being (WHO, 1986). A community includes any collection of people with common interests and shared values. The healthy communities movement embraces the idea that communities working collaboratively in a partnership arrangement with mutual support, shared responsibilities, and shared benefits can bring about an improved state of health and well-being. Common characteristics of healthy community groups include multisectored representation that attempts to meld a diversity of interests and concerns and a focus on community-based needs in the broadest sense. Typical issues of concern include health and mental health services, social services, economic development, education (at all levels), public safety and protection, environmental quality, housing and food, transportation, culture, and recreation.

At the international level, the WHO sponsors healthy cities projects in over thirty-five European cities and eighteen national networks in Western and Eastern Europe, North America, and Australia. At the national level, the U.S. Public Health Services, American Hospital Association, Healthcare Forum, National Civic League, and the Kellogg Foundation have established projects in hundreds of cities and communities throughout the United States. Two states (California and Indiana) have established state-level healthy communities agencies. In Oregon and southwest Washington, there are at least six healthy community groups including Portland, Washington County, Bend, Salem, Clark County, and Cowlitz County. Dr. Dowd, currently chair of the Washington County Healthy Communities Task Force, is forming a regional consortium to address issues of common interest among the other groups. This Consortium for Building Healthier Communities will include representatives from local healthy communities groups and other key organizations to support collaboration in education, research, advocacy, communications, and information systems development.

A key assumption in bringing about a healthy, nurturing community or system is that groups and institutions concerned with health and human services needs in the community, acting collaboratively with focus and knowledge, can be empowered to bring about significant change for the resolution of targeted issues of relevancy to the community. These groups and institutions will form collaborative alliances and, in concert with broader community interests, identify and articulate critical issues, assess community health and social needs, develop and prioritize objectives, formulate strategic alternatives, select and implement feasible strategies, establish benchmarks, and assess progress and results. These collaborative alliances will, in turn, establish and maintain a planning, implementation, and assessment structure and process that involves engagement in concerted and sustained activities designed to empower those collaborating groups and institutions to bring about a healthy, nurturing community.

Nurturing communities and systems that embrace common ground will focus on creating a sense of purpose and shared vision that binds people together and inspires them to fulfill their deepest aspirations. The formulation of a common vision and mission and a mutual set of values and principles will set the stage for defining critical issues of concern and will provide the framework for development of strategies and actions that will ultimately bring about desired changes in the lives of residents, workers, and constituents. Collaborative efforts by communities and systems are constructive responses to creating and maintaining a nurturing atmosphere that provides a safety net for children, youth, and families.

Successful collaboration involves both structure and process. The National Network for Collaboration has developed a model that is useful to consider in the formulation of criteria for judging the efficacy of collaborative efforts. This model is based on the premise that collaboration is a process of participation through which people, groups, and organizations work together to achieve desired results. The capacity to work together is determined by the nature and strength of relationships among collaborating parties. The first step in developing a collaboration framework is building and sustaining relationships of trust wherein expectations are clearly understood by all participating individuals. Positive relationships lead to a common vision and provide the values and principles that allow concerted action to achieve mutually supported outcomes. The collaboration framework provides common elements relating to structure and process that should be incorporated into any effort designed to bring about nurturing communities or systems. These elements include grounding, core foundation, outcomes, and process of contextual factors.

All collaboration framework elements are grounded in valuing and respecting diversity, that is, respect for each other's ideas, talents and uniqueness and appreciation for other's interests and concerns. Valuing and respecting diversity will result in openness, understanding, and sharing. Mutual aspirations and commitment to a common cause can only come about when a collaborating group is somehow represented in the planning and decision making process. Furthermore, an effective collaboration requires open, uninhibited communication that comes from grounding in valuing and respecting diversity, which supplies the knowledge and skills required to effectively cause change and realize intended outcomes.

The core foundation represents the common base of understanding that binds individuals together for a common cause. Development of the core foundation centers on defining the purpose of the collaboration (mission), an image of the overall desired future of the community or system (vision), and a set of beliefs or values and principles that provide the foundation for working relationships and describe how the organization intends to operate on a continuing basis.

A healthy community supports and enables its citizenry or constituents to achieve optimal health, well-being, and quality of life in an environment which enhances livability and affordability, fosters uninhibited access to health and human services and community strength.

Work undertaken by Dr. Ron Dowd in Oregon has led to a focus on three critical issue areas of concern. Dr. Dowd is currently professor of public administration and public health at Portland State University in Portland, and he has extensive experience planning, organizing, and assessing health and human service delivery systems.

1. *Community livability and affordability* as these relate to quality of life with respect to employment, housing, living environment, and land use. *Dimensions* of this issue area would include housing, employment/income, economic development, ability to secure basic services, and land use. *Contradictions* to a nurturing community or system would be inadequate housing, insufficient income and employment, poor economic development, lack of basic services, and suboptimal land use.

2. *Access to human and health services* as this relates to the ability of the health and human services delivery system to provide appropriate and quality services in a timely and responsive manner to those in need. *Dimensions* of this issue area would include information and awareness, consumer barriers, provider barriers, organizational delivery system, and disenfranchised population. *Contradictions* to a nurturing community or system would be inability to access and understand information, inability to reduce consumer barriers, inability to reduce provider barriers, malfunctioning delivery system, and the existence of disenfranchised populations.

3. *Family health, development, and support* relates to empowerment, self-esteem, and supportive families to resist addictive and dysfunctional behaviors in families, children, and youth. *Dimensions* of this issue would include family physical and mental health, integrated/comprehensive services, education and personal development, environmental quality, and recreational/social opportunity. *Contradictions* to a nurturing community or system would be poor family health, lack of integrated services, limited choices for development, degrading quality of life, and inadequate social and recreation outlets.

Nurturing communities and systems will enable effective action in two areas:

1. *Collaboration and integration* as a means to achieve results. *Dimensions* in this area would include community or system environment and customs, collaborating group characteristics, groups connectedness and communication patterns and resources. *Contradictions* to a nurturing community or system would be lack of

historical collaborative working relationships, inadequate representation in decision making, lack of mutual respect and trust, inhibited and limited communication, and insufficient financial and human resources.

2. *Capacity building and empowerment* as a means to enable focus and progress. *Dimensions* in this area would include leadership, knowledge of the community or system, skills in community or system development, ability to function as a team, research and evaluation capacity, and sustainability. *Contradictions* to a nurturing community or system would be poor, or absent, leadership, insufficient information about the community or system, absence of learning venues to expand knowledge and skills, inability to work together with common purpose and commitment, insufficient technical assistance to plan, implement, and evaluate interventions, and inability to sustain group effort.

The above outcomes can be viewed as end results, or goals, to be anticipated in healthy communities and systems. Outcomes are either impact outcomes or process outcomes. Impact outcomes address community livability and affordability, access to health and human services, and family health, development and support. Process outcomes address effective action—collaboration and integration and capacity building and empowerment. Goals are further refined into a hierarchy of subgoals and objectives that express the eventual outcome as a sequence of desired changes in related dimensions that, taken as a whole, are expected to result in the eventual outcome—a healthy community. The outcome envisioned here is to bring about a situation in the community and among its systems that provides community livability and affordability, access to health and human services and family health, development and support *through a process* of collaboration, integration, capacity building, and empowerment. The eventual outcome will be achieved if all subgoals and related objectives are achieved. In short, we have a healthy community when communities and systems are enabling its citizenry or constituencies to take effective action to achieve optimal health, well-being and quality of life in an environment which enhances livability and affordability, fosters uninhibited access to basic health and human services and encourages a focus on the family as the basic unit for wellness and community strength.

OTHER APPROACHES

Environmental management is becoming a multidisciplinary subject that is now emerging in several contexts in higher education. Using an ecological definition of health and a broader concept of environmental quality, a comprehensive practical approach to environmental management can be developed using a community-based model which embodies the concept of a health care management continuum and the concept of an environmental management continuum.

Health Care Management Continuum

Achieving a complete state of health, with due consideration to ecological factors requires attention to four interactive components of a health care management continuum. These are:

1. curative or treatment services, including surgery
2. health education to enable people to make decisions concerning their health
3. environmental management to strike at the roots of eco-pathological conditions and to reduce environmentally preventable illnesses and the cost of treatment
4. education research in order to strengthen the scientific basis of policy making and decisions

These interacting elements serve as the basis for an integrative management approach to health care management. Aside from issues related to cost reduction, the continuum represents an innovative approach to achieving public health rather than continuing with an illness model of medical care.

Environmental Continuum

The environmental continuum approach was developed by El-Ahraf and Hanson as a conceptual framework that represents the full spectrum of human needs and ecology. It has the following characteristics:

*   It employs environmental health as its primary organizing concept and utilizes its potential.
*   It includes socioenvironmental considerations in addition to the physical and biological environmental arrangements.
*   It accommodates different lifestyles and responds to environmental concerns of different social strata, extending from concerns about poor housing to conservation of natural resources and pure ecological considerations.
*   It uses a programmatic approach to environmental management where environmental improvement can be the end result or just a mechanism to reach another social or economic end.
*   It emphasizes a community approach to environmental management.
*   It avoids environmental polarization and environmental dichotomy in the community.

In addition, the concept of environmental continuum is simpler than the ecosystem approach and, as such, is easier to translate into public policy.

A community approach to environmental management utilizes two potent forces: the potential of environmental health in both the health continuum and in the environmental continuum, and wise utilization of human resources. This is particularly significant in the case of developing countries. The concept of the environmental continuum was used by El-Ahraf and Hanson as the conceptual basis for a successful environmental management model in the Willowbrook neighborhood of the South Central area of Los Angeles, California, and such it was tested under field conditions.

The Willowbrook Model Neighborhood Program was a part of the larger national effort of the Model Cities Program designed to improve urban conditions through the infusion of federal funding to generate citizen and local government involvement in dealing with urban decay and the array of social ills, environmental deterioration, poor health and depressed economic conditions associated with it. While the concept of the Model Cities Program was an innovation in itself, the Willowbrook Model Neighborhood Program went a step further by developing the local capacity to involve the community in its own affairs through exercising the empowerment of citizens of all ages to act on their own behalf in a team approach with the environmental health professional. School children were involved in environmental education programs with a wide range of objectives ranging from enhancing/creating a sense of environmental aesthetics to understanding the biology of rats in order to control them in one of the poorest neighborhoods in the nation. Children at one school shared their experience with children from other schools and taught them the essentials of environmental education.

Youth were involved in activities that took them away from identification with gangs and into the realm of positive impact on their environment including cleanup campaigns, control programs known as cockroach crusades, and recycling.

Mature adults were involved in block clubs where they represented a socio-environmental movement to create a better environment under what would be discouraging human conditions. Professional organizations, the county board of supervisors, local universities, and the news media joined together with the Willowbrook community to provide support and encouragement. Dr. El-Ahraf and Mr. Hanson were invited to appear before President Nixon's Committee on Health Education to describe the innovative techniques used in the Willowbrook Model Neighborhood Program. Since Willowbrook was in the County of Los Angeles and not the city, the term Model Neighborhood was employed rather than the more common Model Cities designation.

Human Settlement Approach

The human settlement approach, as illustrated by the Doxiadis Theory of Ekistics which embodies urban and regional planning. It is a theory of action, and its realization assumes an ongoing environmental administration of the total in accordance with verified ecological understanding. Doxiadis argued that under-standing the whole range of human settlements from the primitive to the most developed is essential to acquiring proper knowledge of the individual cities, towns, and villages where people live. Human settlements represent a complex system of fine elements (i.e., nature, humans, society, buildings, and networks). As such, the complexity of the system is illustrated by the fact that it is a system of man-made as well as natural, social, and political elements. These can be seen from social, political, economic, cultural, and technological points of view. The widest and most comprehensive view is needed to fully understand the subject of human settlements. Doxiadis stated that "to achieve the needed knowledge and to develop the science of human settlements we must move from an interdisciplinary approach to a condisciplinary science; making links between different disciplines is not enough. If we have one subject we need one science, and this is what ekistics, the science of human settlements has tried to achieve" (Doxiadis 1970: 393).

Yet this science is not entirely new. Ancient civilizations must have possessed this science in order to build the marvelous cities they built. Successful human settlements are judged as such when they achieve a balance between humans and their human-made environment. In creating human settlements, humans have obeyed general principles and laws that represent an extension of man's biological characteristics and their subsequent linkage to the biology of larger systems. Five specific principles have shaped human settlements. These are:

1. maximization of man's potential contacts with the elements of nature, with the work of humans and with other people.
2. minimization of the effort required for achieving actual and potential contacts with these elements.
3. optimization of human's protective space to avoid physical harm or psychological discomfort.
4. optimization of the quality of humans' relationship with their environment including nature, society, networks (i.e., roads and various forms of telecommunication) and shells (i.e., buildings for residential or work uses).
5. achieving optimum synthesis of the previously listed four principles.

When appropriate balance is achieved, successful human settlements are created now and into the future. Using scientific principles, ekistics emphasizes that human settlements are subject to systematic investigation and are most successful when a balance between humans and the surrounding ecology is achieved. Within this context one can appreciate the work of Doxiadis and its impact on broader environmental issues.

Problem Shed Approach

The problem shed approach employs economics as its primary organizing concept, but it also incorporates data from other sciences, especially engineering and physical sciences, to analyze a particular environmental problem for which specific boundaries can be identified. This approach has been applied principally to water quality management. This is best illustrated by the fact that this approach "employs economics as its primary organizing concept, but incorporates physical sciences, engineering and all other data relevant to the analysis of particular environmental problems for which specified boundaries can be identified." (Caldwell 1971: 16).

Ecosystem Approach

The ecosystem approach as symbolized by the Spaceship Earth model emphasizes an ecological concept in which the life-support system is basically closed. Therefore, "to approach environments as ecosystems means that the totality of interacting entities and systems, physical and social, that comprises every environment must be taken in any decision regarding the environment" (Caldwell 1971: 18). The complexity of the system makes it a formidable task to convert it into public policy. Yet it is of utmost importance to incorporate this concept in administrative and scientific discussions concerning environmental quality and health.

New International Scientific Order (NISO)

In addressing the issue of United Nations (UN) agencies and global science, Dittmann prepared a paper that addresses the issue of the New International Scientific Order (NISO). In the context of the impact of science, economics, energy and other factors on the global environment and the requirement for a new approach among UN agencies and countries he noted "the formulation of a New International Scientific [and Technological] Order (NISO) should incorporate, but not be restricted to, the relevant elements of the New International Economic Order. The New International Information and Communication Order, the UN Conference on Science, Technology and Development (UNCSTD) and other international agreements which have been by-and-large agreed upon, such as those achieved in the UN Conference on the Environment and Development (UNCED), and the Cairo Conference on Sustainable Development and Population" (Dittmann 1999: 1). Dittmann further noted that developing countries in particular have requested access to technology that is environmentally safe and energy-efficient.

CONCLUSION

El-Ahraf and Hanson's ecological definition of health provides a philosophical basis for global environmental management with environmental health as an organizing concept. An integrative approach should synthesize a number of environmental management approaches, that is, health care management continuum, environmental management continuum, Ekistics, problem shed, and the ecosystem approach. Mathematical modeling, including techniques used by the Club of Rome, should also be considered. The implication of these broadened scopes and definitions of environment and health is clear: those attempting to solve environmental problems must have equivalent depth, breadth, and ability to synthesize the diverse technical material in a manner that is useful to public policy makers and the public at large in the decision making process.

A comprehensive and integrated approach to analyzing current environmental activities on a national and global basis and predicting their future impact on land use, should replace the crisis-oriented, segmented approach. The two objectives of understanding the value of ecologically sustainable development and the importance of the health implication of environmental factors then can be integrated into a global environmental management model. The ultimate goal is to develop a sustainable land use model where public policy supports environmental quality and public health.

Appendix A
U.S. Geological Survey Environmental Inventory Checklist

I. Physical and Chemical Characteristics

    A. Earth

        1. Mineral resources
        2. Construction material
        3. Soils
        4. Landform
        5. Force fields and background radiation
        6. Unique physical features

    B. Water

        1. Surface
        2. Ocean
        3. Underground
        4. Quality
        5. Temperature
        6. Recharge
        7. Snow, ice and permafrost

    C. Atmosphere

        1. Quality such as gases, particulate, etc.
        2. Climate (micro and macro)
        3. Temperature

D.   Processes

    1.   Floods
    2.   Erosion
    3.   Deposition such as sedimentation, precipitation, etc.
    4.   Solution
    5.   Sorption such as ion exchange, complexing, etc.
    6.   Compaction and settling
    7.   Stability such as slides and slumps
    8.   Stress-strain (earthquakes)
    9.   Air movement

II.   Biological Conditions

A.   Flora and Fauna

    1.   Trees
    2.   Shrubs
    3.   Grass
    4.   Benthic organisms
    5.   Insects
    6.   Microfauna
    7.   Endangered species
    8.   Barriers
    9.   Corridors

III.   Cultural Factors

A.   Land Use

    1.   Wilderness and open spaces
    2.   Wetlands
    3.   Forestry
    4.   Grazing
    5.   Agriculture
    6.   Residential
    7.   Commercial
    8.   Industrial
    9.   Mining and quarrying

B.   Recreation

    1.   Hunting
    2.   Fishing
    3.   Boating
    4.   Swimming
    5.   Camping and hiking
    6.   Picnicking
    7.   Resorts

C. Aesthetics and Human Interest

1. Scenic and human interest
2. Wilderness qualities
3. Open space qualities
4. Landscape design
5. Unique physical features
6. Parks and reserves
7. Monuments
8. Rare and unique species or ecosystems
9. Historical or archaeological site and objects
10. Presence of misfits

D. Cultural status

1. Cultural patterns (lifestyle)
2. Health and safety
3. Employment
4. Population density

E. Construction facilities and activities

1. Structures
2. Transportation network (movement and access)
3. Utility networks
4. Waste disposal
5. Barriers
6. Corridors

IV. Ecological Relationships

A. Salinization of water resources
B. Eutrophication
C. Disease-insect vectors
D. Food chains
E. Salinization of surficial material
F. Brush encroachment
G. Other items

Appendix B
San Diego State University
Final Environmental Impact Report

This EIR addresses the procurement of roughly 300 acres of the former Prohoroff Ranch in Northern San Diego County for the purpose of building the San Diego State University North County Center. The proposed land lies within the city limits of the city of San Marcos and was bounded by Twin Oak Valley Road from the east, Myrtle Road-Barham Drive from the south, and La Moree Road from the east. During the time the EIR was being conducted, this particular area was lightly populated, but future projections indicated a rapid growth. This is one of the reasons why the trustees of California State University were very much interested in moving relatively quickly, since the availability of sizable contiguous land parcels was diminishing rapidly.

The California State University interest was based on the projected enrollment increase at the San Diego State University campus coming from the northern parts of San Diego County. Since San Diego State University's main campus had exceeded its master plan enrollment, in order to meet additional enrollment growth, a center in the northern edge of the county was needed. The study evaluated various aspects such as site geology including seismicity, soil conditions, active or inactive faults, projected demographics and predicted population growth, and the economic viability of the area. Moreover, essential factors such as infrastructure issues relating to water, gas, electricity, sanitary sewer, solid waste, law enforcement, fire protection, health services, and telecommunication services were evaluated. A separate section of the report examined both public and private transportation issues relating to existing and proposed circulation routes. This included the adverse impact of added vehicular traffic on ambient air quality, noise level, and sound levels.

The project found a number of significant environmental impacts. These included the loss of about 200 acres of existing open space, modification of existing land, increased urbanization of the area, increased vehicular traffic, and deterioration of the ambient air quality for the area. A number of recommendations were proposed to mitigate and/or minimize the environmental impacts. The recommendations included minimizing the loss of open spaces, maintaining most of the current steep slope areas in their current natural states, and designing the massing of buildings in such a way as to minimize their impact to the environment.

As required in every EIR, the report examined a variety of different common alternatives. The first alternative was to have no project. This alternative was deemed nonresponsive in meeting the educational needs of the local community. The second alternative was to acquire less than the proposed 306 acres. This option would hamper the potential growth of the campus unnecessarily, it was rejected. The fourth alternative was to acquire the land for the purpose of building the center. This was found to be responsive to the needs of the community and the legislative mandates of the California State University system.

The EIR has an extensive set of appendices that may be requested from the University. However, Appendix A represents the portion most relevant to issues examined here. Eventually, the San Diego State University North County Center became California State University, San Marcos (CSUSM), one of the newest campuses in the CSU system.

SAN DIEGO STATE UNIVERSITY

Final Environmental Impact Report

NORTH COUNTY CENTER

SAN MARCOS CAMPUS LAND ACQUISITION

SEPTEMBER 1987

SCH. # 87072904

THE CALIFORNIA STATE UNIVERSITY
OFFICE OF THE CHANCELLOR
400 GOLDEN SHORE, LONG BEACH, CALIFORNIA 90802-4275

TABLE OF CONTENTS

EIR FOR SDSUNCC CITY ACQUISITION

Notice of Completion Form
List of Abbreviations
Abstract

THE FOLLOWING ABBREVIATIONS AND ACRONYMS WERE USED IN THE TEXT OF THIS REPORT

ADT	Average Daily Traffic
CPEC	California Postsecondary Education Commission
cfs	Cubic Feet per Second
city	City of San Marcos, California
creek	San Marcos Creek
CSU	California State University
EDU	Equivalent Dwelling Unit
EJPSA	Ensinas Joint Powers Sewer Agency
FTE	Full-time Equivalent

I-15	Interstate Route #15
I-5	Interstate Route #5
JAC	Joint Advisory Committee
LOC	Level of Capacity
mgd	Million Gallons Per Day
MLWRP	Meadowlark Water Reclamation Plant
NCSA	North County Service Area
NCTD	North County Transit District
NSDCCSSS	North San Diego County Campus Site Selection Study
PG	Postgraduate
Partnership	Bieri and Avis Partnership
Ranch	Prohoroff Poultry Ranch
SANDAG	San Diego Area Governments
SCMWD	Southern California Metropolitan Water District
SDCDS&FC	San Diego County Department of Sanitation and Flood Control
SDCRTC	San Diego County Regional Transportation Commission
SDCWA	San Diego County Water Authority
SDG&E	San Diego Gas and Electric
SDSU	San Diego State University
SDSUNCC	San Diego State University North County Center
SMCWD	San Marcos County Water District
SMFPD	San Marcos Fire Protection District
SML	San Marcos Landfill
SR-78	State Route 78
TA/DL&P	Tadlock Associates/Deems Lewis and Partners
Trustees	Trustees of the California State University

ADDITIONS TO THE TABLE OF CONTENTS
DEIR REVIEW PERIOD DOCUMENTS

A.   Advertisement for Public Hearing
B.   Copy of Public Hearing Transcript
C.   Comments from Paul Malone (City of San Marcos)
D.   Copies of correspondence during review period numbered 1 through 11 plus response
     to letters
E.   List of Federal Endangered Species

Public Notice for a Final Environmental Impact Report

SCH #87072904

In accordance with the California Administrative Code,

CAMPUS: San Diego State University North County Center held a public hearing on

the Draft Environmental Impact Report for

PROJECT TITLE: Land Acquisition, SDSUNCC

which is to be located on the campus of: North County Center

on (or at) STREET OR LOCATION OF PROJECT: 800 W. Los Vallecitos, San

Marcos, California

Date: September 16, 1987 Time: 7:00 p.m. Room: 97 Building: Administration

A Final Environmental Impact Report has been filed with the State and local clearinghouses.

Copies of the Final Environmental Impact Report are available for public review at the Reference Desk of the campus library and the office of the Director of Facilities Planning and Management at the University located at the following address:

Address of Campus: SDSUNCC San Diego State University North County Center
                       800 W. Los Vallecitos, San Marcos, CA 92069

THE TRUSTEES OF THE CALIFORNIA STATE UNIVERSITY
Ben L. Prewitt, Chief
Design and Construction
P.O. Box 92229
Long Beach, Calif. 90809-2229

Rev. 5/22/87

SCH #87072904

Trustees of the California State University

Office of the Chancellor

ABSTRACT
FINAL ENVIRONMENTAL IMPACT REPORT (FINAL EIR)
SAN DIEGO STATE UNIVERSITY NORTH COUNTY CENTER (SDSUNCC)

I. SCOPE OF THE PROPOSED ACTION

This Final Environmental Impact Report (Final EIR) is in accordance with the guidelines of the Trustees of the California State University (Trustees) and the Office of Space and Real Estate Services, State Department of General Services. The Trustees are the lead agency for the proposed acquisition of 304 acres of land. This Final EIR addresses the purchase of approximately 304 acres of the former Prohoroff Ranch (Ranch) in the North San Diego County city of San Marcos (city) as the site for the San Diego State University North County Center (SDSUNCC). The Trustees will file an appropriate California Environmental Quality Act (CEQA) action for future projects including a campus Master Plan.

II. LOCATION OF THE PROPOSED SDSUNCC

The proposed land acquisition for SDSUNCC is in the Barham/Discovery neighborhood within the San Marcos city limits east of Twin Oaks Valley Road, south of Myrtle Road-Barham Drive and east of La Moree Road. The area is approximately midway between California State University, Fullerton and San Diego State University. The site is in an area that was thinly populated but is now infilling at a very rapid rate. The proposed acquisition is shown on Map #2 of this report. The proposed location will be an excellent site for SDSUNCC. The site is under one ownership, the HSL-BA Joint Venture I Bieri and Avis Partnership (Partnership), except for one small parcel near the intersection of Myrtle and Twin Oaks Valley Road.

III. FEASIBILITY OF COMPLETING THE ACQUISITION FOR SDSUNCC

The Trustees, in conducting a search for an SDSUNCC site, are complying with a legislative mandate. The Trustees reviewed the concept of a north San Diego County center located on the former Partnership's land on July 9, 1986.

The Partnership has indicated to representatives of the Chancellor's staff a willingness to sell a portion of their holdings to the State of California for SDSUNCC and that the small parcel outside their ownership could be acquired along with the major land segment. The Partnership also owns approximately 400 acres southwest of the proposed acquisition.

The Partnership has indicated that they would include a portion of that ownership in the proposed SDSUNCC site if such additional land would enhance the possibility of producing a design of high quality for SDSUNCC. The city of San Marcos is also desirous of having SDSUNCC located within their corporate boundaries.

The Trustees have considered acquisition of the property for the SDSUNCC and have included funding for this action in their 1987/88 Capital Outlay Budget. On February 2, 1987, the California Postsecondary Education Commission (CPEC) endorsed acquisition of the site and the construction of SDSUNCC. The 1987 Budget Act, passed by the Legislature and signed by the Governor, included funding for the acquisition of the property for SDSUNCC.

The following actions remain: The Trustees must approve this EIR and the acquisition. The Public Works Board may authorize the Office of Space and Real Estate Services, State Department of General Services, to proceed with the proposed land acquisition.

IV. ALTERNATIVES TO THE PROPOSED ACTION

Five alternatives were examined for this report. These are:

A. No project.
B. A larger acquisition of land.
C. A smaller acquisition of land.
D. The acquisition of another site.
E. The acquisition of the proposed site.

No Project

This alternative is not responsive to the educational desires of the citizens of North County Service Area (NCSA) nor the Legislative mandate and, therefore, is not a viable alternative.

A Larger Acquisition of Land

This alternative would not reflect a proper cost-benefit ratio and would remove land not essential for SDSUNCC from the public tax rolls. A larger acquisition of land is, therefore, not a viable alternative.

A Smaller Acquisition of Land

This alternative could adversely impact the growth and final character of SDSUNCC and inhibit its development into a quality institution. This is not a viable alternative.

The Acquisition of Another Site

This alternative was evaluated in detail by the "North San Diego County Campus Site Selection Study" by PRC Engineering, San Diego, California, dated May 1986. That report is made a part of this Final EIR. It concludes that the present site is superior.

The Acquisition of the Proposed Site

The acquisition of the Ranch as the site for SDSUNCC is the most viable course of action. This site is responsive to the legislative mandate, meets the criteria established by the Trustees and approved by CPEC and is well located in relation to the NCSA.

V. FINDINGS

The Trustees have evaluated the proposed SDSUNCC site acquisition to determine if this action could cause significant impacts under provisions of the California Environmental Quality Act (CEQA) and their guidelines. The following four significant impacts were identified by this Final EIR:

A. There will be a loss of about 200 acres of existing open space in the central and southeastern corner of the site.
B. There will be modification to the existing landforms in the central one-third of the site.

C.   Locating SDSUNCC in the San Marcos area will tend to accelerate urbanization and growth of the area.
D.   There will be an increase of vehicle emissions due to student, faculty and staff accessing SDSUNCC. Combined with the increased ADT on SR-78, there could be a decrease in the ambient air quality after 1995.

VI. MITIGATIONS PROPOSED

The following are proposed as mitigations to impact "A" above:

1.   To maximize the retention of open space and to minimize the loss of open space in the extreme southeastern quadrant, severe slopes should be kept open and future landscaping should include indigenous plants as a priority.
2.   Open space within the SDSUNCC shall be landscaped in a manner which enhances the aesthetic quality of the area.

SDSUNCC will be an occupancy that will retain the significant open space through a campus environment with the proposed mitigation. The educational, humanistic and cultural benefits that will accrue from placing SDSUNCC on the Ranch will outweigh the loss of open space.

The following is proposed as a mitigation to impact "B" above:

1.   That the site development and grading be sensitive to the extent possible to existing landforms. It is further recommended that the design and massing of future buildings be carefully coordinated to enhance the remaining landforms and minimize the alterations.
2.   To enhance the aesthetics of the area, it is recommended that all existing structures, debris and utilities on or over the proposed site be removed.

There are no mitigations to impact "C" except that the overriding consideration of the educational. cultural and humanistic values of SDSUNCC outweighs the urbanizing and growth-inducing impacts. The project in fact is designed as a service to meet demands from existing growth patterns. The following is proposed as a mitigation to "D" above.

1.   To minimize vehicle emissions, a program recommended to promote car and van pooling would contribute to the mitigation of traffic congestion. The reduction of motor vehicle trips would reduce emissions of automobile-related pollutants in the area.

VII. CONCLUSIONS

This report has considered the environmental, cultural, historical, biotic, natural and economic elements that could be adversely impacted by the acquisition of the property owned by the Partnership in the city of San Marcos for SDSUNCC. Based on fully informed and publicly disclosed findings, it is concluded that: acquisition of this property by the Space and Real Estate Division, Department of General Services and the transfer of jurisdiction to the Trustees for the SDSUNCC will have three significant adverse environmental impacts which cannot be entirely mitigated.

The Trustees have specifically identified the following expected benefits which will result from establishing SDSUNCC in San Marcos and these outweigh the environmental impacts of this act.

    A.   Increase the postsecondary educational possibilities in the NCSA.
    B.   Increase the cultural opportunities in the NCSA.
    C.   Meet the humanistic expectations of the citizens of the NCSA.

The growth-inducing impacts cannot be assumed to be necessarily detrimental. The rapid population growth of the NCSA is the reason for the legislative mandate to the Trustees to select a site for SDSUNCC in that area.

VIII.   DOCUMENT PREPARATION STAFF

This Final EIR was prepared under the direction of Mr. Ben L. Prewitt, Director of Design and Construction, with the assistance of Mr. William Chatham, Chief of Planning, Mr. Steven Lohr, Principal University Facility Planner, Chancellor's Office, The California State University; and Mr. Anthony Fulton, Director, Facilities Planning and Management, San Diego State University.

SAN DIEGO STATE UNIVERSITY NORTH COUNTY CENTER (SDSUNCC) FINAL ENVIRONMENTAL IMPACT REPORT (FINAL EIR)

1.00   DESCRIPTION AND JUSTIFICATION FOR THE PROPOSED ACTION

This Final Environmental Impact Report (Final EIR) is in accordance with the requirements of the California Environmental Quality Act (CEQA), Public Resources Code (PRC), Section 21000 et seq., and the guidelines of the Trustees of the California State University (Trustees) and those of the Office of Space and Real Estate Services, California State Department of General Services.

1.01   EIR PROCESS

This Final EIR addresses the purchase of approximately 304 acres of the former Prohoroff Ranch (Ranch) in the North San Diego County city of San Marcos (city) as the site for the San Diego State University North County Center (SDSUNCC). The Trustees, as the lead agency for the proposed 304-acre land acquisition, must complete the EIR process prior to the purchase. When the Trustees receive jurisdiction of the land, they will continue planning for a facility and file an appropriate CEQA action for development of the facility.

This proposed land acquisition east of Twin Oaks Valley Road in the city of San Marcos will be a suitable location for the future SDSUNCC. The site is almost halfway between California State University, Fullerton and San Diego State University, an area which until recently was relatively sparsely settled but which now is expanding very rapidly.

1.02   LOCATION OF THE PROPOSED SDSUNCC LAND ACQUISITION

The proposed 304-acre acquisition (Ranch) is within the Barham/Discovery neighborhood of the city. The proposed land acquisition is in portions of Sections 13, 14, 23 and 24, Range 3W, Township 25S, San Bernardino Base and Meridian. The area is on the border of the Santa Fe and San Marcos quadrangle maps. The proposed site for SDSUNCC is shown on Map #2 of this report. The Ranch site for the proposed SDSUNCC is in north San Diego County and within the San Marcos city limits. The Ranch lies one-half mile south of State Route (SR-78), east of Twin Oaks Valley Road, south of Myrtle Road-Barham Drive and east of La Moree Road. The southern boundary of the acquisition is an east-west property line drawn approximately 3,000 feet south of the corner of Twin Oak Valley Road and Myrtle Avenue.

1.03   CHARACTERISTICS OF THE PROPOSED ACTION

The proposed action is for the acquisition of a permanent site for SDSUNCC to function as an upper division/postgraduate facility. The initial planned occupancy on the site will be for that function. Eventually, the site could be used for a complete postgraduate and graduate state university program. CSU and SDSU are planning the initial complement of buildings and facilities using the enrollment figures of 2,000 FTE. These are target figures for the years of 1994/95. The target year is two years beyond the date of the opening of the center on the Ranch. The academic programs at the present off-campus center in San Marcos are scheduled to be expanded to meet the target year commitments. The planned opening complement of facilities to house the expanded curricula and increased enrollment is being carefully coordinated by the CSU academic and physical planning staffs. CSU has used the center stratagem at least five times in the past as a means to facilitate the opening of new four-year universities. Off-campus centers in areas of increasing population experience enrollment growth and curricula expansion to the stage where it is prudent to establish a four-year university. CPEC foresaw this eventuality and in January 1987 provided for the conversion possibility of the SDSUNCC to a four-year campus. This conversion would take place two years after CSU notifies CPEC that it proposes to convert SDSUNCC to a four-year autonomous university.

The proposed land acquisition is for a permanent site for SDSUNCC to function as an upper division/postgraduate off-campus center of SDSU.

1.04   JUSTIFICATION FOR THE PROPOSED ACQUISITION

The justification for the proposed acquisition of land is to provide the citizens of the north San Diego and south Orange counties with a quality institution of higher education. This is in compliance with the direction of Senate Bill 1060 authored by Senator William Craven during the 1985 session of the Legislature. This bill called for the Trustees to conduct activities that would establish a permanent off-campus center in the northern portion of San Diego County. On March 1, 1986, Tadlock & Associates/Deems Lewis and Partners (TA/DL&P), under contract to CSU, submitted a report entitled "Demographic/Market Analysis for Off-Campus Center, San Diego State University, Northern San Diego County." The report is made a part of this Final EIR of this reference. The TA/DL&P report outlined the NCSA and also made the following recommendations:

A.   That NCSA include the San Diego County region northward from Del Mar, North City and Poway, plus the Capistrano-San Clemente area of Orange County and the Rancho California-Corona area of Riverside County.

B.   That NCSA population through 2010 be assigned to replicate the population mix currently found county wide.

C.   That SDSU's current enrollment be used as the model for additional NCSA programming.

D.   That CSU plan for a comprehensive campus in the NCSA to house a minimum of 14,000 and a maximum of 21,000 FTE by the year 2010.

E.   That CSU acquire a site as soon as possible because the rapid commercial and residential growth in the NCSA is depleting the availability of good sites and acquisition costs are increasing.

F.   That CSU should locate the site on the SR-78 corridor or its connections to I-15 to obtain optimum ease of access for a maximum number of NCSA residents.

G.   That particular attention be given to meet the following major educational needs: education, business, health service, general services operations, information services and systems and general education.

The following report by CSU, dated September 1986, is also made a part of this Final EIR: "Land Acquisition and Planning for New Off-Campus Centers: Northern San Diego County and Ventura County, Program Justification Documentation, Fiscal Year 1987-88."

1.05   OWNERSHIP OF THE PROPOSED ACQUISITION

The proposed land acquisition is under one ownership, HSL-BA Joint Venture I led by Bieri and Avis Partnership (Partnership), except for one small, approximately two and one-half acre parcel near the intersection of Myrtle and Twin Oaks Valley Roads, which is owned by Shubin/Tolmochoff.

The Partnership also owns approximately 400 acres south of the proposed acquisition. The Partnership has indicated a willingness to include a portion of the 400 acres into the proposed site acquisition if the design quality of SDSUNCC would be enhanced by the additional land. The Partnership expressed to members of the Chancellor's staff that they would prefer to sell the northern portion of their land for SDSUNCC rather than develop a residential community on the site. The city, through its officials, also expressed a strong desire to have SDSUNCC locate on the Ranch which is within their corporate boundaries.

1.06   EASEMENTS ON OR OVER THE PROPOSED ACQUISITION

The proposed SDSUNCC site has some street, underground utilities and above ground electrical power line easements which are on or over the lower and middle portions. The street easements which may impinge are Twin Oaks Valley Road on the west, and La Moree Road on the east. There has been a formal vacation of Barham Drive from Twin Oak Valley Road on the west to La Moree Road, the proposed eastern boundary of the acquisition.

The site has a network of underground utilities for water, sewer and gas lines. San Diego Gas and Electric (SDG&E) has a 20-foot wide easement for a wooden pole line running in a southeasterly direction from near the corner of Myrtle and La Moree to about where Barham Drive intersects Twin Oaks Valley Road from the west. SDG&E has indicated that it will relocate their overhead line across the property at their expense.

SDG&E served the site with a three-inch gas line and there are onsite gas services to the former poultry facilities and fertilizer production areas. The onsite water distribution and sewer collection systems were the property owner's responsibility. The surface drainage followed natural declivities and, as a rule, was not intercepted and put into channels or conduits.

Existing onsite utility easements on or over the proposed land acquisition will not have significant adverse impacts to the acquisition of the site or the subsequent development of a high quality design for SDSUNCC.

1.07   SITE GEOLOGY

The site of the proposed acquisition for the SDSUNCC is underlain by the Southern California Batholith granitic and gabbroic rocks formed about 100 million years ago during the Cretaceous Period. These are coarse-grained igneous rocks which suggest an oceanic crust. Gabbros have a high specific gravity, are hard, and have high strength and elasticity values. The bedrock is overlain with a relatively thin soil covering. Gabbros and granitic rock weather slowly, producing shallow soils with low percentages of clay particles and exhibiting moderate expansive characteristics. The exposed weathered rocks are a series of rounded grayish knobs rising above the thin soil cover. Removal of these rock knobs will be difficult. It will also be difficult to conduct extensive trenching operations associated with utility lines or to construct large underground spaces such as building basements. The site geology will be a significant determinant in the design of the utilities distribution systems and the foundation and below grade areas of structures.

1.08   SITE GEOLOGIC HAZARDS

The proposed acquisition has varying slopes and rock outcrops on its surface. The materials that make up the slopes are a complex physical, chemical and biological system whose stability can vary greatly over a relatively short time span. A slope may fail in one or more of several modes. The susceptibility to slope failure depends on the nature of the materials involved, the moisture content and the steepness of the slope. A slope may slide, fall, flow or subside. In a sliding failure, a cohesive mass moves along a weakened or lubricated slip plane. Flow or mass wasting is water related and has a lobate failure pattern and can occur on relatively shallow slopes and usually has a large horizontal component. Rockfalls usually occur on steep slopes when unstable blocks of rocks are dislodged by natural forces.

Subsidence is a downward transport of material usually due to the withdrawal of pore fluids or, at times, by underground flows washing the fines out from under an area. The proposed site does not exhibit any pronounced or incipient evidence or geologic hazards. The slope wash that occurs is a natural ongoing process. Geologic hazards will not create significant adverse impacts upon SDSUNCC constructed on the Ranch site.

1.09   FAULTS

No active or inactive faults have been identified in the area of the proposed acquisition. This is not a guarantee that there are no faults in the immediate area, only that none have been identified. An active fault is defined by the Alquist-Priolo Special Studies Zone Act, Public Resources Code, Section 2621 et seq., as one which has had no surface displacement within the Holocene time (11,000 years). There are two active fault zones more than 10 kilometers to the east—the Elsinore and the San Jacinto. The Newport/Inglewood Fault on the north and the Rose Canyon Faults on the south are offshore to the west and may be continuations of the same fault lines. Both of these faults are more than 10 kilometers from the proposed acquisition. The site of the proposed acquisition is as well situated in regard to faults as can be expected in California.

1.10   SEISMICITY

All of California is in a seismically active zone and earth tremors are frequent, but fortunately the intensity of most varies from low to moderate. The proposed acquisition lies west of both the Elsinore and San Jacinto fault zones. The State Division of Mines and Geology is of the opinion that, because the proposed acquisition is situated on exposed bedrock for the most part, well-designed structures will not suffer from moderate tremors. In the lower lying areas of alluvium just south of Myrtle Avenue there could be more serious impacts such as momentary liquefaction. This phenomena depends on the wave characteristics of the tremors, degree of saturation percentage of silts and sands and the thickness of the alluvium. If the structures and developments are constructed on the rocky outcrops above the low-lying fill, seismicity will not have a significant impact on the site developments.

2.00   MARKET ANALYSIS, DEMOGRAPHICS AND INTERACTIONS

This section will deal with demographics and the economic effect of SDSUNCC on the city to the year 2010.

2.01   DEMOGRAPHICS OF THE NCSA

San Diego County is, in the minds of most inhabitants, two entities, North County and Greater San Diego. The two areas are topographically separated by the canyons and mesas north of the city, Miramar Naval Air Station and the University of California on the mesa between Torrey Pines and La Jolla. The inhabitants of North County do not wish to be identified with the Greater San Diego Area. For the North County demographics the following areas will be considered as being within the NCSA: North County West—Pendleton, Oceanside, Carlsbad, and San Diequito; North County East—Fallbrook, Pauma, Vista, Valley Center, Escondido and San Marcos. There are three communities to the south that have the North County mentality. These are Poway, North San Diego and Del Mar/Mira Mesa.

Table I
San Diego Regional Population Growth Projections

			YEARS		
SERVICE AREA	**1990**	**1995**	**2000**	**2005**	**2010**
1	100	117	132	153	176
2	279	320	358	436	530
3	283	318	347	422	494
4	210	250	292	316	343
NCSA	880	1,005	1,129	1,327	1,551
5	2,335	2,527	2,699	2,992	3,163
TOTAL	3,215	3,532	3,828	4,319	4,714

The boundaries of NCSA will be the Pacific Ocean on the west; the sparsely populated area parallel to I-15 on the east; on the north, an east-west line drawn south of the San Clemente/Capistrano area in Orange County; and on the south, an east-west line drawn just south of the cities of Poway and Del Mar. San Diego Area Governments (SANDAG) and the California State Department of Finance both have ongoing population projections as a part of their normal procedures. State agencies, including CSU, rely on these projections for their future planning. Table I from the TA/DL&A gives the anticipated population increases for the three areas that will be the major contributors to SDSUNCC plus metropolitan San Diego. These areas are (1) North Transitional Zone, (2) North County West, (3) North County East, (4) South Transitional Zone, and (5) San Diego County. All figures in the table are to be multiplied by 1,000.

The NCSA will have a million inhabitants and San Diego County will have 4,714,000 by the year 1995, only seven and one-half years from now.

2.02   ENROLLMENT AT SAN DIEGO STATE UNIVERSITY (SDSU)

SDSU is the largest institution in the 19-campus CSU system, with a Full-time Equivalent (FTE) enrollment of 25,300, which equates to over 32,000 individual students. The demand for postsecondary education in San Diego County has forced SDSU to operate above its planned capacity. The Vice President for Academic Affairs at SDSU expects to turn away over 1,000 students because of lack of facilities. The SDSU campus, with a total of 207 usable acres out of a total of 283, is impacted by city traffic, bisection of the campus by a major city arterial and topography, plus the need for more parking, residence halls and academic buildings.

For the 1990/91 academic year, SDSU will have a total enrollment potential of 30,800 with 27,049 at the home campus and 3,331 at SDSUNCC. The Trustees' enrollment ceiling for SDSU of 25,000 FTE is based on facility utilization factors of 100 percent. The present usage of many departments and facilities exceeds this factor. It would strain practicality to increase SDSU to accept 2,000–3,000 FTE beyond the enrollment ceiling. SDSU has reached and passed the optimum size for the available land base and circulation. The SDSU home campus would be over-saturated if the enrollment reached 35,000 which is about 1.7 percent of the service area population of 2,100,000.

Table II
CSUNC FTE From 1990 to 2010

YEARS				
1990	**1995**	**2000**	**2005**	**2010**
4,075	4,665	5,200	5,790	6,440

SDSU is in the southwestern corner of its service area, which complicates access by students from the rapidly expanding NCSA. While it is not absolutely impossible, it would be extremely costly and probably unwise to increase the SDSU enrollment by an additional 14,000 to 21,000 FTE on the present SDSU campus. To expand the campus by the acquisition of adjacent land would be extremely costly and borders on the impossible. The Legislature has acted wisely in expediting the implementation of SDSUNCC in the North County Service Area.

2.03   PREDICTED FTE GROWTH FOR SDSUNCC

The rapid population growth in the NCSA is apparent to anyone who is driving through the area. Predicting the average yearly growth by area is essential to orderly planning by the various governmental bodies with interests in NCSA. In Table II is a probable increase in the SDSUNCC FTE on the San Marcos site. These figures are an extrapolation from SANDAG, Department of Finance and CSU.

All of these predictions are based on past demographic experiences, which in 30 years may not be entirely valid. The awakening of the Pacific Rim Nations may be a factor that will skew the social, economic and demographic patterns of the past so they may read as much as 10 percent low.

Table III

	YEAR				
LEVELS	**1990**	**1995**	**2000**	**2005**	**2010**
Upper Division/Lower Division & Postgraduate	3,700	8,200	13,200	17,100	21,400
Lower Division/ Postgraduate	2,700	5,990	9,650	12,500	15,400

SANDAG predicts that the total population of the city of San Marcos will increase from 17,479 in 1980 to 41,277 in the year 2000, an increase of 23,798 or 136 percent. If the same area is held and the same rate of increase continues, by the year 2020 the population will be about 35,000. This would be a good-sized host community for SDSUNCC, which is expected to grow more rapidly. The TA/DL&P enrollment predictions for SDSUNCC with lower division, upper division and postgraduate and with just upper division/postgraduate are given in Table III.

These enrollments are based on the age cohorts of the area and contribution rates as set by SANDAG and CSU.

2.04   INTERACTION OF SDSUNCC AND THE CITY OF SAN MARCOS

Using CSU, Bakersfield, Fresno and Sonoma as models, a predictable result will be that SDSUNCC will be a magnet that will draw future development in its direction. The existence of SDSUNCC may lead to upgrading of the character and types of existing developments in the area. The production of aggregate adjacent to the proposed SDSUNCC site will be an operation that will be eliminated.

SDSUNCC will enrich the cultural life of the San Marcos area and make the city unique in NCSA. By the year 2010, the city will achieve maturity and SDSUNCC will have established its academic role in the area and in the CSU system. There will be few individual entities coming into San Marcos that will have such a pervasive and lasting positive impact on its future.

2.05   ECONOMICS

The acquisition of a portion of the Ranch for SDSUNCC will not have an immediate nor significant impact on the economics of the San Marcos area of influence. As the institution matures, it will be one of the more stable long-term contributors to the economic well-being of the community. A major educational institution is a complex organism and many factors will come into play to produce the total economic interface with its host community. The academic staff will number about 20 percent of the enrollment. This is a relatively well paid group with a middle-class purchasing pattern. The maintenance and operations staff, while not as numerous as the academic, receive the union scale wages for their craft or trade. The percentage of faculty and staff that reside in San Marcos will depend on:

A.   How the local housing costs compare with those in the adjacent areas.
B.   The strength of the sociological identification with the community that can be generated among the faculty and staff.
C.   The quality of community service in the community.
D.   The quality of life in the community compared with that in adjacent areas.

Regardless of where the faculty and staff reside, they will provide tangential economic benefits to the city just because they go there on a regular basis.

Day students who do not live in the area will not be a significant economic asset. They favor trendy purchases, fast foods and entertainment. When and if SDSUNCC becomes an autonomous university with on-campus student housing, the resident students will be more of an economic asset to the community. In general, the economic benefit to an area that students provide is their numbers. According to the law of averages a certain percentage will patronize local establishments.

A large educational institution has a sizable budget for support and operations in addition to the faculty and staff wages. During the formative years, SDSUNCC will have a large capital outlay budget for construction of facilities if the predicted enrollment projections are met. The monetary outlay for the construction is spread widely but there will be benefits to the local area. The state and CSU have consolidated purchasing for many items that are common to several agencies or institutions. This practice will curtail some economic benefits to the local area. There are many services and supplies that will be local procurements and this list will grow in time.

SDSUNCC will have a steady and unspectacular but long-term positive economic impact on the area and the city in particular.

2.06   GROWTH AND URBANIZATION

The proposed SDSUNCC may induce growth and promote urbanization of the local area. According to the state CEQA guidelines, growth itself is not a significant adverse impact. The growth of the area is assured and the city has taken steps to guide the nature of the growth that will occur. The city general plan is the mechanism used for controlling and directing the future growth. Growth does not have positive impacts such as increases in employment, housing opportunity and amenities that a larger population mass can support. SDSUNCC, by its nature, is a cultural, educational and humanistic asset that will override any adverse growth-inducing impact it might have. The city and local area infrastructure can support SDSUNCC. There is a demand for its services and it has legislative support. The area is attracting more of the hi-tech industries and SDSUNCC would complement this trend by preparing people of the area to enter these fields. One example is the San Diego Tribune, which located its production facility and headquarters in the area. The new technologies could not be properly exploited in its former location. With the maturing of computer-related operations and advances in communications, there will be a dispersal of many firms to areas along a good corridor of circulation such as SR-78. SDSUNCC will support these endeavors, which is a positive aspect of modern civilization.

Any adverse impact SDSUNCC might create will be offset by its overriding benefits.

3.00   INFRASTRUCTURE

The city has in place a good basic general plan for its emergence from a largely agricultural area into an industrial and commercial center. The existing infrastructure can easily support SDSUNCC at least to the year 2000. During that period there will be augmentations to all elements which will ensure continuing support.

3.01   WATER

The Southern California Metropolitan Water District (SCMWD) brings water into and turns it over to the San Diego County Water Authority (SDCWA). This body distributes the water to the individual municipalities and water districts. The serving utility for the San Marcos area is the San Marcos County Water District (SMCWD) which is not co-terminus with the city limits. SMCWD is guaranteed an adequate water supply for the near future based upon its past demand. SMCWD has an existing 14-inch water main in Twin Oaks Valley Road running along the western edge of the site. This existing service would be sufficient to meet the SDSUNCC demands to the year 2000. SMCWD has plans for the installation of a 30-inch water main to the corner of Barham Drive and Twin Oaks Valley Road. These two lines would be adequate to serve SDSUNCC up to 12,000 FTE. There will be an adequate water supply for SDSUNCC on the proposed Ranch site.

3.02   ELECTRICITY

The serving utility for electricity in the San Marcos area is San Diego Gas and Electric (SDG&E). The rates for electrical use in the SDG&E service area are the second highest in the country. When the installed loads for electricity, heat and hot water reach the proper ranges, congeneration would be a good investment. There is an existing SDG&E 60 Kv. line parallel to and near the southern boundary of the SDSUNCC site. Adequate electrical service could be provided to the site quickly by increasing the capacity of one of the two existing 12 Kv. lines running from the Escondido or San Marcos substations. The SDSUNCC ultimate load of 20 mega-watts will require a small on-campus substation that could be served from the 69 Kv. line along the southern boundary of the site.

Existing on-site electrical lines and services may be relocated prior to or coincident with the site land acquisition. The future electrical service for SDSUNCC should be underground and the design phased to agree with its growth. There will be no adverse impact to SDSUNCC due to the demands on the electrical service.

3.03   GAS

The serving utility for gas in the San Marcos area is SDG&E. There is an existing 3-inch gas line to the Ranch with many on-site feeder lines used during the poultry and fertilizer operations. This line is sufficient for the immediate future, but would not be sufficient to service SDSUNCC when its demand reaches 35,000 cubic feet per hour (cfh), identified as the ultimate demand in the NSDCCSSS. There is an existing 16 medium pressure gas transmission line at Mission Avenue and Twin Oaks Valley Road.

This location just north of the site would be a logical starting point for augmenting the site gas supply. Bringing additional service to the site could be classed as an augmentation and under present guidelines would be installed by SDG&E at no cost to the consumers. It is recommended that existing on-site gas lines be abandoned and all services for SDSUNCC be in new lines that are protected or resistant to galvanic action. Gas service for SDSUNCC at the Ranch site is available for the near future demands.

3.04   SANITARY SEWER

The serving utility for the sanitary sewer system in the area is the SMCWD. SMCWD uses two treatment plants to process the sewage, Meadowlark Water Reclamation Plant (MLWRP) and the Encinas Joint Powers Sewer Agency (EJPSA). This agency operates through a six member Joint Advisory Committee (JAC) of which SMCWD is one. JAC oversees operation of the Encinas Pollution Control Facility and the network that transports waste water from the various service areas to the Encinas Plant. SMCWD has a capacity quots of 2.8 million gallons per day (mgd), which at plant ultimate capacity of 45.75 mgd, will be increased to 3.2 mgd. The SMCWD is exceeding its quota by about 0.5 mgd and is billed for the excess contribution.

SMCWD operates the MLWRP and the water reclaimed by the facility is used for irrigation of agriculture, land and landscaping in the LaCosta area. The present capacity of the plant is 2.5 mgd, with an ultimate of 22 mgd. The possibility of supplying reclaimed water to the SDSUNCC area is remote because of the uphill pumping costs. The sewer system improvement funding is derived from sewer connection fees on new developments.

The SMCWD has calculated the contribution from SDSUNCC at 15 FTE equals 1 Equivalent Dwelling Unit (EDU). The generation per dwelling is 250 gallons per day (gpd) and for commercial, office and industrial 100 gpd, 200 gpd and industrial 10 gpd, respectively. If SDSUNCC reaches 15,000 FTE its EDU will be 250,000 gpd of waste water. The existing 8-inch line along Twin Oaks Valley Road south of Myrtle can accept the SDSUNCC outfall for the near future.

3.05 SOLID WASTE

Removal of solid waste in the city is provided by a single private contractor with an exclusive franchise. The contractor assesses a monthly service charge and pays a franchise fee to the city for the exclusive franchise rights. The solid waste is transported to the San Marcos Landfill (SML), 201 acre county-owned facility south of Questhaven Road. The facility is operated by a private firm under contract to the county. The San Diego County Department of Public Works (SDCDPW) is responsible for developing new disposal sites. There are several plans for new disposal sites in North County, including a recycling and combustion system. This operation will burn refuse-derived fuel to generate power and reclaim ferrous and non-ferrous metals, glass, plastics, film and paper. It will not be on-line before 1990. The SML is expected to reach capacity by 1991. The solid waste generated from the city is estimated at just under 3000 tons daily. The impact from solid waste disposal will be a persistent problem as in most metropolitan areas. The solid waste disposal will not create any significant adverse impacts.

3.06 LAW ENFORCEMENT

The law enforcement agency for the city is the San Diego County Sheriff's Department. The city is in Sheriff's Beat 13, which is headquartered at 325 South Melrose in Vista. An automated computer-driven dispatch system, which gives emergency calls priority, and dispatches the nearest deputy to the scene is in operation. Emergency response time ranges from 9 to 13 minutes. The service consists of four one-man patrol units working eight-hour shifts seven days a week, and a second unit working five days a week from 5:30 p.m. to 2:00 a.m. There are also three traffic control units with overlapping patrols working 20 hours per day, five days per week. The police coverage in the city equates to one patrol unit for about every 14,000 persons. The cost to the city for law enforcement is over $750,000 a year. SDSUNCC will rely upon the San Diego County Sheriff's Office for police protection. Once the site is occupied and there is a sizable all-day enrollment, State University Police may assume the law enforcement on the site. Law enforcement for SDSUNCC on the proposed Ranch site will not create any significant adverse impacts.

3.07 FIRE PROTECTION

The San Marcos Fire Protection District (SMFPD) services about 33 square miles of area from two fire stations. Station #1 is located at 333 Firebird Lane, less than a mile from the SDSUNCC site. Response time from this station is estimated to be about 3-4 minutes. This is a three-man station with a 1,500 gallon-per-minute pumper and a rescue squad. Station #2 is located at 1250 South Rancho Santa Fe Road, which is about 4.5 miles to the west and response time would be about 10 minutes. The SMFD has three class A pumpers, three grass/brush units and two rescue units.

Twenty full-time employees are used to man the stations for fire suppression and there are about 30 paid on-call volunteers. The total available firefighting force depends on the day of the week and hour of the day. The coverage equates to about 0.30 full-time firefighters per thousand population in the SMFPD service area. There is an Automatic Aid Agreement between the SMFPD and the Vista Fire Protection Service and response time for the proposed SDSUNCC site will be good up to about the year 2000. Around or before that date it must be assumed there will be an increase in both equipment and manpower due to the population growth in the SMFPD. Fire protection for SDSUNCC on the proposed Ranch site will not create any significant adverse impacts.

3.08   HEALTH SERVICES

There are no hospitals within the city limits and the possibility of one being established there is rather remote. This does not imply that health services are not readily available. Palomar Hospital, the closest, is 6.5 miles southeast at 555 East Valley Parkway in Escondido. Tri-City Hospital in Oceanside is 9.8 miles to the west. In case of an emergency, the SMFPD would request an ambulance for transporting the patient to a hospital. There are plans for the construction of the Scripps Memorial Hospital in Carlsbad, and that would be only 5 miles to the west. The ambulance response to an emergency on the SDSUNCC site would be about five minutes. There are many physicians in the area and good medical attention is readily available. Medical services in the large metropolitan areas is generally not closer than 5 to 10 miles. Medical services will not create any significant adverse impacts.

3.09   TELEPHONE AND DATA TRANSMISSION

The serving utility for telephone and data transmission services for the proposed SDSUNCC site is Pacific Bell. There is an existing underground telephone cable along Twin Oaks Valley Road, the westerly boundary of the site. The data transmission speed and quality of this line are unknown. This service would have to be augmented when the enrollment approaches 1,000 FTE. The cost of the augmentation along Twin Oaks Valley Road would probably be borne by Pacific Bell but augmentation of services on the site would probably be the responsibility of SDSUNCC. There is the possibility of locating an earth station to acquire satellites for line-of-sight transmissions on the higher portions of the site with fiber optics ground connections. Acquisitions to the south by an earth station might encounter ground clutter and occlusion by the still higher ground to the south. Telephone and data transmission for SDSUNCC on the proposed Ranch site will not create any significant adverse impacts.

4.00   CIRCULATION

The proposed acquisition is on the border of developed surface traffic circulation routes to the north and relatively rural area to the south. Until Barham Drive is developed there is no east-west circulation route on the northern perimeter of the site. The southern boundary of the site is a property line and any circulation required along that line will probably have to be developed by and within SDSUNCC.

4.01   EXISTING TRAFFIC CIRCULATION ROUTES AROUND
THE PROPOSED SITE

The site is about 1,000 feet south of SR-78 to the east of Twin Oaks Valley Road, which has access to both the east and west lanes of that route. North of SR-78 through the city Twin Oaks Valley Road is a four-lane, 84-foot-wide street over crossing but with no interchange to Mission Road. North of the city it narrows to a two-lane country road. South of Myrtle Avenue, Twin Oaks Valley Road becomes a poorly surfaced two-lane, 24-foot-wide country lane which terminates near South Lake Reservoir. There is access east to Myrtle and Barham Boulevard from Twin Oaks Valley Road but, at present, these are dead ends to the east. Barham Boulevard is being improved from La Moree Road, west over existing Myrtle Avenue, and connecting to Grand Avenue. This will provide east-west access to the site south of SR-78. The city has plans for the development of Twin Oaks Valley Road south as a four-lane road to Questhaven in the Carlsbad area. This would present an alternative route to students, faculty and staff coming or going to that area. This improvement would allow these people to circumvent San Marcos, Grand and Santa Fe Avenue, heavily used city streets.

The city services 96 miles of city streets of all types and has a good plan for the development of circulation. The two routes that are of interest to SDSUNCC are Twin Oaks Valley Road and Barham Drive. La Moree Road could develop into a major arterial along the east side of the site depending on the design of the SDSUNCC parking and entrances. The main city arterials are not in a grid pattern as, in general, they follow the historic agricultural routes that avoided adverse topography. The routes change names as they go from one community to another. As an example, San Marcos Boulevard becomes Encinitas west of Rancho Santa Fe and SR-12 Palomar Airport Road west of Linda Vista. The city circulation plan is viable as a general overall guide, but placing SDSUNCC on the Ranch will require reevaluating average daily trips (ADT) in that area. As a rough guide, SDSUNCC will generate 2.5 ADT per FTE using the experience of other institutions as a guide.

4.02   AVERAGE DAILY TRIPS (ADT) ON EXISTING CIRCULATION ROUTES

The ADT on the main routes near the site are taken from the SANDAG 1986 North San Diego County Area Average Weekday Traffic Volumes. These ADT, as listed in Table IV, are to be multiplied by 1,000.

These ADT are below the capacity of the roads. The maximum number of vehicles SDSUNCC traffic will add is 2.5 times the FTE at any given time. If Twin Oaks Valley Road and Barham Drive are developed to two lanes in each direction, they will have sufficient capacity for the predicted SDSUNCC traffic to the year 2005.

Table IV
Average Weekday Traffic Volume

ROUTE	ADT
1. Twin Oaks Valley Road north of Mission	96.0
2. Twin Oaks Valley Road south of Mission	8.4
3. Twin Oaks Valley Road south of SR-78	2.8
4. Barham - Myrtle north of site	2.0
5. Buena Creek Road	40
6. Mission west of Twin Oaks Valley Road	15.9
7. Mission east of Twin Oaks Valley Road	15.8
8 . San Marcos west of Twin Oaks Valley Road	14.9
9. San Marcos south of SR-78	24.0
10. Barham east of La Moree	5.9
11. Grand to Las Posas	9.7
12. Grand east of Las Posas	5.6
13. Rancho Santa Fe south of SR-78	26.5
14. Rancho Santa Fe south of Encinitas/San Marcos	22.2
15. Santa Fe Avenue west of Mission	15.9

Table V
Street Classifications

STREET	CLASS

Twin Oaks Valley Road north of Mission
    Deer Springs Road to Borden Road — Major
    Borden Road to Applewilde Drive — Prime
    Applewilde Drive to Questhaven Road — Major
Barham Drive
    Twin Oaks Valley Road to Woodland Parkway — Prime
    Woodland Parkway to Mission Road — Secondary
Questhaven Road
Rancho Santa Fe to Twin Oaks Valley Road — Major

4.03   STATE ROUTE 78 (SR-78)

SR-78 is unique in that it is a state route which will be upgraded to interstate standards. The possibility of SR-78 becoming a federal route is not too promising at the present. There is wide support from communities along its route and each terminus for upgrading the route and others in San Diego County. Appendix F of this report is the San Diego County Regional Transportation Commission (SDCTC) information pamphlet on the November 1987 ballot measure for a sales tax increase to fund local transportation routes. SR-78 will be widened to three lanes in each direction from I-5 to I-15. It will also receive improvements to access and exit ramps. Half of the cost for the improvements along SR-78 have been funded by the Federal Department of Transportation. The remainder will be funded equally by Cal Trans and the six communities along the corridor. The upgrading of SR-78 would help to meet the circulation needs of SDSUNCC beyond the year 1995.

4.04   CIRCULATION ELEMENT, STREET CLASSIFICATIONS, CITY OF SAN MARCOS

The existing circulation network of streets in the city has been classified according to its use and capacity. Appendix G of this report is the City of San Marcos Circulation Element Street Classifications which define the main streets near the site as listed in Table V. There is no mention of La Moree Road which until the possibility of SDSUNCC locating in the area, was a residential street accessing the Rancho Coronado development on the hills above the site. In the development of the master plan for SDSUNCC there should be coordination with the city if there is the possibility for increasing traffic on this street.

4.05   PUBLIC MASS TRANSPORTATION

The serving utility for public mass transportation in the area is the North County Transit District (NCTD). The current funding limits the service to areas of high density demand. There is adequate and frequent bus service from both Oceanside and Escondido to San Diego. The NCTD local bus line #341 travels Mission Boulevard/Rancho Santa Fe/Lake San Marcos/San Marcos Boulevard. The Discovery Street stop is the closest service to the proposed site. The Escondido to Oceanside line #302 travels east-west along Mission Boulevard on a 30-minute schedule with stops at Descanso and Rancho Santa Fe. There is consideration for a new local line to serve the Palomar College area north of SR-78, but no definite date for commencement of service has been set due to funding.

San Diego County, in cooperation with the NCTD, has prepared the Escondido-Oceanside Corridor Light Rail Feasibility Study to identify the travel demands in the corridor. The daily trip demand was estimated at just under 500,000, of which about 30 percent were total corridor trips and 70 percent had one of the terminus as a starting or ending point. California state universities, with the exception of San Francisco State University, do not generate a strong public mass transportation demand. Public mass transit to the proposed SDSUNCC site and the prognosis for future improvements are both very poor.

There is a strong proposal to have a light rail line in operation between Oceanside and Escondido for the centennial celebration next year. This would operate over the Santa Fe tracks similar to the operation of the line to the Mexican border. It is hoped that once the line is in operation, public demand will be sufficient to continue operation. If the service is good and there are parking lots at each terminus and at several key stops along the way, it would have great merit and could succeed.

4.06   TRANSPORTATION INTO SDSUNCC

Using the statewide existing CSU facilities as a model, it can be stated that for the foreseeable future, student, faculty and staff access into SDSUNCC will be by private automobile usually carrying only one person. During the formative years, SDSUNCC will probably not have a viable carpool system because most students work part or full-time and their points of origin are scattered. When the enrollment reaches 1,000 FTE, some carpooling will occur but it will be a struggle as the service area is so spread out and thinly populated with severe topographic constraints. Student, faculty and staff transportation into SDSUNCC will have an impact on the existing city traffic and the air quality. As a partial mitigation, it is recommended that from the beginning SDSUNCC should work for a strong carpool program and extension of public mass transportation into the site. If the light rail system becomes operational, SDSUNCC could run shuttles to the nearest station as a means of reducing traffic in the area.

4.07   PARKING

Access to SDSUNCC parking lots will probably be from the east and west along Barham Drive and, from the north, along Twin Oaks Valley Road. SR-78 will be the arterial that most students, faculty and staff will use to get to San Marcos. The site lends itself to establishing the parking on the lower lying north and western quadrants. These areas will have easy and rapid ingress and egress from either Barham Drive or Twin Oaks Valley Road. Once the site is developed, it may indicate that La Moree Road on the east should be increased into a feeder to Barham Drive to relieve pressure on Twin Oaks Valley Road.

The CSU system does not fund parking lots by an appropriation in the annual state budget. CSU has system wide bond issues which fund the construction and maintenance of all campus parking lots and structures. The usual formula for providing additional parking facilities on a campus requires the establishment of a definite need. This is necessary to preserve the integrity of the CSU Parking Bond Program. It may be necessary to advance credit to SDSUNCC toward an initial complement of parking sufficient to meet the enrollment needs. Within five years, SDSUNCC will be able to support its just portion of the parking revenue bond assessments. A parking structure may not be economically feasible at SDSUNCC for the foreseeable future.

Student parking has created some neighborhood problems at times in the surrounding neighborhoods at each of the CSU campuses. This could also occur at SDSUNCC. It is recommended as a mitigation that the city and SDSUNCC cooperate from the beginning and work to prevent student parking along neighborhood streets adjacent to the center. To enforce this action will require adequate and safe parking areas at SDSUNCC.

Parking at SDSUNCC will not create significant impacts in the city's Barham/Discovery neighborhood with the proposed mitigations.

4.08   IMPACT OF SDSUNCC TRAFFIC ON LOCAL AIR QUALITY

The increase in traffic in the vicinity of SDSUNCC may have an incremental impact on the vehicular traffic in the area. It carries 72.8 ADT east of Twin Oaks Valley Road and 49.2 ADT to the west. A listing of the Escondido and Oceanside monitoring data for vehicular pollutants is given in Table VI.

The California State Ambient Air Quality Standards and the federal standards are included in Appendix C. There is no air quality monitoring station in San Marcos but it is assumed that the values there would closely approximate those of Escondido. The low sulfur dioxide data would indicate a high vehicular load and a low heavy industry load.

A mathematical model for the impact of SDSUNCC-related traffic of 1,200 cars per hour was superimposed on the existing conditions and is presented in Appendix C.

Table VI
Air Quality Data
Average Concentration Parts Per Hundred Million (PPH/M)

POLLUTANTS	ESCONDIDO	OCEANSIDE
1. Ozone	7.3	6.1
2. Carbon Monoxide (CO) parts/million	1.3	1.3
3. Nitrogen Dioxide parts/million	3.6*	3.2
4. Nitric Oxide	1.8*	2.4
5. Oxide of Nitrogen (NOx)	4.9	5.0
6. Sulfur Dioxide	7.0	2.0
7. Total Hydrocarbons parts/ten million	20.7*	24.9
8. Particulate No$_3$		2.62
9. Particulate Matter		10.4
10. Total Suspended Sulfates (SO$_4$)		6.48
11. Total Suspended Particulate Matter	64.8	53.60
12. Soiling Index	2.20	2.96

* Insufficient data points per month.

5.00   BIOTIC AND CULTURAL ELEMENTS

This section will treat the natural, cultural and economic elements that might be impacted by construction of SDSUNCC on the former Prohoroff Ranch.

5.01   SITE FLORA

The detritus of civilization and litter that remains on the site testifies to its past long and varied usage. The site is a combination of highly altered lower and middle regions and the almost undisturbed natural habitats in the higher southeastern quadrant. Quoting from the site selection report, "The remaining natural habitats are confined to coastal shrubs, chaparral and grassland." The abutting land in this upper area is for the most part in the natural state, although on the crest of the hills above the site there are houses on estate-sized tracts. This development will continue to grow and usurp more of the apparent natural habitats. There are vehicle tracks throughout this area and, judging from the litter left behind, is well-known to the younger cohorts. No plants identified as rare or endangered were located on the site. It will be necessary to fence the site to prevent trespassing and slope degradation by vehicles. Siting SDSUNCC on the Prohoroff Ranch will not have a significant impact on any rare or endangered species. A list of rare and endangered species of flora and fauna of California are presented as Appendix B of this report.

5.02   SITE FAUNA

The area occupied by the poultry ranch, fertilizer operation and aggregate extraction operation rid this area of most species. The orchards, while not natural habitats, provided nesting areas as well as being a frequent habitat for birds and small mammals. The natural habitat in the higher slopes could and may still be crossed by the larger predators such as coyotes and fox. Several species of smaller mammals still inhabit the area. The Site Selection Report stated that no plant or animal listed as endangered or rare was noted in the area. The impact of construction of SDSUNCC on the subject site will not have any significant impact on any animal or plant listed as a rare or endangered species.

5.03   CULTURAL AND HISTORICAL RESOURCES

The Prohoroff Ranch was used prior to 1890 and this operation significantly altered over 50 percent of the proposed acquisition for the SDSUNCC. The probability of cultural artifacts being found in these sectors is very low. The higher so-called natural habitats could have isolated remnants, but probably never supported a campsite. The most weighty item carried to encampments was water and the carriers managed to have encampment sites selected close to water. Quoting from the Site Selection Report, "One prehistoric isolated artifact was found and four historic sites." The former was collected and the latter were homesites constructed between 1900 and 1930. Three of the structures and the foundation of the fourth remain. The historical significance of these four sites is rather tenuous. In case some stray archeological or historical resource is found during the construction of the SDSUNCC facilities, the appropriate resource person at SDSU will be contacted for procedural guidance on the proper recovery method of the item. Construction of SDSUNCC on the Prohoroff site will not have any significant impact on any known cultural or historical resource.

5.04   CLIMATE

The climate of the San Marcos area is described as Mediterranean with a daily temperature range of about 15 degrees in summer and 20 degrees in the winter. The area is one of low cyclonic storms but is occasionally brushed lightly by the trailing edge of storms traveling northeast from off the coast of Mexico. The annual mean temperature is about 60 degrees. The maximum summer temperatures can exceed 90 degrees during the Santa Ana conditions but the average mean is around 86 degrees. San Marcos is far enough inland so that most of the morning fogs in the winter and spring do not reach that far inland. There is a natural funnel for ocean breezes along San Marcos Creek, however, and the summers are warmer than at Oceanside and the winters a degree or two colder. The area is semi-arid as the normal rainfall averages around 10 inches a year and about 85 percent of that occurs from November to March. Light frosts can occur during winter but they are infrequent. The climate of the area is benign and is conducive to outdoor activities and interactions during most days of the year.

5.05   NOISE POLLUTION

The academic buildings for SDSUNCC will be located one to two hundred feet in elevation above a busy freeway one-half mile to the north. During the middle of the day, the noise from the freeways is not particularly noticeable from the site. The freeway is depressed and bordered with random trees and shrubs which may attenuate the upward and horizontal spread of the vehicular noises. Depending on the intensity and duration, noise may produce psychological or physiological damage. Noise may also interfere with the normal orderly execution of human activities. Noise would be detrimental to the orderly processes in an educational institution and must be kept to about 40 to 45 decibels. At over 65 the ambience would become offensive. There are no national noise standards at present but there are occupational noise standards which are presented in Table VII.

Above a 95 DBA background noise communication is impossible. The following charts regarding the effects of noise are presented in Appendix E:

1. Apparent Sound Levels at Eardrum Due to Traffic
2. Sound Levels at Eardrum and their Corresponding Sound Pressure, Power and Maximum Exposure Time
3. Sound Pressure Level Attenuation Chart

It is recommended that noise abatement with the landscaping be a campus design element. To reduce inward migrating noise the academic buildings must be properly sited and acoustically treated. Shops, central plants, and service buildings should be treated to prevent interior noise from migrating outward. With proper design, external noise should not have a significant impact on the proposed SDSUNCC.

Table VII
Occupational Standards for Noise

DBA	Maximum Exposure Time*
90	8 hours
92	6 hours
95	4 hours
97	3 hours
100	2 hours
102	1-1½ hours
105	1 hour
110	½ hour
115	Less than ½ hour

*These exposure times presuppose that the rest of the work in areas with over 90 decibels would be spent in a more normal reduced noise area.

5.06 SAN MARCOS CREEK

The principal drainage in or near the proposed acquisition is the westerly flowing San Marcos Creek. The stream which is largely unimproved has a maximum capacity of approximately 12,000 cubic feet per second (cfs) which equates to 339 cubic meters per second (cms). The 100-year flood of San Marcos Creek will not affect the area of the proposed acquisition. The Las Posas branch flowing from the north has about the same capacity and enters the creek downstream of the proposed acquisition. San Marcos Creek enters Lake San Marcos, a flood control project completed in 1952. The San Marcos Water District (District) has constructed the South Lake Reservoir south of and in the hill above the creek. A rupture of this reservoir should not affect the proposed acquisition site. The 100-and 500-year floods along San Marcos Creek and its tributaries within the San Marcos city limits will inundate an area on both sides of Twin Oaks Valley Road north of SR-78 and a low-lying area south of Myrtle Avenue and east of La Moree Road. To the west, the area between Bent Avenue on the east and MacMahr Drive on the west along both sides of Discovery Street is subject to flooding during the 100-year flood under the present conditions and level of development of the drainage system. Any development that speeds up the concentration time of the storm water could increase the area subject to flooding.

Paving a significant area will decrease the storm water concentration time parameters as hard paving does not provide an equivalent flow friction to downward migrating waters as vegetation. To mitigate a rapid concentration time and maintain or decrease flooding at the level of the status quo, the channel capacity must be increased. As a natural consequence of development the area storm drainage system will have to be improved to a point where the lower-lying flat area's exposure to the danger of flooding, will be less than the present. The city has plans for the development of the main channel of San Marcos Creek down stream from the Ranch. This work will be completed by 1991.

The site will not be flooded during the 500-year flood level according to the National Flood Insurance Map, Community Panel #060296 0005C.

6.00 FINDINGS, RECOMMENDATIONS AND CONCLUSIONS

This proposed acquisition of 304 acres of land as the site for SDSUNCC will have significant impacts that cannot be fully mitigated and a statement of overriding considerations balancing the benefits namely as described in 6.07 versus the adverse environmental effects will be made.

6.01 ANY ENVIRONMENTAL EFFECTS WHICH CANNOT BE AVOIDED IF THE PROPOSED PROJECT IS IMPLEMENTED

If the proposed action is implemented, the three following environmental effects cannot be completely mitigated:

A. Loss of up to approximately 160 acres of open land.
B. Some modification of landforms on portions of about 165 acres of pre-existing rock knobs and native bedrock.
C. Contribute to the growth and urbanization of the area.

In answer to A: approximately 85 acres of the total 304 to be acquired by SDSUNCC were previously occupied by the poultry and other long-standing operations and, therefore, at most 270 acres could be considered open land. Using the 19 campuses of the California State University as a guide, a probable allotment of acreage by the year 2010 could be as detailed in Table VIII.

Table VIII

	Acres
Academic Core	95
Athletic Fields	50
Residence Facilities	39
Corporation Yard	25
Roads and Circulation	10
Perimeter Landscaped Buffers	10
Parking	75
TOTAL	304

Of the 270 acres that were more or less open land, the 60 acres that will probably be occupied by the athletic fields and landscaped perimeter buffer zones would essentially remain open space. The actual loss of existing open space would be about 160 acres in central portions of the site. There will remain as open space about 110 acres of 41 percent of the original acreage.

Parking will probably occupy as much as 75 acres in the lower-lying ex-Ranch areas. This area cannot be considered as open space as it was occupied and still is by various types of structures. The Corporation Yard, shops, roads and circulation were not counted as remaining open space.

The site will have a master plan architect, who will work closely with the Physical Planning and Development division of the Chancellor's Office and the local SDSUNCC administrators to produce a quality center. Human scale and environmental issues will be important criteria of the SDSUNCC master plan.

To extrapolate on B: There will be modifications to the existing landforms in approximately the central one-third of the site. The most drastic modification will be the site preparation and grading operations necessary to prepare the building sites, utility runs, roads and athletic fields. There have been extensive modifications to this central area, including the construction of high unconsolidated berms, land leveling and excavations.

In answer to B: Photos taken from across SR-78 show that the sensitive land area in the southern and eastern portions have been disturbed by roads and excavations to the top in the past. This portion of the site will not be adversely encroached upon with the exception of fire protection measures. The SDSUNCC occupancy of the Ranch site would be one of the least harmful that could occur relative to the sensitive higher ground. Each phase of the site development and grading will be accomplished as expeditiously as possible. SDSUNCC cannot undertake the more economical landform alteration by a prolonged aggregate recovery operation on the site to establish the rough grades.

Given the premises:

1. The sparse population density of the status quo cannot be maintained in the face of the pressure of population that is building up in NCSA due to immigration.
2. The Partnership has plans for construction of a major residential development on the area and later on the land to the south if the proposed acquisition for SDSUNCC is not consummated.
3. The Legislature has recognized the need for a site for SDSUNCC in the NCSA.

The fact that SDSUNCC may contribute to growth and urbanization is overridden by the educational, cultural and humanistic resources it will provide to the area.

6.02 MITIGATING MEASURES PROPOSED TO MINIMIZE UNAVOIDABLE IMPACTS

The mitigations proposed to minimize the loss of open space will reduce that impact to an acceptable degree. The acquisition of the proposed property by the state for CSU would reserve more open space than any other type of development that is likely to occur in this area.

The alteration of the landform to form the academic core of SDSUNCC will be a relatively difficult and costly operation. The following are the mitigation measures proposed.

A. The grading and site development plan for the academic core should be sensitive to the existing topography and landforms.
B. The master plan design by the massing, orientation, size, textures, architectural palette and materials should contribute towards minimizing the effect of landform alteration. Retaining walls, ramps and other architectural features could use some of the native rock as an exposed material. It is recommended that native rock be one of the elements on an architectural palette of materials. The amount of rock that is removed for construction of SDSUNCC will not present a significant visual impact from off the site.

6.03 THE RELATIONSHIP BETWEEN LOCAL SHORT-TERM USES OF MAN'S ENVIRONMENT AND MAINTENANCE AND ENHANCEMENT OF LONG-TERM PRODUCTIVITY

A large portion of the lower-lying parts of the site was once a major poultry and egg ranch. A collateral operation was the sale of fertilizer produced from chicken droppings and mixed with sawdust and peaty soils. The poultry operation was forced to cease operations for sanitary, health and environmental reasons. It would be impossible to re-establish the operation at the present time. The orchard was abandoned and it would be impossible to re-establish it as a viable economic operation for several reasons. Agriculture is dependent on processing plants and distribution and there are none of these facilities remaining in the area. An orchard abandoned over six years is ruined as an economic entity.

Chicken sheds, housing for employees, miscellaneous machinery and storage bins and buildings cover a quarter of the site. There are indications that sand and gravel were produced or recovered on some of the higher portions of the site. The area has abandoned machinery, vehicles and rotary kilns scattered about. In spite of all the debris that is strewn around and about the area, it does not present a negative visual impact from the roads on the north nor looking down from the heights at the southeast corner of the property.

Above the chicken ranch and fertilizer operation is an apparently abandoned fruit orchard in poor condition. The site presents a rather dramatic visual appearance. Agriculture and allied operations have ceased on the site and, due to the radical change in the character of the San Marcos area, the site will never return to that state; now only the detritus remains.

In place of the detritus there will be the facilities of the well-designed SDSUNCC to serve postsecondary students of the area. This new operation will be both humanistically and culturally superior to the existing abandonments.

**6.04   ANY IRREVERSIBLE ENVIRONMENTAL CHANGES WHICH
         WOULD BE INVOLVED IF THE PROPOSED ACTION SHOULD
         BE IMPLEMENTED**

The only irreversible environmental action that could occur would be the removal of rock to construct building pads and level areas around the building to facilitate student circulation and general congregating. If the buildings were demolished and rock brought back it would not be the same as the native weathered rock that was egested from the earth. This is not a significant impact as the character, use and perception of the area has changed. A university campus would be in many ways analogous to over-covering a cultural site. Placing a campus on the proposed site would preserve as much as 20 percent of the relatively undisturbed areas in the southeast. The irreversible changes are not significant environmentally.

6.05   PUBLIC DISCLOSURE

In accordance with the provisions of the state CEQA guidelines, the Trustees are making this fully informed decision to approve the purchase of the Ranch as a site for SDSUNCC.

There will be a lessening of the first two impacts identified below as relatively significant, but they cannot be avoided and there is no mitigation to the third.

    A.   Loss of open space.
    B.   Alteration of existing landforms.
    C.   Contributing to growth and urbanization.

6.06   FINDINGS

The findings of this Final EIR are as follows:

    A.   The acquisition for CSU of the northern portion of the Ranch in the city of San Marcos by the Space and Real Estate Division of the Department of General Services will have significant impact on the local environment.
    B.   The acquisition of the property will enable the Trustees to carry out their legislative mandate to provide a center for quality education in the North San Diego County area.
    C.   There is no known serious organized opposition to this proposed action.
    D.   There is strong support in the North County area for the SDSUNCC facility.

The Trustees are approving this action because the benefits provided by SDSUNCC override the four environmental impacts identified by this Final EIR.

6.07   CONCLUSIONS

Based on the findings, it is concluded that:

    A.   Selection of an NCSA site for a university in San Marcos is in accordance with the legislative mandate and regional need.
    B.   The proposed acquisition of the subject site for a future state university in the North County Service Area will have positive humanistic, educational and cultural impacts on the area, which override the adverse environmental impacts.

Selected Bibliography

Advisory Commission on Intergovernmental Relations. *Substate Regionalism and the Federal System*. Washington, D.C.: Government Printing Office, 1973.

Advisory Commission on Intergovernmental Relations. *Trends in Metropolitan America*. Washington, D.C.: Government Printing Office, 1977.

American Public Works Association. *National Conference of Solid Waste Disposal Sites*. Chicago, Illinois: American Public Works Association, 1971.

Anderson, Robert. *American Law of Zoning: Zoning, Planning and Subdivision Control*. Rochester, New York: Lawyers Cooperative Company, 1968.

Arbuckle, Gordon J., et al. *Environmental Law Handbook*. Rockville, Maryland: Government Institutes Inc., 1993.

Ashton, John, ed. *Healthy Cities*. Philadelphia, Pennsylvania: Open University Press, 1992.

Ausubel, Jesse H., and R. Herman. *Cities and Their Vital Systems: Infrastructure, Past, Present, and Future*. Washington, D.C.: National Academy Press, 1973.

Babcock, Richard. *The Zoning Game; Municipal Practices and Policies*. Madison, Wisconsin: University of Wisconsin Press, 1966.

Baesel-Tillis, Patricia, and Joan Tucker-Carver. "Garbage and Sewage Disposal from Recreational Boats." *Journal of Environmental Health* 61(1998): 8–17

Basset, Edward, et al. *Model Laws for Planning Cities, Counties and States*. Cambridge, Massachusetts: Harvard University Press, 1935.

Bayley, Peter B., ed. "Understanding Large River-floodplain Ecosystems Restoration." *BioScience* 45(1995): 153.

Bellah, Robert. *Habits of the Heart*. Berkeley: University of California Press, 1985.

Benenson, Abram, ed. *Control of Communicable Diseases Manual*. Washington, D.C.: American Public Health Association, 1995.

Benjamin, Stan. "Utility Land Management." *Electric Perspectives* 13(1989): 28–39.

Bergstrom, Arno, et al. *Collaboration Framework: Addressing Community Capacity*. Columbus, Ohio: National Network for Collaboration, 1994.

Best, Robin Hewitson. *Land Use and Living Space*. London; New York: Methuen, 1981.

Bocking, Stephen. "Visions of Nature and Society: A History of the Ecosystem Concept." *Alternatives* 20(1994): 12.

Bohlen, Curtis C. "Protecting the Coast Column." *BioScience* 40(1990): 243.

Bosselman, Fred P., and David Callies. *The Quiet Revolution in Land Use Control.* Washington, D.C.: Government Printing Office, 1971.

Brookes, Warren. "The Strange Case of the Glancing Geese." *Forbes* September 2, 1991, 104–109.

Buckman, H., and Nyle Brady. *The Nature and Properties of Soils.* 7th ed. New York: The MacMillan Company, 1969.

Burby, Raymond, and Linda C. Dalton. "Plans Can Matter! The Role of Land Use Plans and State Planning Mandates in Limiting the Development of Hazardous Areas." *Public Administration Review* 54(1994): 229–238.

Byrnes, Patricia. "Toward a Tapestry of Lifelands." *Wilderness* 57(1994): 4.

Cahill, Lawrence, ed. *Environmental Audits.* 7th ed. Rockville, Maryland: Government Institutes, Inc., 1996.

Caldwell, Lynton Keith. *Environment, A Challenge to Modern Society.* Garden City, New York: Natural History Museum, 1971.

Caldwell, Lynton Keith. *International Environmental Policy: Emergence and Dimensions.* 2nd ed. Durham, North Carolina: Duke University Press, 1990.

Caldwell, Lynton Keith (Robert V. Bartlett and James N. Gladden, eds.). *Environment as a Focus for Public Policy.* 1st ed. College Station, Texas: Texas A & M University Press, 1995.

Caldwell, Lynton Keith and Robert V. Bartlett, eds. *Environmental Policy: Transnational Issues and National Trends.* Westport, Connecticut: Quorum Books, 1997.

Caldwell, Lynton Keith, and Kristin Shrader-Frechette. *Policy for Land: Law and Ethics.* Savage, Maryland: Rowman and Littlefield Publishers, 1993.

California Environmental Quality Act. Assembly Bill 1888 and Senate Bill 919, 1993.

Canter, Larry W. *Environmental Impact Assessment.* New York: McGraw-Hill, 1977.

Carlin, A.P. *Hazardous Wastes.* Washington, D.C.: U.S. Environmental Protection Agency, 1977.

Carr, F. Housley, and Tom Ichniowski. "Corps' New Policy Could Open Farmlands to New Development (U.S. Army Engineers)." *ENR* 225(1990): 8–9.

Cavazzoni, James, and T. Volk. "Assessing Long-term Impacts of Increased Crop Productivity on Atmospheric CO_2." *Energy Policy* 24(1996): 403–411.

Cebrian, Just, and Carlos M. Duarte. "Plant Growth-rate Dependence of Detrital Carbon Storage in Ecosystems." *Science* 268(1995): 1606–1608.

Chameides, W.L., P.S. Kasibhatla, J. Yienger, and H. Levy II. "Growth of Continental-scale Metro-agro-plexes, Regional Ozone Pollution, and World Food Production." *Science* 264(1994): 74–77.

Christman, R. *State Land Use Programs: Issues and Opinions.* Pittsburgh, Pennsylvania: Land Policy Project, 1975.

Clapham, W.B., Jr. *Natural Ecosystems.* New York: Macmillan, 1973.

Clark, Colin. *Regional and Urban Location.* New York: St. Martin's Press, 1982.

Clawson, Marian. *America's Land and Its Uses.* Baltimore, Maryland: Johns Hopkins University Press, 1972.

Cnossen, Sijbren, and Herman Vollebergh. "Toward a Global Excise on Carbon." *National Tax Journal* 45(1992): 23.

Collier, George A., Daniel C. Mountjoy, and Ronald B. Nigh. "Peasant Agriculture and Global Change." *BioScience* 44(1994): 398.

Collin, Robert W. "Environmental Equity and the Need for Government Intervention." *Environment* 35(1993): 41.

Commoner, Barry. *The Closing Circle: Nature, Man and Technology.* New York: Alfred A. Knopf, 1971.

Cone, Maria. "Owens Valley Plan Seeks L.A. Water to Curb Pollution." *Los Angeles Times,* December 17, 1996, A1, A26.

Coppock, J.T. "Report on Reports: Land Transformation in Agriculture, SCOPE 32." *Environment* 30(1988): 25–27.

Costanza, Robert, and Lisa Wainger. "Ecological Economics (Calculates Value of Ecosystems by Using Coastal Wetlands in Louisiana)." *Business Economics* 26(1991): 45–48.

Costanza, Robert, Lisa Wainger, Carl Folke, and Karl-Goran Maler. "Modeling Complex Ecological Economic Systems Understanding People and Nature." *BioScience* 43(1993): 545.

Council on Environmental Quality. *Environmental Quality—Ninth Annual Report.* Washington D.C.: U.S. Government Printing Office, 1978.

Council on Environmental Trends. *Environmental Trends.* Washington, D.C.: U.S. Government Printing Office, 1989.

Countryman, David. *Guiding Land Use Decisions: Planning and Management for Forests and Recreation.* Baltimore, Maryland: Johns Hopkins University Press, 1982.

Crawford, Martin. *Air Pollution Control Theory.* New York: McGraw-Hill, 1976.

Crutzen, Paul J., and Meinrat Andreae. "Biomass Burning in the Tropics: Impact on Atmospheric Chemistry and Biogeochemical Cycles." *Science* 250(1990): 1669.

Daily, Gretchen C. "Restoring Value to the World's Degraded Lands. Frontiers in Biology: Ecology." *Science* 269(1995): 350.

Dasmann, Raymond F. *Environmental Conservation.* New York: Wiley and Sons, 1968.

Davidson, Donald A. *The Evaluation of Land Resources.* 2nd ed. New York: Longman Scientific and Technical, 1982.

Davis, Kenneth. *Land Use.* New York: McGraw-Hill, 1976.

Deming, David. "Climatic Warming in North America: Analysis of Borehole Temperatures." *Science,* 268(1995): 1576.

Department of Transportation. *Transportation Noise and Its Control.* Washington, D.C.(DOT P5630.1), June, 1972.

Detwiler, R.P., and Charles A.S. Hall. "Tropical Forests and the Global Carbon Cycle." *Science* 239(1988): 42–47.

Dicker, Thomas G., and K.R. Domeny. *Environmental Impact Assessment: Guidelines and Commentary.* Berkeley, California: University Extension, 1974.

Dittmann, Roger. "U.N. Agencies and Global Science." Presented at the AAAS Annual Meeting and Science Innovation Exposition, Anaheim, California, January 22, 1999.

Donohue, Gerry, "Law of the Land: Conflict Between Environmental Concerns and Property Rights." *Builder* 14(1991): 112–115 July Building Green special issue.

Dopper, Frank J. *The Politics of Land Reform.* Madison, Wisconsin: University of Wisconsin Press, 1981.

Douglas, Porter R. "A 50-year Plan for Metropolitan Portland." *Government Finance Review* 12(1996): 13–16.

Dowd, Ronald P. *Critical Issue Areas for Healthy Communities.* Hillsboro, Oregon: Healthy Communities Task Force for Washington County, 1996.

Doxiadis, Constantinos A. "Ekistics, the Science of Human Settlements." *Science* 170(1970): 393–404.

Duel, W.C. *Physicians Guide to Air Pollution.* Chicago, Illinois: American Medical Association, 1973.

Dufour, Darna L. "Use of Tropical Rainforest by Native Amazonians." *BioScience* 40(1990): 652.

Edwards, Sue Snaman. "Consider the Community, Not Just Market Demographics." *Professional Builder* 54(1989): 37.

Ehlers, Victor M., and Ernest W. Steel. *Municipal and Rural Sanitation.* 6th ed. New York: McGraw Hill, 1965.

El-Ahraf, Amer. "The Need for Sub-College Environmental Education Programs." *Journal of Environmental Health.* 34(1971): 167–170.

El-Ahraf, Amer. "The University's Role in Environmental Education." *Journal of Environmental Health.* 44(1981): 32–35.

El-Ahraf, Amer. "Public Health Perspective for the 80s: The Challenges and Strategies." Keynote speech at the Annual Meeting of the Arizona Public Health Association, Yuma, Arizona, September 24, 1981.

El-Ahraf, Amer. *An Ecological Definition of Health as Basis for an Integrative Model of International Environmental Management.* Paper read at Conference on Conservation and Development Implementing the World Conservation Strategy, Ottawa, Canada, May 31–June 5, 1986.

El-Ahraf, Amer, Kavous Emami, and Reza Karkia. "Water Recycling: Considerations for Higher Education and Global Implication." In *Global Business Trends.* Cumberland, Maryland: Academy of Business Administration, 1995, 688–701.

El-Ahraf, Amer, and Donald Hanson. "Action Environmental Health Education Programs: Concepts and Practice." An invitational paper presented before President Nixon's Committee on Health Education, Los Angeles, California, January 29, 1972.

El-Ahraf, Amer, and Al Hearne. "Environmental Health and Its Role in Comprehensive Planning for Health." *Journal of Environmental Health* 41(1979): 224–227.

El-Ahraf, Amer, Al Hearne, and Jack McGurk. *Environmental Health Delivery Within California.* A state/local task force report sponsored by California Conference of Directors of Environmental Health, California Conference of Local Health Officers, and California Environmental Health Association. Sacramento, California: California State Department of Health Services, 1980.

El-Ahraf, Amer, and W. Van Willis. *Animal Waste Management: Environmental Health Problem and Technological Solution.* Westport, Connecticut: Praeger, 1996.

Environmental Protection Agency. *Report to the President and Congress on Noise.* Washington, D.C. (92-63), February, 1972.

Environmental Protection Agency. *A Citizen's Guide to Clean Water.* Washington, D.C., June, 1973.

Environmental Protection Agency. *Public Health and Welfare Criteria for Noise.* Washington, D.C. (550/9-73-002), July, 1973.

Environmental Protection Agency. *A Drop to Drink: A Report on the Quality of Our Drinking Water.* Washington D.C., July, 1976.

Environmental Protection Agency. *Los Angeles County Noise Ordinance Protective Noise Levels.* Washington, D.C. (550/9-79-100), November, 1978.

Eronn, Robert. *The Natural Step.* Stockholm, Sweden: Swedish Institute, 1993.

Fabos, Julius. *Land Use Planning: From Global to Local Challenge.* New York: Chapman and Hall, 1985.

Federal Highway Administration. *Noise Standards and Procedures.* U.S. Department of Transportation (90-2), Washington, D.C. February, 1973.

Franklin, Jerry F., Caroline S. Bledsoe, and James T. Callahan. "Contributions of the Long-term Ecological Research Program." *BioScience* 40(1990): 509.

General Plan Guidelines. Office of Planning and Research, Governor's Office, State of California, 1990.

Gilbert, Gregory S., and Stephen P. Hubbell. "Plant Diseases and the Conservation of Tropical Forests: Conservation Planners Need to Consider the Roles Disease Plays in Natural Communities." *BioScience* 46(1996): 98.

Gomez-Pompa, Arturo, and Andrea Kaus. "Taming the Wilderness Myth: Environmental Policy and Education are Currently Based on Western Beliefs about Nature Rather Than on Reality." *BioScience* 42(1992): 271.

Goodkin, Sanford R. "The Strengths and Weaknesses of the Nation-state California." *Professional Builder and Remodeler* 56(1991): 40.

Gottdiener, Mark. *The Social Production of Urban Space.* 1st ed. Austin: University of Texas Press, 1985.

Gurwitt, Rob. "To See the Impact on Land Use." *Governing* 6(1993): 21–22.

Hagman, Donald G. *Urban Planning and Land Development Control Law.* St. Paul, Minnesota: West Publishing, 1971.

Harden, Jennifer W., Eric T. Sundquist, Robert F. Stallard, and Robert K. Mark. "Dynamics of Soil Carbon During Deglaciation of the Laurentide Ice Sheet." *Science* 258(1992): 1921.

Harney, Kenneth R. "Owners Win Their Days in Court (Rights of Property Owners Vis-à-vis Environmental and Land-use Controls)." *Barron's* 72(1992): 61.

Harris, David, and John Thompson. "Legal Separation Leads to a Happy Marriage: A Story of Green Acres." *Public Management* 78(1996): 17–19.

Harrison, Fred. *The Power in the Land: An Inquiry into Unemployment, The Profits Crisis, and Land Speculation.* New York: Universe Books, 1983.

Hayden, B.P., R.D. Dueser, J.T. Callahan, and H.H. Shugart. "Long-term Research at the Virginia Coast Reserve; Modeling a Highly Dynamic Environment." *BioScience* 41(1991): 310.

Healthcare Forum. *Building Community Capacity: The Potential of Community Foundation.* Minneapolis, Minnesota: Rainbow Research, 1994.

Healy, Robert. *Land Use and the States.* Baltimore, Maryland: Johns Hopkins Press, 1976.

Heimlich, Ralph E. "Costs of an Agricultural Wetland Reserve." *Land Economics* 70(1994): 234–246.

Henderson, Donald. *Effects of Noise on Hearing.* New York: Raven Press, 1976.

Henrik, Robert. A presentation at the Systems Thinking Conference, Boston, Massachusetts, September, 1995.

Hogue, Teresa. "Community Based Collaboration: Community Wellness Multiplied." Oregon State University: Oregon Center for Community Leadership, 1993.

Houghton, Richard A. "The Worldwide Extent of Land-use Change." *BioScience* 44(1994): 305–313.

Hulme, Mike, and Mick Kelly. "Exploring the Links Between Desertification and Climate Change Research on the Sahel Region of Africa." *Environment* 35(1993): 4.

Hunsaker, Carolyn T., and Daniel A. Levine. "Hierarchical Approaches to the Study of Water Quality in Rivers." *BioScience* 45(1995): 193–203.

Inhaber, Herbert. "Of LULUs, NIMBYs, and NIMTOOs (Locally Unwanted Land Uses: Approaches for Settling Disputes over Sites for Hazardous and Radioactive Wastes)." *The Public Interest* 107(1992): 52–64.

Jacobs, Lynn. *Waste of the West: Public Ranching.* Tucson, Arizona: Lynn Jacobs, 1992.

Johnson, Barry L., William B. Richardson, and Teresa J. Naimo. "Past, Present and Future Concepts in Large River Ecology: How Rivers Function and How Human Activities Influence River Processes." *BioScience* 45(1995): 134–141.

Kaplan, O. Benjamin. "Health Input in Land Use Planning: Experiences in a Land Use Program." *AJPH* 68(1978): 489–491.

Kaufman, Les. "Catastrophic Change in Species-rich Freshwater Ecosystems: The Lessons of Lake Victoria." *BioScience* 42(1992): 846.

Kauppi, Pekka E., Kari Mielikainen, and Kullervo Kuusela. "Biomass and Carbon Budget of European Forests." *Science.* 256(1992): 70.

Kempton, Willett, and Paul P. Craig. "European Perspectives on Global Climate Change." *Environment* 35(1993): 16.

Kerr, Richard A. "The Carbon Cycle and Climate Warming: Learning How Carbon Cycles Through the Environment, With and Without Human Intervention, Is Crucial to Predicting the Greenhouse Effect." *Science* 222(1983): 1107.

Kitto, William, and F. Burns. "The ABCs of NEPA Regs." *Planning* June, 1980.

Kline, Jeffrey, and Dennis Wichelns. "Using Referendum Data to Characterize Public Support for Purchasing Development Rights to Farmland." *Land Economics* 70(1994): 223–233.

Knopman, Debra S., and Richard Smith. "20 Years of the Clean Water Act Federal Water Pollution Control Act Amendments of 1972." *Environment* 35(1993): 16.

Koren, Herman. *Handbook of Environmental Health and Safety: Principles and Practices.* Volume 1. New York: Pergamon Press, 1995.

Koren, Herman. *Handbook of Environmental Health and Safety: Principles and Practices.* Volume 2. New York: Pergamon Press, 1980.

Kosobud, Richard F., Thomas A. Daly, David W. South, and Kevin G. Quinn. "Tradable Cumulative CO_2 Permits and Global Warming Control." *Energy Journal* 15(1994): 213.

Kosowatz, John J. "Developers Gain in Wetlands Pact." *ENR* 224(1990): 8–9.

Lake, Robert W. *Resolving Locational Conflict.* New Brunswick, New Jersey: Center for Urban Policy Research, 1987.

Langs, Michael. "Financing in a Growth-managed Environment." *Mortgage Banking* 52(1992): 71–72.

Leung, Hok Lin. *Land Use Planning Made Plain.* Kingston, Ontario, Canada: Ronald P. Frye, 1989.

Leveson, David. *Geology and the Urban Environment.* New York: Oxford University Press, 1980.

Liptak, Bela, ed. *Environmental Engineers Handbook.* Radner, Pennsylvania: Chilton, 1974.

Lounsbury, John F., L. Sommers, and E. Fernard. *Land Use: A Spatial Approach.* Dubuque, Iowa: Kendall/Hunt, 1981.

Luckmann, William H., and Robert L. Metcalf. *Introduction to Pest Management.* New York: Wiley & Sons, 1975.

Lundgren, Lawrence. *Environmental Geology.* Englewood Cliffs, New Jersey: Prentice Hall, 1986.

Lyle, John Tillman. *Design for Human Ecosystems: Landscape, Land Use and Natural Resources.* New York: Van Nostrand Reinhold, 1985.

MacNeill, Tim, E. John, and Ian Jackson. "Sustainable Development—The Urban Challenge." *Ekistics: The Problems and Science of Human Settlements* 58(1991): 348–349.

Marsh, William M. *Landscape Planning: Environmental Applications.* Reading, Massachusetts: Addison-Wesley, 1983.

Maskell, Kathy, Irving M. Mintzer, and Bruce A. Callander. "Basic Science of Climate Change." *Lancet* 342(1993): 1027.

Mather, Alexander S. *Land Use.* Somerset, New Jersey: Wiley & Sons, 1986.

Matson, P.A., and P.M. Vitousek. "Ecosystem Approach to a Global Nitrous Oxide Budget." *BioScience* 40(1990): 667.

Mattessich, Paul W., and Barbara Monsey. *Collaboration: What Makes It Work.* St. Paul, Minnesota: Amherst H. Wilder Foundation, 1992.

Mayer, Steven E. *Building Community Capacity: The Potential of Community Foundation.* Minneapolis, Minnesota: Rainbow Research Inc., 1994.

McAllister, Donald M. *Environment: A New Focus for Land-Use Planning.* Washington, D.C.: National Science Foundation, 1973.

McCoy, Charles. "U.S. Forest Service Finds Itself Bedeviled by Hells Canyon Plan (Feud Between River Rafters and Power Boaters)." *Wall Street Journal,* August 18, 1994, A1.

Meyer, Alden. "Cutting Energy Consumption is the Key to Averting Global Warming's Impacts." *The Oil Daily,* 9481, April 18,1990, 4.

Mihie, Lories, Jr. *The Balance of Nature.* New York: Alfred E. Knopf, 1969.

Miller, G. Tyler., Jr. *Living in the Environment.* 10th ed. New York: Thomas Publishing Company, 1998.

Miller, Richard F., and Peter E. Wigand. "Holocene Changes in Semiarid Pinyon-juniper Woodlands: Response to Climate, Fire, and Human Activities in the U.S. Great Basin." *BioScience* 44(1994): 465.

Mooney, Harold A., Peter Vitousek, and Pamela A. Matson. "Exchange of Materials Between Terrestrial Ecosystems and the Atmosphere." *Science* 238(1987): 926.

Morgan, Mark D. "Acidification of Freshwater Ecosystems: Implications for the Future." *BioScience* 45(1995): 296.

Muller, Frank. "Mitigating Climate Change: The Case for Energy Taxes; Energy Tax Proposals Aimed at Slowing Climactic Change." *Environment* 38(1996): 12.

Nathanson, Jerry A. *Basic Environmental Technology.* New York: John Wiley & Sons, 1986.

National Heart, Lung and Blood Institute. *Respiratory Diseases Task Force Report on Prevention, Control and Education.* Washington, D.C.: U.S. Department of Health Education and Welfare, Public Health Service, 1977.

National Institute for Occupational Safety and Health. *Practical Problems and Policy Issues Arising from Exposure to Hazardous Chemicals and Physical Agents in the Workplace.* Washington D.C.: Subcommittee on Labor, Senate Committee on Human Resources, 1977.

Natural Resources Defense Council. *Land Use Controls in the United States: A Handbook on the Legal Rights of Citizens.* New York: Dial Press, 1977.

Natural Resources Defense Council. *Transportation Controls for Clean Air.* Natural Resources Defense Council, 1973.

Neue, Heinz-Ulrich. "Methane Emission from Rice Fields Special Section: International Agricultural Research." *BioScience* 43(1993): 466.

Office of the Chancellor, California State University. "Final Environmental Impact Report. San Diego State University North County Center. San Marcos Campus Land Acquisition." Long Beach, California: California State University, 1987.

Ojima, D.S., K.A. Galvin, and B.L. Turner. "The Global Impact of Land-use Change." *BioScience* 44(1994): 300–304.

Oppenheimer, Michael. "Context Connection and Opportunity in Environmental Problem Solving. The Earth Day Series." *Environment* 37(1995): 10.

Ortega, Bob. "Portland, Oregon Shows Nation's City Planners How to Guide Growth." *Wall Street Journal,* December 26, 1995, A1–A2.

Papaioannou, John G. "Scale Perception in Ekistics." *Ekistics: The Problems and Science of Human Settlements* 60(1993): 309.

Patch, Steven, Richard Maas, and Jason Pope. "Lead Leaching from Faucet Fixtures Under Residential Conditions." *Journal of Environmental Health* 61(1998): 18–21.

Phelan, Michael J. "Environmental Health Policy Decisions: The Role of Uncertainty in Economic Analysis." *Journal of Environmental Health* 61(1998): 8–12.

Phillips, Jonathan D. "Land Management Effects on Innate Soil Erodibility." *Focus* 40(1990): 36.

Posey, Darrell A. "People, Property, and Bioprospecting." *Environment* 38(1996): 6.

Powers, Mary. "Battle Looms in Louisiana." *ENR* 224(1990): 12–13.

Public Land Law Review Commission. *One-Third of the Nation's Land.* Washington, D.C.: U.S. Government Printing Office, 1970.

Pulliam, H. Ronald. "The Birth of a Federal Research Agency. National Biological Service Special Supplement: Biodiversity Policy." *BioScience* 45(1995): S91.

Qayoumi, Mohammad. "Managing Environmental Issues." *Facilities Management* 8(1993): 3–4.

Qayoumi, Mohammad. "Chloroflourocarbons." Presentation at the Association of Physical Plant Administrators Institute, Newport Beach, California, 1993.

Qayoumi, Mohammad. "The Environmental Condition of Central Asia." Presentation at the Conference on Central Asia, Ohio State University, March, 1994.

Rau, John G., and David C. Wooten, eds. *Environmental Impact Analysis Handbook.* New York: McGraw-Hill, 1980.

Ravo, Nick. "Saving Taxes and Open Spaces, Too (Large Landowners Using Conservation Easements and Limited Development Plans)." *New York Times*, late New York edition, August 29, 1993, 1.

Real, Leslie A. "Sustainability and the Ecology of Infectious Disease: Diseases and Their Pathogenic Agents Must be Viewed as Important Parts of Any Ecosystem Management Strategy." *BioScience* 46(1996): 88.

Reiger, George. "The Resource Revolution." *Field & Stream*, May, 1988, 21.

Reiger, George. "The Resource Revolution." *Field & Stream*, June, 1988, 14.

Reiger, George. "Death and Taxes." *Field & Stream*, April, 1989, 18.

Reitze, Arnold. *Environmental Law.* Washington, D.C.: North American International, 1972.

Relph, Edward. *The Modern Urban Landscape.* Great Britain: John Hopkins University Press, 1987.

Rhind, David, and R. Hudson. *Land Use.* London; New York: Methuen, 1980.

Richey, Jeffrey E., Carlos Deser, and Clara Nobre. "Amazon River Discharge and Climate Variability." *Science* 246(1989): 101.

Roberts, Roc A., and Jeff Corkill. "Grass Seed Field Smoke and Its Impact on Respiratory Health." *Journal of Environmental Health* 60(1998): 10-15.

Root, Terry L., and Stephen H. Schneider. "Ecology and Climate: Research Strategies and Implications. Frontiers in Biology: Ecology." *Science* 269(1995): 334.

Ross, Lester. "The Next Wave of Environmental Legislation Special Report: China's Environment." *The China Business Review* 21(1994): 30.

Sarkar, Sahotra. "Ecological Theory and Anuran Declines." *BioScience* 46(1996): 199.

Schlosser, Isaac J. "Stream Fish Ecology: A Landscape Perspective." *BioScience* 41(1991): 704–712.

Seattle [Chief]. "Where is the Eagle Gone." Chief Seattle to President Franklin Pierce, 1855. Eugene, Oregon: Western Graphics Corporation, 1976.

Senn, Charles L. "Syllabus in Environmental Health." Los Angeles, California: University of California, School of Public Health, 1970.

Senn, Charles, Amer El-Ahraf, and Donald Hanson. "Modern Roles of the American Public Health Association in Housing." Presented at the American Public Health Association's Annual Meeting, Atlantic City, New Jersey, 1972.

Servary, Raymond F., Jr., and D.B. Neubert. "An Agricultural Land Preservation Program that Developers Can't Match." *Government Finance Review* 7(1991): 17–20.

Short, Henry L. and Jay B. Hestbeck. "National Biotic Resource Inventories and GAP Analysis." *BioScience* 45(1995): 535–539.

Siegel, Paul B., and Thomas G. Johnson. "Break-even Analysis of the Conservation Reserve Program: The Virginia Case." *Land Economics* 67(1991): 447–461.

Simonson, Richard. "How to Stop Development on the Urban Periphery." *Real Estate Review* 25(1995): 88–93.

Sisk, Thomas D., Alan E. Launer, Kathy R. Switzky, and R. Paul. "Identifying Extinction Threats." *BioScience* 44(1994): 592–604.

Skole, D.L., W.H. Chomentowski, and W.A. Salas. "Physical and Human Dimensions of Deforestation in Amazonia." *BioScience* 44(1994): 314–322.

Smart, J. Eric. *Recreational Development Handbook.* Washington, D.C.: Urban Land Institute, 1981.

So, Frank S. *The Practice of State and Regional Planning.* Chicago, Illinois: American Planning Association, 1986.

So, Frank S. *The Practice of Local Government Planning.* Washington, D.C.: International City Management Association, 1988.

Sprout, Harold, and Margaret Sprout. *The Context of Environmental Politics.* Lexington, Kentucky: University Press of Kentucky, 1978.

Stavins, Robert N., and A.B. Jaffe. "Unintended Impacts of Public Investments on Private Decisions: The Depletion of Forested Wetlands." *The American Economic Review* 80(1990): 337–352.

Stebbing, J.H. "Effect of the Pittsburgh Air Pollution Episode on Pulmonary Function in School Children." *Journal of Air Pollution Control Association* 26(1976): 547–553.

Stone, Richard. "Long-term NSF Network Urged to Broaden Scope National Science Foundation Long-term Ecological Research Network." *Science* 262(1993): 334.

Stoss, Frederick W. "Environment Online: The Greening of Databases." *Database* 14(1991): 13.

Sullivan, Thomas F., ed. *Environmental Law Handbook.* 14th ed. Rockville, Maryland: Government Institutes, Inc., 1997.

Swain, Edward B., Daniel R. Engstrom, Mark E. Brigham, Thomas A. Henning, and Patrick L. Brezonik. "Increasing Rates of Atmospheric Mercury Deposition in North America Lakes of Minnesota and Wisconsin." *Science* 257(1992): 784.

Swan, James, and William Stopp, eds. *Environmental Education: Strategy Towards a More Livable Future.* New York: Sage Publications, 1974.

Tevis, Cheryl. "Family Converting Land." *Successful Farming* 90(1992): 41.

Thiesenhusen, William C. "Implications of the Rural Land Tenure System for the Environmental Debate: Three Scenarios." *Journal of Developing Areas* 26(1991): 1–23.

Thompson, Anne M. "The Oxidizing Capacity of the Earth's Atmosphere: Probable Past and Future Changes." *Science* 256(1992): 1157.

Turk, Jonathan. *Environmental Science.* 4th ed. Philadelphia, Pennsylvania: Saunders College, 1988.

Turner, Monica G., Robert H. Gardner, and R. O'Neill. "Ecological Dynamics at Broad Scales: Ecosystems and Landscapes. Special Supplement: Biodiversity Policy." *BioScience* 45(1995): S29.

Turner, R. Eugene, and Nancy N. Rabalais. "Changes in Mississippi River Water Quality This Century." *BioScience* 41(1991): 140.

Turnock, Bernard J. *Public Health What it is and How it Works*. Gaithersburg, Maryland: Aspen Publishers, Inc., 1997.

Tyvoll, John L., Elichia A. Venso, Michael E. Folkoff, Brent R. Skeeter, and Asif M. Shakur. "Ozone Exposure in Rural Maryland's Lower Eastern Shore." *Journal of Environmental Health* 61(1998): 14–20.

U.S. Department of Agriculture. *Stratification of Forest Lands for Timber Management Planning*. Washington, D.C.: U.S. Government Printing Office, 1971.

U.S. Department of Agriculture. *Our Land and Water Resources: Current and Prospective Supplies and Uses*. Washington, D.C.: U.S. Government Printing Office, 1974.

U.S. Department of Energy. "Energy Information Administration." *Annual Energy Review 1990*, DOE EIA-0384 (90), May, 1991.

U.S. Department of Housing and Urban Development. *A New Partnership to Conserve America's Communities: A National Urban Policy*. Washington, D.C.: U.S. Government Printing Office, 1978.

U.S. Department of the Interior. *Range Condition Report*. Washington, D.C.: U.S. Senate Committee on Appropriations, January, 1975.

U.S. Department of Transportation. *Airport Master Plans*. Washington, D.C.: U.S. Government Printing Office, 1971.

United Nations Conference on Environmental Development. *United States of America National Report*. Washington, D.C.: Council on Environmental Quality, 1992.

van Kooten, G. Cornelis. "Bioeconomic Evaluation of Government Agricultural Programs on Wetlands Conversion." *Land Economics* 69(1993): 27–38.

Vine, Marilyn, Darrah Degnan, and Carol Hanchette. "Geographic Information Systems: Their Use in Environmental Epidemiologic Research." *Journal of Environmental Health* 61(1998): 7–15.

Walker, D.A., P.J. Webber, E.F. Binnian, K.R. Everett, N.D. Lederer, E.A. Nordstrand, and M.D. Walker. "Cumulative Impacts of Oil Fields on Northern Alaskan Landscapes." *Science*. 238(1987): 757–761.

Walter, John. "Taking the Pulse of the Land (Soil Conservation Service's Natural Resources Survey)." *Successful Farming* 92(1994): 24.

Walter, John. "Top Farmland's in Shadow of the City." *Successful Farming* 85(1987): 10.

Warner, David. "Expanding the Wilderness." *Nation's Business* 81(1993): 66–67.

Watkins, T.H. "Community." *Wilderness* 58(1995): 9.

Weiss, Marc A. *The Rise of the Community Builder*. New York: Columbia University Press, 1987.

Willgoose, Carl E. *Environmental Health: Commitment for Survival*. Philadelphia, Pennsylvania: W. B. Saunders, 1979.

World Bank. *Environmental Assessment Sourcebook*. Washington, D.C.: World Bank, 1991.

World Health Organization. "Constitution of World Health Organization." *Chronicle of World Health Organization*. Geneva, Switzerland: World Health Organization, 1947, 29–43.

World Health Organization. *Ottawa Charter for Health Promotion*. Geneva, Switzerland: World Health Organization, 1986.

Zimmerer, Karl S. "Soil Erosion and Social Discourses in Cochabamba, Bolivia: Perceiving the Nature of Environmental Degradation. Theme Issue: Environment and Development." Part 1. *Economic Geography* 69(1993): 312.

Index

About the Authors

AMER EL-AHRAF is President of Southern California International College and President of the degree-granting division of the International Education Corporation. He served as University Advancement Vice President, Executive Vice President, and Professor of Environmental Quality and Health, California State University, Dominguez Hills. Past president of various important state and national associations in public health, he has served as a trustee and governor of several community based organizations, and has spoken at conferences and national and international symposia. He also serves on the editorial boards of journals in his field and is recipient of The Walter Mangold Award and the Walter Snyder Award, both for his contributions to the field of environmental health.

MOHAMMAD QAYOUMI is Vice Chancellor for Administrative Services at University of Missouri-Rolla. He served for many years on the faculties of the University of Cincinnati and San Jose State University. He has published more than 50 articles, two books, and is on the editorial board of a respected manual on facilities management.

RON DOWD is Professor of Public Administration and Health Care Administration at Portland State University. He has served as a consultant to various health and social organizations and institutions in strategic planning, management development, facilities management, systems and organizational development and other fields. He also serves on task forces and other administrative bodies nationwide and particularly in Oregon.

ISBN 1-56720-065-6

EAN

9 781567 200652

90000>

HARDCOVER BAR CODE